FREEDOM BOUND I

FREEDOM BOUND I

Documents on women in
colonial Australia

edited by
Marian Quartly,
Susan Janson and Patricia Grimshaw

ALLEN & UNWIN

First published 1995
Allen & Unwin Pty Ltd
9 Atchison Street, St Leonards, NSW 2065 Australia

National Library of Australia
Cataloguing-in-Publication entry:

Freedom bound. I, Documents on women in colonial Australia.

Bibliography.
Includes index.
ISBN 1 86373 735 9.

1. Women—Australia—History—Sources. 2. Women—
Australia—History—Sources. I. Quartly, Marian, 1942– .
II. Janson, Susan. III. Grimshaw, Patricia, 1938– .
IV. Title: Documents on women in colonial Australia.

305.420994

Set in 10/12 pt Garamond by DOCUPRO, Sydney
Printed by Kim Hup Lee Printing, Singapore

10 9 8 7 6 5 4 3 2 1

Contents

Introduction   ix
Acknowledgements   xi

Part 1   Women in convict society 1788–1840   1

1.1   The Colonial Office sketches a plan to establish a penal
      colony in New South Wales   2
1.2   An English journal prints a 'human interest' story about
      convicts bound for Botany Bay   6
1.3   An Officer of the Marines struggles to control some
      refractory convict women   9
1.4   An English gentleman attempts to understand Aboriginal
      women and Aboriginal family life   12
1.5   An English lady discovers the natural wonders of New
      South Wales   14
1.6   An emancipated convict considers her life in the colony   18
1.7   A sea captain remembers the labours of Aboriginal
      women in the sealing trade   19
1.8   A gentry wife works to maintain family ties   21
1.9   A lonely immigrant seamstress writes home   23
1.10 An Aboriginal woman gives evidence of her
      exploitation in the sealing trade   26

1.11   A woman tries to escape from a violent husband   28
1.12   A woman poet imagines the feelings of an Aboriginal
       mother   31
1.13   Women convicts riot at the Launceston Female Factory   34

Part 2   Women in a masculine democracy 1840–1860   36

2.1   A newspaper reports the Governor's views about female
       intemperance   37
2.2   A missionary despairs of converting the Aborigines   39
2.3   A lady reformer finds a working man a wife   43
2.4   A wife chronicles an unhappy marriage   45
2.5   A wife perseveres in a grim marriage   47
2.6   A Mechanics' Institute discussion class debates the
       inferiority of woman's intellect   51
2.7   A husband asks his wife to join him in the colonies   55
2.8   A middle-class sister and brother consider their career
       options   59
2.9   A young lady seeks economic independence   61
2.10   A woman asks for the vote for women   64
2.11   A wife advises her husband on raising sheep   66
2.12   Parliamentarians approve a divorce bill   68
2.13   A young lady finds that men are vile   71

Part 3   Frontiers—rural and urban 1860–1885   74

3.1   A white Queensland girl observes Aborigines   75
3.2   A lady reformer on the tensions of city life   79
3.3   A widow persists in asking for charity   82
3.4   A sister keeps house in Queensland   86
3.5   A politician with a radical view of women's rights   90
3.6   A woman remembers selectors living in poverty   93
3.7   A man puts the case for women's higher education   96
3.8   A journalist reports on prostitutes and charity workers 100
3.9   A woman speaks out on women's rights   104
3.10   Aboriginal women describe living conditions on a
       reserve   106
3.11   Working women take industrial action   111
3.12   A woman imagines a feminist utopia   115
3.13   Wives are told how to achieve marital bliss   118
3.14   A journalist observes the white Australian girl   122
3.15   A novelist remembers women's power in the family   125

Part 4   Seeking social solutions 1886–1901   129

4.1   An Aboriginal woman tells of mission life   130
4.2   A male missionary tells of white male cruelty to
       Aboriginal women   132
4.3   The making of a woman temperance advocate   136
4.4   A journal opposes a feminist's views on marriage   139
4.5   A new journal claims a new voice for women   141
4.6   A clergyman's wife describes their plight   144
4.7   A judge supports the battle for contraception education   146
4.8   Women who are not members of trade unions are
       questioned about their work   150
4.9   A woman chemist advocates contraception   154
4.10   A worker for women's suffrage reports on the progress
       of the cause   156
4.11   A male journalist discusses the woman question and
       the social question   159
4.12   A woman replies to another woman's doubts about
       suffrage   163
4.13   Women and children still struggle for subsistence   166
4.14   A woman writer claims a national identity for
       Australian women   169
4.15   The Federal Constitution inscribes citizenship for some
       women   173
4.16   A feminist embraces women's citizenship   177

Notes   179
Select bibliography   186
Index   190

Introduction

The task of bringing women's voices from the past into the present has its rewards, and its frustrations. The rewards are displayed on these pages. Women (and some men) speak about women's experience in eighteenth-century and nineteenth-century Australia. Their language is sometimes unfamiliar, but the voices are generally direct enough to give the reader a sense of immediate access to the past.

Readers in the late twentieth century are not of course the intended audience of these documents; we merely eavesdrop on a past and have to imagine its meaning. Women wrote for family and friends, or occasionally for the readers of a journal or newspaper, and it is only at the very end of our period that women spoke from platforms to people they did not know personally. The changing form of the documents gathered here, from family letters to published poems and novels to public addresses, illustrates the movement of women into public life, which is one of our major themes.

The frustrations come from knowing what is missing from these pages. Aboriginal women and white working-class women are not adequately represented here. The problem reflects the previous century's distribution of power and knowledge in society. Poor people generally had little book learning. They wrote slowly and painfully and had nowhere to keep what they wrote, so the few letters from working-class families presented here are uncommon survivals. We have also included legal documents and interviews that record the spoken words of poor white women and Aboriginal women, but they come to us framed and shaped by official knowledge and practice. Powerful families had a near monopoly on both public and private writing and on the preservation of what was written. Our collection speaks mainly in voices that are well educated and white.

Several excellent collections of documents recording Australian women's history were published during the 1970s and 1980s. Each reflected the preoccupations of the years that produced it. The editors of these collections went to the past with questions about the status of women, paid and unpaid work, the marginalisation and institutionalisation of women, and women's relations in the family—all issues that concerned the women's movement in those decades. And all in various ways were looking to find women working together in the past, on behalf of themselves and other women.

Writing in the 1990s, we are working in the same tradition as these earlier collections. Like those earlier editors, we are mainly concerned to rediscover female experience in the past, to make it available to the queries of the present. Like them we understand that histories excluding women have also tended to ignore large areas of masculine experience. So we look to refocus the historical gaze to include those areas of experience that are ignored when women are omitted: private life and all its emotions; reproduction and its demographic, economic and political effects.

Perhaps we differ from earlier editors by self-consciously placing ourselves in that tradition. In shaping the volume we wanted to include particular themes and even particular documents whose significance is established in a mature historiography. Women's history is now a confident and well-defined area of study in Australia; the paths are there for us to follow.

Inevitably, however, our concerns are also different; we reflect a different present. Earlier histories took up the concerns and the debates of women who, despite those differences, understood themselves to be part of a single movement, based upon shared female experience. Today many women argue that differences in class, colour, ethnicity, culture and generation deny that common experience. Others disagree, but no-one can claim now to speak in the name of all women.

So our greatest difference from earlier document collections lies in the way that we approach the historical mobilisation of women. Historians have tended to accept the view of their historical subjects, that women naturally have interests in common, and that these only need to be discovered to form a basis for common action. We understand such common interest and common action as the products of a particular time and place. Women created their sense of group identity within a specific social and political context. Thus nineteenth-century feminism was made in reaction to, and from the same ideological materials as, a liberalism grounded in the assumed rationality and equality of middle-class men. And twentieth-century feminism flowered from the proposition that white women, and not women of colour, were the true citizens of Australia, the mothers of the race. To include, to create group identity, it seemed necessary to exclude, and to denigrate.

So we bring you these documents not as evidence of the unfolding of some inevitable historical process, but as weapons retrieved from an ideological battleground. Almost every document was written or recorded in order to make something happen—to persuade, to unite, to divide. A close reading of these rich texts will bring the past into a focus that is at once more narrow and more complex than earlier ways of seeing. Listen to the voices with equal measures of scepticism and sympathy, and you will discover the past in true perspective; that we are of it and not of it.

Acknowledgements

We thank Merilyn Bourke for her typing, and Sara Aveling, Ben Aveling, Katharine Grimshaw and Catherine Welch for their critical readings of the manuscript.

The editors have made every effort to obtain and acknowledge copyright. Copyright permissions have been generously granted by Fremantle Arts Centre Press, Harper Collins Publishers Australia, Melbourne University Press, Oxford University Press, Penguin Books Australia Ltd, Reed Books Australia and University of New South Wales Press.

Part 1
Women in convict society 1788–1840

To pragmatists among the men planning the convict colony at Botany Bay, women were a necessary evil: a means of satisfying male lust that would otherwise break out in worse forms of disorder. Convict women, Aboriginal women, even women from the Pacific Islands, were all thought of as serving this purpose. To idealists, and to pragmatists in optimistic moments, women represented the future: the means by which the country would be settled by industrious families. 'Settling' carries a great weight of meaning in the Australian lexicon; it embraces at once the location of unruly populations, the domestication of the natural environment, and (by implication) the dispossession of the Aborigines—and women are at the heart of it.

So from the beginnings of the convict colonies, officials acted upon the assumption that a woman's place was in the home. A convict woman who chose to marry, or in the early years merely to cohabit, effectively lost her convict status, having passed from the control of the government to the control of her husband. There was a certain masculine gallantry in this, a sentimental idealisation of female vulnerability apparent also in early characterisations of Aboriginal women. But there was also a masculine arrogance, an assumption that the proper function of women, white and black, was to serve male

1

needs, and women who denied male authority were characterised as prostitutes and whores.

Most women probably accepted this masculine authority most of the time, in public and in private. Mostly they had little choice. There were some areas of Aboriginal women's lives in which men traditionally did not interfere, but these hardly survived the dislocation of Aboriginal culture before the white invasion. Convict women found that the acceptance of a husband's authority was necessary to survive in the colonies; Margaret Catchpole was exceptional in her ability to live alone. And while work as a wife and mother was generally less unpleasant than labouring for the government or an assigned master, a husband's authority could be violently enforced without community disapproval.

Women did challenge male authority, but usually when they were gathered in company: in ships, on assignment, especially in the female factories where they worked or were punished for colonial crimes, or merely for pregnancy. More often than men, women in institutions were moved to quite violent revolt, often by a shared sense of injustice. Female solidarity was arguably more evident than male solidarity among the convicts.

On the other hand there was little sense of sisterly feeling between different kinds of women in the colonies. Convict women and servants are invisible in the accounts of gentry women's lives, or mentioned only as colonial oddities. A lady like Elizabeth Macarthur was interested in Aboriginal women as women and especially as mothers, but it is their difference that she stresses. Only at the end of our period is any kind of common femaleness suggested, with Eliza Dunlop's poetic assertion of the essential humanity and femininity of 'The Aboriginal Mother'.

Document 1.1 The Colonial Office sketches a plan to establish a penal colony in New South Wales

The documents recording the decision to found Australia are hardly glorious—a handful of begging letters from adventurers wanting to set up and govern commercial colonies, and a few office memos and committee reports documenting the slow progress of the British Government towards the reluctant decision that New South Wales was the only possible destination for the thousands of convicts sentenced to transportation whose labour could no longer be sold in the rebellious North American colonies. This draft—just the preliminary

points of a plan—was included in a proposal sent on 18 August 1786
by the Home Secretary, Lord Sydney, to Treasury officials charged
with costing the scheme.

Although women made up only a small proportion of those
sentenced to transportation, this and similar documents show that
those planning the colony considered their presence important. The
proposal to fetch additional women from the Pacific Islands was
included in the instructions given to Captain Arthur Phillip as Gov-
ernor of New South Wales, but was never carried out.[1]

August 1786

Heads of a plan for effectually disposing of convicts, and rendering their
transportation reciprocally beneficial both to themselves and to the State,
by the establishment of a colony in New South Wales, a country which,
by the fertility and salubrity of the climate, connected with the remoteness
of its situation (from whence it is hardly possible for persons to return
without permission) seems peculiarly adapted to answer the views of
Government with respect to providing a remedy for the evils likely to
result from the late alarming and numerous increase of felons in this
country, and more particularly in the metropolis.

It is proposed that a ship of war of a proper class, with a part of her
guns mounted, and a sufficient number of men on board for her navigation,
and a tender of about 200 tons burthen, commanded by discreet officers,
should be got ready as soon as possible to serve as an escort to the convict
ships, and for other purposes hereinafter mentioned.

That, in addition to their crews, they should take on board two
companies of marines to form a military establishment on shore (not only
for the protection of the settlement, if requisite, against the natives, but
for the preservation of good order), together with an assortment of stores,
utensils, and implements, necessary for erecting habitations and for agri-
culture, and such quantities of provisions as may be proper for the use of
the crews.

As many of the marines as possible should be artificers, such as
carpenters, sawyers, smiths, potters (if possible), and some husbandmen.
To have a chaplain on board, with a surgeon, and one mate at least; the
former to remain at the settlement.

That these vessels should touch at the Cape of Good Hope, or any
other places that may be convenient, for any seed that may be requisite
to be taken from thence, and for such live stock as they can possibly
contain, which, it is supposed, can be procured there without any sort of

difficulty, and at the most reasonable rates, for the use of the settlement at large.

That Government should immediately provide a certain number of ships of a proper burthen to receive on board at least seven or eight hundred convicts, and that one of them should be properly fitted for the accommodation of the women, to prevent their intercourse with the men.

That these ships should take on board as much provisions as they can possibly stow, or at least a sufficient quantity for two years consumption; supposing one year to be issued at whole allowance, and the other year's provisions at half allowance, which will last two years longer, by which time, it is presumed, the colony, with the live stock and grain which may be raised by a common industry on the part of the new settlers, will be fully sufficient for their maintenance and support.

That, in addition to the crews of the ships appointed to contain the convicts, a company of marines should be divided between them, to be employed as guards for preventing ill consequences that might arise from dissatisfaction amongst the convicts, and for the protection of the crew in the navigation of the ship from insults that might be offered by the convicts.

That each of the ships should have on board at least two surgeons' mates, to attend to the wants of the sick, and should be supplied with a proper assortment of medicines and instruments, and that two of them should remain with the settlement.

After the arrival of the ships which are intended to convey the convicts, the ship of war and tender may be employed in obtaining live stock from the Cape, or from the Molucca Islands, a sufficient quantity of which may be brought from either of these places to the new settlement in two or three trips; or the tender, if it should be thought most adviseable, may be employed in conveying to the new settlement a further number of women from the Friendly Islands, New Caledonia, etc., which are contiguous thereto, and from whence any number may be procured without difficulty; and without a sufficient number of that sex it is well-known that it would be impossible to preserve the settlement from gross irregularities and disorders.

The whole regulation and management of the settlement should be committed to the care of a discreet officer, and provision should be made in all cases, both civil and military, by special instructions under the Great Seal or otherwise, as may be thought proper.

Upon the whole, it may be observed with great force and truth that the difference of expence (whatever method of carrying the convicts thither may be adopted) that this mode of disposing of them and that of the usual ineffectual one is too trivial to be a consideration with the Government, at least in comparison with the great object to be obtained by it, especially now the evil is increased to such an alarming degree, from the inadequacy of all other expedients that have hitherto been tried or suggested.

It may not be amiss to remark in favour of this plan that considerable advantage will arise from the cultivation of the New Zealand hemp or flax-plant in the new intended settlement, the supply of which will be of great consequence to us as a naval power, as our manufacturers are of opinion that canvas made of it would be superior in strength and beauty to any canvas made of the European material, and that a cable of the circumference of ten inches made from the former would be superior in strength to one of eighteen inches made of the latter. The threads and filaments of this New Zealand plant are formed by nature with the most exquisite delicacy, and may be so minutely divided as to be manufactured into the finest linens.

Most of the Asiatic productions may also without doubt be cultivated in the new settlement, and in a few years may render our recourse to our European friends for those productions unnecessary.

It may also be proper to attend to the possibility of procuring from New Zealand any quantity of masts and ship timber for the use of our fleets in India, as the distance between the two countries is not greater than that between Great Britain and America. It grows close to the water's edge, is of size and quality superior to any hitherto known, and may be obtained without difficulty . . .

ESTIMATE OF CLOTHING TO SERVE A MALE CONVICT FOR ONE YEAR

	No.	Value each.	
Jackets	2	s. d.	£ s. d.
Woollen drawers	4	4 6	0 9 0
Hat	1	2 0	0 8 0
Shirts	3	2 6	0 2 6
Worsted stockings	4 pr.	3 0	0 9 0
Frocks	3	1 0	0 4 0
Trousers	3	2 3	0 6 9
Shoes	3 pr.	2 3	0 6 9
		4 6	0 13 6
			£2 19 6

The expence of clothing female convicts may be computed to amount to the like sum.

Document 1.2 An English journal prints a 'human interest' story about convicts bound for Botany Bay

Scot's Magazine *presented the following story to its middle-class readers late in 1786, while the convict transports bound for New South Wales were still loading their human cargo. The young convict couple at the centre of the story are Susannah Holmes and Henry Kable. Both had been convicted of robbery. Kable was about 21 years old in 1786, and Holmes perhaps a little older.*

The sentimental readers of Scot's Magazine were so moved by this story that they donated twenty pounds' worth of books and clothing to the couple. Most of the people who were literate enough to read magazines had ideas about love and marriage that differed from those of the rest of the population, and Holmes and Kable would have barely recognised themselves—and their relationship—in the story as told. But they did choose to marry as soon as they arrived in New South Wales, and prospered with the colony.[2]

November 1786

NARRATIVE RELATING TO A CONVICT ORDERED TO BE TRANSPORTED TO BOTANY BAY

In consequence of the late determination of government to send some convicts to Botany Bay, with a design of establishing a colony in New South Wales, an order lately came down to the keeper of Norwich Gaol to send such female convicts as were then in prison to Plymouth, to be in readiness to go upon that expedition. Three unhappy women, who had been a long while in the castle under sentence of transportation, were accordingly sent, and were committed to the care of Mr Simpson, turnkey of the prison. One of these unfortunate females was the mother of an infant about five months old, a very fine babe, whom she had suckled from its birth. The father of the child was likewise a felon under similar sentence, and had been in prison more than three years. He had repeatedly expressed a wish to be married to this woman, and though seldom permitted to see the child, he discovered a remarkable fondness for it; and that the mother's only comfort was derived from its smiles, was evident from her particularly tender manner nursing it. When the order came down for her removal, the man was much distressed, and very importunate to attend the woman, and application was made to the minister to permit him to go; but so many similar applications having been made, this could not be complied with. The miserable woman was therefore obliged to go without the man, who offered to be her husband, that he might be her companion and protector during a long and melancholy voyage, and in a distant and unknown land. The child, however, was still her property, as the laws of England, which are distinguished by the spirit of humanity which framed them, forbid so cruel an act as that of separating an infant from its mother's breast.

When Mr Simpson arrived at Plymouth with his party, he found that they were to be put on board a hulk, which lies there till the ship which goes to the South Sea is ready to take them. He therefore took a boat, and went to the vessel to deliver up his prisoners. Some forms, which the gaoler of Norwich had not been apprised of, having been omitted, the Captain of the hulk at first refused to take them, and these miserable creatures were kept three hours in an open boat, before they were received into their new abode of wretchedness. And when they were admitted, the Captain, finding that one of them had an infant, peremptorily refused to take it on board, saying, that he had no orders to take children; neither the intreaties of Mr Simpson, not the agonies of the poor wretch, could prevail upon the Captain even to permit the babe to remain until instructions could be received from the minister. Simpson was therefore obliged to take the child; and the frantic mother was led to her cell, execrating the cruelty of the man under whose care she was now placed, and vowing to put an end to her life as soon as she could obtain the means. Shocked at the nonparalleled brutality of the Captain, and his humanity not less affected by the agonies of the poor woman, and the situation of the helpless babe, Mr Simpson resolved still, if possible, to get it restored to her. No way was left but an immediate personal application to Lord Sydney; and having once before been with his Lordship on a business of humanity, he was encouraged to hope that he should succeed, could he but have an interview with him. He therefore immediately went back to Plymouth, and set off in the first coach to London, carrying the child all the way on his knee, and feeding it at the different inns he arrived at as well as he could.

When he came to London, he placed the child with a careful woman, and instantly posted to Lord Sydney's. Neither his Lordship nor his secretary were to be spoken to, at least this was told him when he addressed the person in waiting at the office: but humanity will not be restrained by forms; acting under the influence of a superior power, it moves forward, unchecked by the fear of offending any earthly one. Mr Simpson was denied admittance, but in vain; for he pressed forward into one of the offices, and told his story to one of the secretaries, who attended very properly to it, and promised to do all in his power to promote the object of his humane petition, but feared it would be impossible for him to see Lord Sydney for several days; he begged, however, of this gentleman to prepare an order for the restoration of the child, and determined to wait in the hall for the chance of seeing his Lordship pass, that he might prevail on him to sign it. Fortunately, not long after, he saw Lord Sydney descend the stairs; he instantly ran to him; his Lordship very naturally shewed an unwillingness at first to attend to an application made to him in so strange and abrupt a manner, but Mr Simpson immediately related the reason of his intrusion, and described, as he felt, the exquisite misery he had lately been witness to, expressing his fears, lest, in the instant he was pleading for her, the unhappy woman, in the wildness of her despair, should have deprived herself of existence. Lord Sydney was greatly affected, and paid much attention to the particular circumstances of his narration, and instantly promised that the child should be restored, commending, at the same time, Mr Simpson's spirit and humanity. Encouraged by this, he made a further appeal to his Lordship's humanity in behalf of the father of the child, which proved equally successful; for his Lordship ordered that he likewise should be sent to Plymouth to accompany the child and its mother, directing at the same time, that they should be married before they went on board, and adding, that he himself would pay the fees.

One of his Lordship's secretaries wrote immediately to Plymouth, that the woman might be informed of the success of Mr Simpson's application; and he, after visiting the child, and giving directions that it might be taken care of in his absence, set off for Norwich, and communicated the glad tidings to the unhappy father of the child. The poor man, who is a fine healthy young fellow, seemed very grateful to Lord Sydney and to Mr Simpson, and was made very happy by this change of circumstances; and it is to be hoped that he may, notwithstanding his past situation, turn out a useful individual of the new community. He set off for Plymouth, accompanied by Mr Simpson, who, after the fatigues, anxieties, and vexations of his first journey to that place, having travelled three days and nights without sleep, no doubt will be amply recompensed by the satisfaction he must experience, in thus having been the means of rescuing two unhappy people from a situation of distress scarcely to be equalled.

It is proper to observe, that Captain Phillips, who is to go out with the convicts to Botany Bay, is a man of very different disposition to the person alluded to in this narrative; but he, unfortunately, had no power to interfere.

The conclusion of the above relation cannot be more properly given, than in the words of Mr Simpson himself, who wrote the following letter a few days ago to a gentleman in Bath:

Dear Sir,

It is with the utmost pleasure that I inform you of my safe arrival with my little charge at Plymouth: but it would take an abler pen than mine to describe the joy that the mother received her infant and her intended husband with. Suffice it to say, that their transports, that the tears that flowed from their eyes, with the innocent smiles of the babe, on the sight of the mother, who had saved her milk for it, drew tears likewise from my eyes; and it was with the utmost regret that I parted with the child, after having travelled with it on my lap for upwards of 700 miles backwards and forwards. But the blessings I received at the different inns on the road have amply repaid me.

—I am, with great respect, your humble servant,

John Simpson
Plymouth Nov. 16

Document 1.3 An Officer of the Marines struggles to control some refractory convict women

The following are extracts from the journal that Ralph Clark, Officer of the Marines, wrote on board the transport ship Friendship, *which carried men and women convicts to Botany Bay in 1787. They describe his dealings with those of the convict women who continually defied the authority of the officers. Clark's hostility towards these women was partly due to the fact that as officer in charge of security aboard* Friendship *he was responsible for keeping them in good order. His view was also coloured by a strong attachment to an ideal of chaste and modest femininity; he kept a portrait of his young wife under his pillow and kissed it solemnly once a week. The refractory women were a minority of those aboard* Friendship—*about eight out of twenty—but Clark tended to generalise all the women on board and indeed all convict women as 'damned whores'.*

Before the fleet sailed the crew broke through the reinforced bulkhead dividing their quarters from those of the women, and four of the women were discovered in the men's hammocks. At the point where the extracts begin, the crew were refusing to sail the ship—a powerful threat—unless they got more meat in their rations.

Clark's lack of punctuation and shaky grammar suggest that he enjoyed only a brief period of education.[3]

18 May 1787

. . . I never met with a parcel of more discontented fellows in my life they only want more provisions to give it to the damned whores the convict women of whom they are very fond since they broke through the Bulkhead and had connection with them. I never could have thought that there were so many abandoned women in England, they are ten thousand times worse than the men Convicts, and I am afraid that we will have a great deal more trouble with them . . .

19 June 1787

. . . Meredith put the four convict women Elizabeth Dudgeon, Margaret Hall, Elizabeth Pulley, Charlotte Ware out of irons, whom I had put in irons the 9th of this month for fighting, there were never three great whores living than they are, and the four of them that went through the bulk-head while we lay at the Mother Bank, I am convinced that they will not be long out of them they are a disgrace to their whole sex, Bitches that they are, I wish the women were out of the ship . . .

3 July 1787

Was called up by the Captain of the ship last night informing us that his men had broke through the Women's Convicts Bulkhead again and that he had caught four of the women in the men's place, four of the number that had gone through while we lay at the Mother Bank and two of them that I had put in irons for fighting. I thought as I have said before that these Damned troublesome whores would not be long before they got there again. Made the signal to speak to the Commander the Capt went on board. The Commander who ordered the men that the women were with to be brought on board of him, sent the Carpenter, the Boatswain, the Steward and one of the seamen to, being the four men that Elizabeth Dudgeon, Elizabeth Pulley, Elizabeth Hackley, Sarah McCormick were with, whom the commander ordered flogged, except the Carpenter, and ordered the four women to be kept in irons all the way. If I had been the Commander, I should have flogged the four whores too.

5 July 1787

[Elizabeth Dudgeon was flogged] . . . she has been long fishing for it, which she has at last got, until her heart's content.

18 July 1787

[Elizabeth Barber, not one of those involved in breaching the bulkhead, was] . . . abusing the doctor in a most terrible manner and said he wanted to f—k her, and called him all the names she could think of . . . [the Captain held an inquiry, and Barber insisted on her charges] . . . she was very much in liquor, she was ordered on a pair of big irons, when she was getting them on she began to abuse Captain Meredith in a much worse manner than she had done the Doctor, she called him everything but a gentleman and said she was no more a whore than his wife . . . in all the course of my days I never heard such expressions from the mouth of a human being. The Captain ordered her hands to be tied behind her back and to be gagged to prevent her making any noise. She hoped and she was certain that she should see us all thrown overboard before we got to Botany Bay. From the bottom of my heart I dont think that the Doctor Mr Arundell ever offered any such thing to the brute. She desired Meredith to come and kiss her C—t for he was nothing but a lousy rascal as we were all, I wish to God she were out of the ship . . .

24 July 1787

It blew hard in the night, the Fleet being all in company. Put Mrs Macnamara both legs in irons for being impertinent to the Convict cook, put also again Elizabeth Barber in Irons who was let out when Margaret Hall was yesterday, she being handcuffed with her, handcuffed her with Elizabeth Tackney and put big irons on Elizabeth Pulley who was handcuffed with Elizabeth Tackney before . . .

25 July 1787

Blew very hard in the night . . . Shipped several in the course of the day, the Doctor begged that S MacCormick might be put out of irons she being very unwell . . .

26 July 1787

The doctor desired that Elizabeth Pulley might be put out of irons she being very ill, having a blister upon her . . .

1 August 1787

. . . Captain Meredith put Elizabeth Barber and Elizabeth Tackney in irons together and Elizabeth Dudgeon and Elizabeth Pulley together, the doctor having reported them well again, except Sarah MacCormick, the damned whore, the moment they got below fell a fighting amongst each other and Captain Meredith ordered the Serjiant not to report them but to let them fight it out, which I think he is very wrong in letting them do so . . .

Document 1.4 An English gentleman attempts to understand Aboriginal women and Aboriginal family life

David Collins collected his observations of the Koori women living around Sydney Harbour in an appendix to his journal describing the first years of the British colony. The journal was published in London in 1798. Collins and the other educated men in the colony took what they believed to be a scientific interest in Koori life and culture, and especially in Koori women. In the first incident described here, Collins asked some European women to attend an Aboriginal birth so that they could tell him what happened; one of them took an active and unwanted part. Warreweer, Boorrong, Goroobarrooboollo, Bennilong, and others of the Karingal people lived easily among the white invaders at this period, regarding them as friends and equals. Collins appears to write here as an objective observer, but he assumes throughout that European women have a more honourable place in European society than Koori women do in Koori society.[4]

c.1791

During the time of parturition these people suffer none but females to be present. War-re-weer, Bennillong's sister, being taken in labour in the town, an opportunity offered of observing them in that critical juncture, of which some of our women, who were favourites with the girl, were desired to avail themselves; and from them we learned, that during her labour one female, Boo-roong, was employed in pouring cold water from time to time on the abdomen, while another, tying one end of small line round War-re-weer's neck, with the other end rubbed her own lips until they bled. She derived no actual assistance from those who were about her, the child coming into the world by the sole efforts of nature; neither did any one receive it from her; but having let it drop, one of our women divided the umbilical cord; after which, she retired to a small hole which had been prepared for her, over which she sat until the after-birth took place. The person who cut the navel-string washed the child, which she readily permitted, though Boo-rong and the other natives objected to it. She appeared much exhausted, and being faint, fell across a fire that was in the place, but without receiving any injury.

I saw Bennillong's wife a few hours after she had been delivered of a child. To my great surprise she was walking about alone, and picking up sticks to mend her fire. The infant, whose skin appeared to have a reddish cast, was lying in a piece of soft bark on the ground, the umbilical cord depending about three inches from the navel. I remained with her for some time, during which she was endeavouring to get it off; to effect which she made use of the small bone of the kangaroo, round the point of which Bennillong had rolled some punk, so that it looked not unlike the button of a foil. She held it every now and then to the fire, then applied and pressed it to the navel until it cooled. This was persevered in, till the mother thought the cord sufficiently deadened, and then with a shell she separated it.

[Collins added a footnote here: 'I find in my papers a note, that for some offence Bennillong had severely beaten this woman in the morning, a short time before she was delivered.']

The infant thus produced is by the mother carried about for some days on a piece of soft bark; and, as soon as it acquires strength enough, is removed to her shoulders, where it sits with its little legs across her neck; and taught by necessity, soon catches hold of her hair to preserve itself from falling.

The reddish cast of the skin soon gives place to the natural hue, a change that is much assisted by the smoke and dirt in which, from the moment of their existence, these children are nurtured. The parents begin early to decorate them after the custom of the country. As soon as the hair of the head can be taken hold of, fish-bones and the teeth of animals are fastened to it with gum. White clay ornaments their little limbs; and the females suffer the extraordinary amputation which they term mal-gum [removal of the first two joints of the little finger of the left hand] before they have quitted their seat on their mother's shoulders . . .

At an early age the females wear round the waist a small line made of twisted hair of the opossum, from the centre of which depend a few small uneven lines from two to five inches long, made of the same materials. This they term bar-rin, and wear until they are grown into women and are attached to men.

The union of the sexes takes place at an earlier period than is usual in colder regions. We have known several instances of very young girls who have been much and shamefully abused by the males.

From their earliest infancy the boys are accustomed to throwing the spear, and to the habit of defending themselves from it. They begin by throwing reeds at each other, and are soon very expert. They also, from the time when they can run, until prompted by manhood to realize their sports, amuse themselves with stealing the females, and treat them at this time very little worse than they do then . . .

Chastity was a virtue in which they certainly did not pride themselves; at least, we knew women who, for a loaf of bread, a blanket, or a shirt, gave up any claim to it, when either was offered by a white man; and many white men were found who held out the temptation. Several girls, who were protected in the settlement, had not any objection to passing the night on board of ships, though some had learned shame enough (for shame was not naturally inherent in them) to conceal, on their landing, the spoils they had procured during their stay. They had also observed that we thought it shameful to be seen naked; and I have observed many of them extremely reserved and delicate in this respect when before us; but when in the presence of only their own people, perfectly indifferent about their appearance . . .

I had long wished to be a witness of a family party, in which I hoped and expected to see them divested of that restraint which perhaps they might put on in our houses. I was one day gratified in this wish when I had little expected it. Having strolled down to the Point named Too-bow-gu-lie, I saw the sister and the young wife of Bennillong coming round the Point in the new canoe which the husband had cut in his last excursion to Parramatta. They had been out to procure fish, and were keeping time with their paddles, responsive to the words of a song, in which they joined with much good humour and harmony. They were almost immediately joined by Bennillong, who had his sister's child on his shoulders. The canoe was hauled on shore, and what fish they had caught the women brought up. I observed that the women seated themselves at some little distance from Bennillong, and then the group was thus disposed of—the husband was seated on a rock, preparing to dress and eat the fish he had just received. On the same rock lay his pretty sister War-re-weer asleep in the sun, with a new born infant in her arms; and at some little distance were seated, rather below him, his other sister and his wife, the wife opening and eating some rock-oysters, and the sister suckling her child, Kah-dier-rang, who she had taken from Bennillong. I cannot omit mentioning the unaffected simplicity of the wife: immediately on her stepping out of her canoe, she gave way to the pressure of a certain necessity, without betraying any of that reserve which would have led another at least behind the adjoining bush. She blushed not, for the cheek of Go-roo-bar-roo-bool-lo was the cheek of rude nature, and not made for blushes. I remained with them until the whole party fell asleep.

Document 1.5 An English lady discovers the natural wonders of New South Wales

Elizabeth Macarthur (1766–1850) came to New South Wales in 1790 with her husband John, an army officer. The document below is an

extract from a very much longer letter, written over the months
between sailings to England. Mrs Macarthur is writing as much to
amuse herself as to inform her lady friend about New South Wales.
There is no woman in the colony she can talk to as a friend: the
clergyman's wife is not really a lady; the Koori women are no more
than interesting curiosities; the convict and servant women who keep
her house and tend her children do not rate a mention, though it is
their labour that makes possible her leisurely way of life. In later years
Elizabeth Macarthur became a pioneer farmer and sheep breeder;
here her energies are constrained by the demands of genteel femi-
ninity and a chronically sick husband.[5]

Sydney, Port Jackson, N.S.Wales,
March 7th, 1791

To Miss Kingdon.

. . . I shall begin my relation now of things more immediately occurring
to myself. It will be unnecessary to go over the chit-chat of my last letter,
such as the state of our house, the attentions we met with, etc., etc.

We passed our time away many weeks cheerfully if not gaily—gaily
indeed it could not be said to be. On my first landing everything was new
to me, every Bird, every Insect, Flower, etc.; in short, all was novelty
around me, and was noticed with a degree of eager curiosity and pertur-
bation, that after a while subsided into that calmness I have already
described. In my former letter I gave you the character of Mr Dawes, and
also of Captain Tench. These Gentlemen and a few others are the chief
among whom we visit. Indeed we are in the habit of intimacy with Captain
Tench that there are few days pass that we do not spend some part of
together. Mr Dawes we do not see so frequently. He is so much engaged
with the stars that to mortal eyes he is not always visible. I have had the
presumption to become his pupil and meant to learn a little of astronomy.
It is true that I have had many pleasant walks to his house (something
less than half a mile from Sydney), having given him much trouble in
making orreries, and explaining to me the general principles of the
heavenly bodies, but I soon found I had mistaken my abilities and blush
at my error. [Ladylike education lacked the necessary mathematics.] Still,
I wanted something to fill up a certain vacancy in my time which could
neither be done by writing, reading or conversation. To the two first I did
not feel myself always inclined, and the latter was not in my power, having
no female friend to unbend my mind to, not a single woman with whom
I could converse with any satisfaction to myself, the Clergyman's wife

being a person in whose society I could reap neither profit or pleasure. These considerations made me still anxious to learn some easy science to fill up the vacuum of many a solitary day, and at length under the auspices of Mr Dawes I have made a small progress in Botany. No country can exhibit a more copious field for botanical knowledge than this. I am arrived so far as to able to class and order all common plants. I have found great pleasure in my study; every walk furnished me with subjects to put in practice that Theory I had before gained by reading, but alas my botanical pursuits were most unwelcomely interrupted by Mr Macarthur being attacked by a severe illness. In December he got better, and in January we were removed into a more convenient house . . .

Of my walks around Sydney the longest has not extended beyond three miles, and that distance I have I believe, only ventured upon twice: once to a farm which Captain Nepean has for his Company, to which we sent our tea equipage and drank tea on the turf, and once to a hill situated between this and Botany Bay where I could command a prospect of that famous spot. Nor do I think there is any probability of my seeing much of the inland country until it is cleared, as beyond a certain distance round the Colony there is nothing but native paths, very narrow and very incommodious. The natives are certainly not a very gallant set of people, who take pleasure in escorting their ladies. No; they suffer them humbly to follow Indian file like. As I am now speaking of the natives, I must give you an account of how we stand with them. [Here she gives a long account of relations between the Koori people and the invaders, culminating in the spearing of Governor Phillip, and the peaceful cohabitation that followed that event.]

. . . since that period the natives visit us every day, more or less. Men, Women and children, they come with great confidence, without spears or any other offensive weapons. A great many have taken up their abode entirely amongst us, and Bannylong and Coleby, with their wives, come in frequently. Mrs Coleby, whose name is Daringa, brought in a new born female infant of hers for me to see, about six weeks since. It was wrapped up in the soft bark of a tree, a specimen of which I have preserved; it is a kind of mantle not much known in England I fancy. I ordered something for the poor woman to eat, and had her taken proper care of for some little while. When she first presented herself to me she appeared feeble and faint; she has since been regular in her visits. The child thrives remarkably well, and I discover a softness and gentleness of manner in Daringa truly interesting. We do not in general encourage them to come to our houses, as you may conceive there are some offensive circumstances which make their company by no means desirable, unless it be those who live wholly with us. A good deal of their language (if it may be so called) is now understood, but we can learn nothing from them respecting the interior part of the country. It seems they are as much unacquainted with it as ourselves. All their knowledge and pursuits are confined to that of procuring for themselves a bare subsistence. They chiefly abide about the sea coast, the women appear to be under very great subjection. They are employed in the most laborious part of their work; they fish and also make the lines and hooks, and indeed seem very little otherway than slaves to their husbands. They weave their lines from the bark of a certain tree, which we call May from the perfume the flower has which strongly resembles the White thorn that blows in that month in England. Their hooks they grind into form from a shell; they perform this with great dexterity upon any rough stone. Their canoes are made of the bark of some of their gum trees, taken off in a particular form for that purpose. These they paddle about the caves and bays very dexterously. The weapons they use are a spear, a wooden sword, a stone adze or axe, and fish gig; the latter is wholly used in spearing fish in the water. The spears which they aim and discharge with wonderful ingenuity at a great distance are some of them most dangerous weapons, having many barbs in them and sharpened shells, but they are still under such terror of our firearms that a single armed man would drive a hundred natives with their spears, and we take care not to venture walking to any distance unarmed, a soldier or two always attending when we make any excursion. I have never yet met a single native in the woods . . .

My spirits are at this time low, very low, tomorrow we lose some valuable members of our small society and some very good friends. In so small a society we sensibly feel the loss of every member, more particularly those that are endeared to us by acts of kindness and friendship. From this circumstance and my former letters you may be led to question my happiness, but this much I can with truth add for myself, that since I have had the powers of reason and reflection I never was more sincerely happy than at this time. It is true that I have some wishes unaccomplished, but when I consider this is not a state of perfection I am abundantly content.

Adieu,

E. Macarthur

Document 1.6 An emancipated convict considers her life in the colony

The ability of Margaret Catchpole (1762–1819) to write this letter to friends in England of itself makes her exceptional among convict women, and the details of her life confirm this. She was transported to New South Wales for the unfeminine crime of horse-stealing, committed in a vain attempt to assist her lover, a smuggler. After earning her ticket of leave she seems to have decided to live independently, whereas the great majority of women took partners, legal or otherwise, to help them survive. Margaret Catchpole's letters reveal a woman with great strength of mind and body, and an uncertain grasp of spelling, corrected in this letter. She did not see her English home and friends before she died.[6]

2 September 1811

I am not [married] and almost fifty years old nor do I intend. I hope to see home once more and to see dear Cousin Charles weigh a pound of tea for me and that fine strong young man Samuel make me a pair of shoes and poor Lucy to thread my needle, for my eyes are not so good as they were, but thank God I can do so well as I do. I rent a little farm, about fifteen acres, but half of it standing timber and the cleared ground I hire men to put in my corn and I work a great deal myself. I have got thirty sheep and forty goats, thirty pigs and 2 dogs, they take care of me for I live all alone, not one in the house. There is a house within twenty roods of me [about 100 metres], I have a good many friends that I go to see when I think proper, such as I have nursed when they lay in [in childbirth] cannot do without me, I am looked upon very well thank God. I hope to get a few pounds to come home with. The white frosty mornings is just the saving of us, it has been very cold indeed this winter, but nothing like your snow—that was very shocking indeed. I am very sorry to hear that you have lost your friend and I am very sorry that I have lost a good friend like Mrs Slorgin for she sent me this time 12 yards of Irish cloth, 3 yards of ribbon, 3 good books and writing paper and this is some of it. Mrs Cobbold sent me a very handsome present 2 pieces for nine caps four lace ones, one just as it came off her own head which I thought more of than anything I put it on directly and many more things too long to mention. My dear Aunt, your hair is kissed and cried over, I will always keep it and I have the other by me that you sent and hope the next time you send you will send some of Lucy's and Charles' hair. Dear Uncle, you must think I can walk well for when I heard there was a box for me,

I set off and walked fifty miles in two days. You cannot tell the happiness it gave me, and tell my friends I was overjoyed to hear of it, now this will give me great happiness for a long time and I hope Lucy will always be dutiful to her mother as my dear aunt must be getting into years, for I do not grow younger myself and have lost all my front teeth, I can stir about as briskly as ever and am in good spirits. Dear uncle I hope when you write again you will send me word of all friends and thank you for the newspapers, and I wish I could send you some, but there is no time, the ship is going to sail directly so I must conclude with my sincere love to you and all my cousins and pray to God to keep his Bliss upon you all and not forgetting myself adieu.

Margaret Catchpole

I am very proud of my dear Charles' letter and sorry I had not time to answer it but I will the next time. James will soon get a rich man I think if he minds Samuel and I hope will overtake them. By taking care this place is getting very plentiful, but everything is very dear, beef mutton and pork 15 to 18 pence per pound, wheat from 12 to 15 shillings per bushell, butter five shillings per pound.

On March the fourteenth is my birthday, then I am fifty years old.

Document 1.7 A sea captain remembers the labours of Aboriginal women in the sealing trade

James Kelly was an English seaman, employed during the 1810s by a Hobart trader to collect seal skins from the European and Aboriginal sealers who worked along the coasts and islands of Bass Strait. Women made up the workforce supporting this operation and many lived with the convict sealers. Later observers represented these women as slaves, exploited by black and white men both; Document 1.10 presents evidence supporting this view. Kelly's women are certainly not slaves, but his account of them was written many years later and had a case to argue. The version presented here was published in The Hobart Town Courier *in 1854.*[7]

18 January 1816

The natives asked if we would bring over more seals on the following day. Briggs [an ex-convict] informed them that they were getting scarce and shy of being caught. Tolo [Tolobunganah, the leader of the Aboriginal group] considered that we had better take some women over to the island to assist in catching them, as they were very dexterous at sealing. This of course being agreed to, Tolo ordered six stout women into the boat. They obeyed with alacrity, evidently delighted with the prospects of the trip. The wind being fair, we ran over to the island, hauled the boat up, and pegged out the kangaroo skins to dry. The women, perceiving some seals on the outer rocks, were anxious to commence operations.

We gave the women each a club that we had used to kill the seals with. They went to the water's edge and wet themselves all over their heads and bodies, which operation they said would keep the seals from smelling them as they walked along the rocks. They were very cautious not to go windward of them, as they said 'a seal would sooner believe his nose than his eyes when a man or woman came near him'. The women all walked into the water in couples, and swam to three rocks about sixty yards from the shore. There were about nine or ten seals upon each rock, lying apparently asleep. Two women went to each rock with their clubs in hand, crept closely up to a seal each, and lay down with their clubs alongside. Some of the seals lifted their heads up to inspect their new visitors and smell them. The seals scratched themselves and lay down again.

The women went through the same motions as the seal, holding up their left elbow and scratching themselves with their left hand, taking and keeping the club in their right ready for the attack. The seals seemed very cautious, now and then lifting up their heads and looking around scratching themselves as before and lying down again; the women still imitating each movement as nearly as possible. After they had lain upon the rocks nearly an hour, the sea occasionally washing over them (as they were quite naked, we could not tell the meaning of their remaining so long) all of a sudden the women rose up in their seats, their clubs lifted at arms length, each struck the seals on the nose and killed him; in an instant they all jumped up as if by magic and killed one more each. After giving the seals several blows on the head, and securing them, they commenced laughing aloud and dancing. They each dragged the seal into the water, and swam with it back to the rock upon which we were standing, and then went back and brought another each, making twelve seals, the skins of which were worth one pound each in Hobart Town. This was not a bad beginning for the black ladies, who now ascended to the top of the small hill, and made smokes as signals to the natives on the main that they had taken some seals. The smokes were soon answered by smokes on the beach. We skinned the seals and pegged them out to dry. The women then commenced to cook their supper, each cutting a shoulder off the young seals weighing about three or four pounds. They simply threw them on the fire to cook, and when about half done commenced devouring them, and rubbed the oil on their skins, remarking that they had had a glorious meal.

Document 1.8 A gentry wife works to maintain family ties

Christiana Jane Blomfield (1802–1852) wrote this affectionate letter to her husband's brothers and sisters whom she had never met. The task of maintaining the channels through which emotional and often financial support flowed from Britain usually fell to wives, whatever the class of the family. Like Elizabeth Macarthur (Document 1.5), Christiana Blomfield depended greatly on the work of women convict servants, mentioned here only in their compulsory attendance at family prayers. Unlike Macarthur, she enjoyed some feminine support in the battle of the sexes.[8]

Newcastle, Hunter's River,
2nd June, 1825

My dear Sisters and Brothers,—About a month ago we secured your welcome packet, and although it contained some melancholy intelligence yet we were happy to hear when the latest letters were written that all our dear friends were well, and I hope we shall hear continual good accounts of my brother Edward's and my niece Louisa's health. I am glad you were all pleased at my letter, and as you say you like my way of writing I shall be most happy to become a correspondent. I am a bad one generally, as I cannot bear formal letters and I scarce ever write to anyone but my own family, but now I know you all I shall feel equal pleasure in writing to you, so will begin and tell you what has passed since I last wrote. I believe I told you that I was expecting your brother, as he had written to me to tell me that he wished to see his wife, so as I was anxious to see him he came up to fetch me down to Newcastle, as he was offered the Government cottage to live in while our own house was building. It is only three miles from our farm, and in June last he came up for us. Just about the same time we received Edwin's letter, which enabled us to draw our money, and after making many necessary purchases we left my father's house on the 24th of last August to come down here, but we were unavoidably detained in Sydney a few weeks, very much against our will, for want of a vessel, and I was beginning to be very anxious, when fortunately we got a passage in a very comfortable vessel and were only ten hours at sea. On the 21st of September we were comfortably settled in this cottage. You will not wonder at my being anxious when I tell you that on the 27th October I was confined, and another little boy made his appearance, and a very fine little fellow he is . . .

Now . . . I'll tell you how we employ our time. In summer time we rise early, but at this time of the year we get up about 7 o'clock. The children are awake at daylight and are soon dressed and running about. After we are dressed we have family prayers. Thomas reads them to myself, the children, and one or two female servants, and both Thomas and Richard kneel by their father and are quiet all the time. After prayers we get our breakfast. Richard and Thomas sit up with us, Richard by me and Thomas by his papa, and when they have drunk their tea and eaten their bread and butter they are in a hurry to get down, so after 'Thank God for my good breakfast' away they skip to play with their wheelbarrows, which is their chief amusement. After breakfast Thomas's mare is saddled and he goes to the farm, where he remains until 4 o'clock. In the meantime I sleep my baby, see the house is put to rights, give out what is wanted for dinner, teach little Tom to read, and Richard comes for his lesson, which is generally P for papa and M for mama, and C for Cow or Onginge, as he calls orange. Tom is much amused and says 'Poor little thing, he don't know better; when he is as big as me he will say it right, won't he ma?' We do not dine until five, as Thomas cannot leave the farm sooner, or there would be little work done. After dinner the children are washed, have their tea, and go to bed, after which Thomas and I walk in the verandah until it is dark, and he tells me what he has been doing at the farm. We get our tea comfortably together and enjoy an hour or two in quiet. I generally work and he reads to me, or we talk of the improvements we intend making when we get to 'Dagworth'. At nine or ten o'clock we have evening prayers and go to bed, and if the children will let us, sleep very soundly. As we are 20 miles from any church we read the church service on Sunday to our servants twice a day and Bland's sermons or some other religious book. I dare say it will not be very long before we have a church and clergyman in the neighbourhood, as it is becoming a very populous district, and as I have always been used to attend public worship regularly, I shall be very glad when I can do this again, and take my children. Dear little Tom is always asking questions. The other day I had been telling him that if he was good and said his prayers that God would love him and give him everything. He said directly, 'What, lots of pancakes and sugar?' Poor little innocent fellow, that is his idea of everything that is good, but he will, I hope, soon know better. He was four years old on the 26th of last month, and he fancies himself a very tall fellow . . . He is very fond of horses, and is always talking about them. I think he will be clever. He has such a good memory, and is always thinking of what he used to do and say when he was at his grandfather's. He also talks of his England grandfather and aunt, as we teach him to think of you. He is much taken with the name of Aunt Louisa, and never forgets to drink your health. He remembers you all also when he says his prayers on going to bed. Richard also says his prayers prettily . . .

I do not know whether I told you that Mr Close had settled at Hunter's River. He was amongst the first people who took their land on the river. He was fortunate in getting a fine grant of land from Governor Macquarie, and has now a very comfortable house, a good barn, etc. He married a particular friend of mine. It was rather singular that Thomas and he, who were such good friends, should happen to marry us, who were playmates. Mrs Close is a very amiable young woman, but very delicate. We often meet, and while our two husbands are talking over their olden times in the Peninsular and bragging of the number of sweethearts, of all the victories they have had, we are also talking of some of our romping days when we were wild little girls. Now, do you not think it is very impudent of these gentlemen talking about their sweethearts before their wives? But between you and I, I think they only want to make us think the more of them and believe it is stories of their own making. Whenever Thomas begins I get quite angry and give him a good talking, which is the only way I have of revenging myself . . .

C. J.B.

Document 1.9 A lonely immigrant seamstress writes home

In 1833 Isabella Gibson came to New South Wales as an immigrant assisted by the government. She expected a young man (a brother? a lover?) to follow her, but heard nothing from him nor from her family. As a seamstress Miss Gibson was more skilled and more literate than most women immigrants. Her long and mostly unhappy letter gives an excellent account of both employment and marriage prospects for women in Sydney at this time. It demonstrates, too, the contraints and isolation imposed upon a single woman determined to retain her respectability.[9]

I send this by the Cognac Packet
Sydney, Jamieson Street,
19th June 1834.

Dear Sister

I wrote home on the 17th of Febry last which letter I hope will reach London about this time informing you that we arrvd at Sydney on the 16 Decr and that I had engaged here with a Mr Hunt to do his apholstary needle work, salery to be 8£ a year For several months after landing I

was afflicted with the scurvy and other complaints from which I have now
got quite better of and at present in good health I am much surprised and
disappointed at receiving no letter from you considering how strictly I
charged you to write soon and how faithfully you promised to do so It is
now ten months since I left home yet no letter from any of you I regularly
enquire at the post office every Packet that comes from England and as
often return home disappointed I can get no intelligence of the Mail Brigg
the ship Richard was to come by it is conjectured here that the owners
of it must have failed and in consiquence of that the ship will not come
here at all at this time but if so it is strange he has not come out by any
other ship whither he has changed his mind and is not coming at all or
what has become of him I cannot assertain I form numberless conjectures
but all in vain every day adds to my anxiety—I still remain at Mr Hunts
and at the end of the first quarter had my wages raised from 2£ to 3£ 10
which is 14£ a year this is the most they will give they are well satisfied
with me or they would not have advanced it so much but in addition to
my needlework I now have to make 8 beds and sweep out 6 rooms every
morning If I was assured that Richard would never come I would endeavour to return home as soon as possible if I could find it at all practicable
but I doubt whether it will ever be in my power Today I requisted the
editor of a newspaper to advertise me to engage with any family that was
going to England and wanted a female servant he said he might do so but
that I would find it a difficult matter to succeed there were such numerous
applications of the same kind by people that were disappointed in their
expectation of endeavouring to return home. he said that by advertising
he thought I might procure a bigger salary if I could undertake to be a
governess but in no other capacity accordingly I am going to advertise
for a nursery governess (that is to begin young children and take the charge
of them) free immigrants are sometimes allowed the privilege of inserting
an advertisement gratis in this newspaper so mine is at this time to be put
in free of expence, but I do not well know what is best to do ther are so
very few places that is any way tolerable here that I am afraid to risk
leaving Hunts they are such quiet people and have never once found fault
with me since I came to their house But I trust that providence will direct
me for the best for I have none either to care for or assist me Shop work
of any kind is rarely to be had here what is sold in the shops is mostly
all brought from London ready made Millinary and dressmaking are I
understand better paid for than what the dressmakers made me to believe
when I was trying amongst them for imployment they charge from three
shillings to 12 for making gowns and from 4 to 7 shillings for covering
a silk or Velvet bonnet willow for bonnet shapes 1/6d per sheet and 2/6

or 3 sh when made into a shape it is mostly gause ribbon that they are trimmed with here and that is about 2 sh per yd I lay out as little as possible on clothing but the family I am in require that their servants well dressed so I am obliged to do so I had my straw bonnet cleaned and pressed lately for which I paid 2/6 I regret that I have no person to live with me that I could trust to or I would take a room and make bonnets and frocks and sell a few toys, penny dolls sell here for 6d each or take in apolstering needlework Miss Veich the Scotch woman is the only person I could put any confidence in and I understand she is expecting to be married soon to a farmer about 150 miles up the country—A farmer and his family that came out with us in the ship went to live at that place and a few of his neighbour farmers employed him to return to Sidney and bespeak wives for them among the free women that he could recommend he fixed on Miss V for one and she has had two letters from the man saying that he intends to come to Sidney soon when if they approve of each other at sight they will be directly married If I was to give the least hint of such a thing being agreeable to me I believe I might have the same opportunity but I could not bring my mind however destitute I may be to think of marrying any person I had no regard for on this account I declined accepting of one offer I have had already from a man who has lived a while in this family as cook and butler an Englishman about 45 years of age he has been most of his life time a soldier and has now a pension of 15£ a year and a house and 20 acres of land from government about 70 miles from Sidney he has now left his service here and gone to live at his little property A number of the women that came out with me have married prisoners—Dear H I hope you will not on any account delay writing to me immediately on receiving this. on my account I would like to see you here but for my fathers sake and your own I could not advise you to come because I am consious by doing so you would run the risk of suffering more hardships than I would like to see any of you subjected to I hope Christina is continuing better that my father is keeping his health and that all of you are well let me know if the cholera has been in London this summer. being so close confined here I have almost no opportunity of hearing any news or seeing any of my ship acquaintances One of the elders of the Scotch kirk here is a shoemaker from Glasgow his wife is also a scotswoman she came here about 2 years ago as a ladies maid they are both very fine people and I have been in their house two or three times Mr Pinkerton the minister died lately after being long ill of a liver complaint. I am at present makeing my tweeded muslin gown that I brought out with me I do this in the evening after I leave of work and I am just now wearing the norwich crape one I got from you it has been

very useful to me and is not thought old fashioned here it is now the
middle of winter here and is very little colder than it is in the middle of
summer at home it is I think both the healthiest and the pleasantest time
of the year I dread the coming of the warm weather again If I could come
home I would not wish to remain here longer than the month of Feby
next. if so I might have time to have an answer to this letter from you
before I left here at all events if you are alive and well do not be so long
in writing to me again I now conclude by sending my best wishes to you
all and remain Dear Helen your affectionate sister Isabella Gibson

If I leave Mr Hunts soon or if anything of consiquence occur to me
I will write to you soon again

Direct to be left at the Post office Sidney till called for.

Document 1.10 An Aboriginal woman gives evidence of her exploitation in the sealing trade

*Sarah was brought from a sealers' camp to Flinders Island, established
by the government as a refuge (and gaol) for the few surviving
Aboriginal Tasmanians. Two Aboriginal women were sent to persuade
her to come in. Two days after her arrival she was interviewed by
George Augustus Robinson, the 'Commandant' of the Flinders Settlement, who had spent the last decade rescuing women from the sealers'
camps. Robinson's questions and Sarah's answers were recorded by
a missionary employed on the island. Like the sealer's reminiscence
in Document 1.7, the interview was not entirely objective.*[10]

3 June 1837

Sarah an Aboriginal Female of New Holland about twenty years of age
has been living with the Sealers for some time past arrived at this
Settlement on the night of the 1st June at 10 p.m. accompanied by the
Corporal and two women belonging to the Settlement and who had been
despatched the day previous to Wooddy Island in the Settlement Boat upon
this particular duty.

Question	Where is your country
Answer	Close to Kangaroo Island
Q	Who took you away
A	James Allen a Sealer and Bill Johnson was in company with him
Q	What age was you
A	Was a big Girl when they took me away

Q	How did they take you away
A	They tied me round the neck and led me like a dog
Q	Where did you go then
A	We stopt in the bush one night when they tied my hands and tied my feet
Q	What did you do in the morning
A	They took me in the Boat and took me to Kangaroo Island
Q	Was there anymore women
A	Plenty—All run away—James Allen and two blackfellows took me the other man looked after the boat
Q	What did you do then
A	I stopt at Kangaroo Island a long time with James Allen

After she had been living at Kangaroo Island for some time the Schooner 'Henry' John Griffith Master and bursar came to the Island and by and by Johnson stole her from Allen he tied her up and put her on board the Schooner with Harry Wally. They took her sealing and came to the Straits Johnson then gave her to Bill Dutton with whom she cohabited—Dutton about 12 months since/ie. Plenty of moons (The Commandant counted with his fingers 12 the number of moons she said it was since Dutton left her) took away her little girl and left her, in the Straits on Wooddy Island and married a white woman and she understands he had gone whaling— She does not like to stop at Wooddy Island—likes to stop here best—does not like the Sealers—would like to go to her own country.

Q	Does the sealers beat the women
A	Yes Plenty—the Sealers cut off a boys ear and the boy died and they cut a piece off a womans buttock
Q	Did Dutton ever beat you
A	Dutton beat me with a rope
Q	Who made you
A	I never heard him
Q	Who is Jesus Christ
A	I never heard him
Q	Would you like to hear about God
A	Yes would like to hear it
Q	Who made the trees the grass the sea
A	Dont know

Would like to learn book and hear about God. She did not get plenty to eat with the sealers only got a little one. The Sealers get drunk plenty and women get drunk too. The statement she says is true.

Document 1.11   A woman tries to escape from a violent husband

This document is a deposition—a statement given before a magistrate and used as evidence in cases brought to trial. It was sworn before a magistrate in Windsor, New South Wales, by Elizabeth Power. Her words, taken down by the magistrate's clerk, were often 'improved', but her voice can still be heard in the pace and phrasing of the statement. The additional information is taken from other depositions, and from further evidence given in court.

Elizabeth Power had been living for about twenty years with an ex-convict farmer, married for most of that time. Michael Power believed that they got on well enough: 'we were always very comfortable; scolding is nothing between man and wife; I have often struck her, but that is nothing between man and wife'. Elizabeth Power put it differently: 'My husband is a very passionate man, and he beats me sometimes'. Late in 1837 he hit her hard enough to cut her head badly, and she decided to leave, taking with her the orphan girl who helped her in the house and more than £500 in banknotes, profits that Power had made by fattening cattle for the Sydney market.

Her statement describes her efforts to make her way to the Derwent River in Tasmania where her married daughter lived. Elizabeth Power had no book learning. She could not read or write, needed help in counting large sums of money, and was not too sure about the days of the month. Schedules and timetables were beyond her ken; she needed help to catch the coach and steamship that would take her to Tasmania. The people from whom she sought help refused her, or in the end cheated her, and the neighbours who cleaned up her wounds called her husband to take her home—perhaps they too believed that blows were 'nothing between man and wife'.[11]

21 December 1837
County of Cumberland

To wit

Elizabeth Power having duly sworn maketh oath and Saith; I am the Wife of Michael Power of Wilberforce, about five or six weeks ago, I do not remember the day of the month, but I know it was on a Sunday My Husband was absent from home, about 3 Oclock in the Afternoon. I went to his Box, it was locked and he had the Keys with him, I took out the bottom of the Box, and took out some money which I knew he had there, it was a Bundle of Bank Notes and one cheque and some Silver My

Husband had placed it in the Box the night before, it was in a Blue Bag, and I took the whole of it, but cannot Say how much was in it—

After I got the money I left My Husbands house taking with me my little girl, Bridget Welsh who lives with me, we called at Patrick Craigans at Freeman's Reach, but only for a short time [for a drink of water], and then came to the Public house of Edward Coffee in Windsor, I got something to drink there and went to Bed with the girl Bridget Welsh. The next morning we Breakfasted at Coffees and remained there the whole day. I told Coffee that I had left my Husband in consequence of his illtreatment of me and intended going to the Derwent [in Tasmania, where she had a grown daughter living]. I told him that I had taken my husbands Money and I began to count it in Coffees presence laying some of it on his knee as I Counted it. [Coffee said that a friend, Dennis Dwyer, helped her count it.] I recollect counting to the amount of Three hundred and forty or fifty pounds, there was a good deal more to count but I was tired and did not finish counting them. I gathered them up and put them into the Bag again, Coffee promised to assist in getting me to the Derwent Said he would get a Box to forward my Clothes to Sydney next day and advised me to go to Sydney by the Mail that night, which I agreed to do, but drank too Much and was unable to proceed. Some time during the night the Constables came to the House to look for me [her husband had reported the theft] and Coffee . . . woke me and . . . by his advice went away taking the Girl with me. I had given Coffee at the time we were Counting the Money two ten pound notes which I have never got since, they were given to him in consequence of his promising to assist me in getting to the Derwent—After leaving Coffees I went to Michael Rafters ['a single man, a gossip of mine' according to her husband] . . . I asked him to get up and let me lay down, he did so . . . About the Break of day my Husband came with Mr. Hodghen the chief constable and Constable Armfield Mr Hodghen said he had a Warrant for me and I got up. Previous to their coming I had placed the Money under the pillow but they never Searched for it there or anywhere else, nor did they Search me . . . I was taken to the Watch house, it was then clear day.

[Bridget brought her the money at the watch house, but could not give it to her unseen.] At ten Oclock I was taken to the Police Officer, and after being examined by the Magistrate I was remanded, it was late in the day when I was sent back to the Watch house, passing Rafters I asked Mr Hodghen permission to go in there for Something I had left, he sent Horan the Watch house Keeper on with the remainder of the Prisoners, and he Mr Hodghen followed me into the Bed Room where the Girl Welsh was. I said to her 'Biddy where is that', She pointed to a corner and there

I found it, Mr Hodghen being present, we then left the house the Girl being with me, As we turned the Corner Mr Hodghen Said 'I see you have got it'. I nodded as much as to say I had, I desired the Girl to walk on before and I then said to Mr Hodghen, that if he would not deceive me I would make him a very handsome present he promised faithfully he would not, we were then near his house which was in our Road to the watch house, he asked me in . . . Hodghen pulled off his Hat and laying it on the Table Said here put it in the Hat, which I did, the money was there in the little Bag . . . he said you will want some change in the Watch house, I put my hand in the Bag and took out a half Crown a Shilling and a Penny. We then had some Tea together and a Glass of Brandy, after which he took me to the Watch house, it was then after Sun set . . .

[Hodghen took her back to his house next morning.] Before we sat down to Breakfast Mr. Hodghen gave me two half Crowns to send out for some Brandy, I sent out for a half a Pint [she told the court 'we took the brandy in our tea, which is the way poor people like it in the morning'] . . . at ten Oclock the Watch house Keeper called and took me to the Police Officer where I was discharged [it was impossible to charge a wife with stealing from her husband, the two being regarded as one person in law, with the wife having no legal identity] and my husband compelled me to go home with him . . .

After going home my Husband treated me very cruelly to compel me to say where the money was . . . [She told the court he 'beat me in a most unmerciful manner so that I had to keep to my bed for two or three days' after which she escaped to a neighbour] who washed the blood from off me. My husband came there and in consequence of his promises I returned home with him, but the next morning I found he had left the House taking with him all my clothes . . . I borrowed some clothes and after night fall on the day following I came into Windsor and went to Mr. Hodghens . . . Hodghen told me I could stop there, that there was no fear of me, and he should see by the Newspapers when there was a Ship going to Launceston . . . [A few days later they got the mail coach to pick her up.] Mr. Hodghen had given me a roll of notes tied up with red tape, I asked him how much was there He replied 'Your regulars' [she told the court 'I thought it was half, I did not expect the whole as I had promised him a handsome present']. When we arrived at Parramatta I determined to Stay there on account of my face being so much bruised ['. . . I was ashamed my face was so much disfigured . . .'] I went to the house of a friend one John Brown, a Cow Keeper, where I went into the garden and counted the notes and found Eighty three one pound notes, making in all Eighty four pounds I had received from Mr. Hodghen . . . When I had

been at Browns about three days my husband came there and took the
money from me . . . I accompanied him home, and remained with him
until he again illtreated me and I again left him, this was on a Tuesday
and I think last Tuesday fortnight I went to Mr. Hodghens . . . [Hodghen
again sent her in the mail coach to Sydney, this time with his daughter
and Mrs Power's friend Dennis Dwyer, but gave her no more money and
called his daughter back to Windsor after a week.] . . . I said I would go
with her as I could not stay there without money. We arrived the night
before last and . . . I got a friend to write a letter to Mr. Hodghen
demanding the money to which I have not received any answer . . .

Sworn to before me on 21st Dec. 1837	her
S. North J.P.	Elizabeth × Power
	mark

*The deposition above was sworn before the magistrate Samuel North
because, as Mrs Power later told the court, 'my husband hearing I
was in Windsor came to me and I went to Mr North and told him
everything'. Then she went home with her husband. Mr Hodghen and
his daughter were found guilty of conspiracy, and sentenced to two
years gaol.*

Document 1.12 A woman poet imagines the feelings of an Aboriginal mother

*During the second half of 1838, Sydney society opinion was divided
over the trials of twelve white stockmen for the murder of about thirty
Aborigines, many of them women and children, near Myall Creek in
northern New South Wales. Sections of the press argued that it was
wrong to try white men for the murder of creatures who were no
more than 'a set of monkies'. Eliza Hamilton Dunlop wrote the poem
below to make a very different case. It presents the Aborigines as
noble people, with family ties and feelings identical to those admired
by middle-class colonists. She also uses Aboriginal terms in an attempt
to present an Aboriginal understanding of the catastrophe. The detail
of the poem—the slaughter with swords rather than guns, the grisly
burning of the bodies, even the escape of a single woman—is drawn
from a close reading of newspaper accounts of the trials.*[12]

The Australian, 13 December 1838

Songs of an Exile (No. 4)
The Aboriginal Mother (from Myall's Creek)

Oh! hush thee—hush my baby,
I may not tend thee yet.
Our forest-home is distant far,
And midnight's star is set.
Now, hush thee—or the pale-faced men
Will hear thy piercing wail,
And what would then thy mother's tears
Or feeble strength avail!
Oh, coulds't thy little bosom,
That mother's torture feel,
Or coulds't thou know thy father lies
Struck down by English steel;
Thy tender form would wither,
Like the *kniven* on the sand,
And the spirit of my perished tribe
Would vanish from our land.
For thy young life, my precious,
I fly the field of blood,
Else had I, for my chieftain's sake,
Defied them where they stood;
But basely bound my woman's arm,
No weapon might it wield:
I could but cling round him I loved,
To make my heart a shield.
I saw my firstborn treasure
Lie headless at my feet,
The gore upon this hapless breast,
In his life-stream is wet!
And thou! I snatched thee from their sword,
It harmless pass'd by thee!
But clave the binding cords—and gave,
Haply, the power to flee.
To flee! my babe—but whither?
Without my friend—my guide?
The blood that was our strength is shed!
He is not by my side!

Thy sire! Oh! never never,
Shall *Toon Bakra* hear our cry:
My bold and stately mountain-bird!
I thought he could not die.
Now who will teach thee, dearest,
To poise the shield, and spear,
To wield the *koopin*, or to throw
The *boommerring*, void of fear;
To breast the river in its might;
The mountain tracks to tread?
The echoes of my homeless heart
Reply—the dead, the dead!
And ever must the murmur
Like an ocean torrent flow:
The parted voice comes never back
To cheer our lonely woe:
Even in the region of our tribe,
Beside our summer streams,
'Tis but a hollow symphony—
In the shadow-land of dreams.
Oh hush thee, dear—for weary
And faint I bear thee on—
His name is on thy gentle lips,
My child, my child, he's gone!
Gone o'er the golden fields that lie
Beyond the rolling clouds,
To bring thy people's murder cry
Before the Christian's God.
Yes! o'er the stars that guide us,
He brings my slaughter'd boy:
To shew their God how treacherously
The stranger men destroy;
To tell how hands in friendship pledged
Piled high the fatal pire;
To tell—to tell of the gloomy ridge!
And the stockman's human fire.

E.H.D.

Document 1.13 Women convicts riot at the Launceston Female Factory

This official report was presented to a government committee inquiring into 'Female Convict Discipline' in Tasmania. During the sixty years of female transportation to Australia, some of the men charged with keeping control of women convicts agreed with Ralph Collins' comment in 1787 (Document 1.3) that their behaviour was many times worse than that of the men. Certainly women convicts were more ready than the men to unite against authority, especially in cases where they believed that authority to be unjust. Here the solidarity of the women is particularly striking, especially in comparison with the willingness of the men convicts to scab.[13]

1841

On the morning of that day Catherine Owen represents that she is unwell and demanded upon that ground to be released from solitary confinement. The Colonial Assistant Surgeon visited the same morning but did not find her in any way indisposed and her confinement therefore continued. In the afternoon the Sub Matron visited her and immediately upon the cell being unlocked a number of the females in the crime class yard seized and held the Sub Matron while others conveyed Owen from the cells to the Mess Room, and then bid defiance to the authorities in the factory. One and all stating that they would not allow her to serve the remainder of her sentence in the Cells.

The Superintendent ordered the Ringleaders of this disturbance to be brought before him, this order the whole class resisted and having (85 in number) barricaded themselves in the Ward, it became necessary to procure some Constables to take the parties into Custody, but upon this being attempted the police were beaten off by the women who had armed themselves with the spindle, and leg, from the spinning wheels, bricks taken from floors and walls of the building, knives, forks etc and also Quart Bottles in which some of them had received medicine. From the great excitement the women were in the Superintendent thought it advisable to leave them to themselves for a time giving directions to the Keeper of the House of Correction not to supply them with food or water.

In the evening the women expressed a wish to see the Superintendent who therefore proceeded to the Factory and was told by them, that if he would give them their Rations and promise not to send the prisoners who had been rescued from the Cells again to punishment and also not try the Ringleaders of the women who took her out of the Cells they would submit. The Superintendent of course refused to enter into such conditions, but required the immediate submission of the whole party at the same time every effort in his power was used by remonstrance and persuasion to induce them to submit but without effect.

On the following morning at daylight the prisoners became very outrageous breaking the Furniture and windows and attempting to burn the Building. The Superintendent then determined to temporise no longer and ordered about fifty men from the prisoners' Barracks to proceed to the female House of Correction and having been sworn in special Constables and furnished with sledge Hammers and Crow bars with the assistance of some constables, the Crime Class ward was forced, the most refractory and violent of the female prisoners were captured and removed to Cells in the Male House of Correction and Gaol. The utmost resistance was offered and every description of Missile that could be procured was brought into operation by the females nothing but the extreme forbearance and proper Conduct of the Men employed prevented in the opinion of the Superintendent very serious results.

The Ringleaders of this riot were subsequently brought to trial and punished by sentences of hard labour to the House of Correction at Hobart Town. These offenders even upon their trial exhibited the most outrageous Conduct abusing and threatening the Magistrates to their face.

Part 2
Women in a masculine democracy 1840–1860

During the 1830s the Australian colonies were known to the world as penal settlements. By the 1860s they were mostly self-governing democracies. The transformation reflected the ending of transportation to New South Wales and Tasmania (though Western Australia continued to accept convicts during the 1850s and 1860s, and chose to delay democracy); the acceleration of assisted immigration and the founding of new non-convict colonies in Victoria and South Australia; and the rush of many thousands of unassisted immigrants to New South Wales and Victoria in search of gold during the 1850s. The transformation was achieved by a transfer of power from autocratic governors, first to appointed councils, then to councils elected on a high property franchise, and finally to parliaments whose lower houses were elected by all men neither bad nor mad enough to be institutionalised, and settled enough to have a permanent address.

Within these male democracies the roles of men and women became more sharply defined. The political world was enlarged to include all men, and fenced around to exclude all women. Informal political activity took place in pubs, from which respectable women were barred. The theory of democracy—that all men were equal because all had equal powers of reason—was assumed to exclude women, on the grounds that they were naturally irrational; as the Swan River Mechanics' Institute discussion class decided in 1853, 'Women would not possess the same amount of Intellect as men if they had the same advantages'.

One of the Swan River debaters asserted that women were 'incapable of equalling the man and taking the reins of government into their own hands and ruling over the man—domestically or otherwise'. Women's exclusion from the masculine world of politics does not seem to have bothered them, but their capacity to rule—or at least to equal the man—*domestically* was a different matter. Men interested in moral reform were beginning to argue that women had an inherent capacity to influence men for good or evil, and Caroline Chisholm told women to expect power within the home—power gained through love.

Middle-class women's journals and letters of this period suggest that the assertion of male authority at home had begun to emerge as a problem. Working-class women like Susannah Mapleson seem to have been less concerned, perhaps because their role was still understood as a partner in a joint family enterprise. But educated women like Helen Spence were looking for a double solution to the problem of male authority: to civilise marriage through love, and to give women a chance of economic independence outside marriage should love fail. In posing the problem as they did, they took their cue from the masculine democrats, and spoke in the name of all women.

Document 2.1 A newspaper reports the Governor's views about female intemperance

The Temperance Advocate *reported the Sixth Annual Meeting of the New South Wales Temperance Society in triumphal tones. The cause of temperance—the movement to stamp out drunkenness—had been much advanced in the colony by the attendance of Governor and Lady Gipps. The editor of the* Advocate *and the Governor, in his speech to the meeting, both made much of the role of women in the temperance movement. They put forward an argument new to the colony—that women by their very nature had power to civilise men.*[1]

21 April 1841

This gratifying meeting was held on Friday evening last. The hall of Sydney College was nearly full before the commencement of the proceedings; and shortly afterwards, hundreds went away from the door, unable

to gain admittance. His Excellency the Governor arrived at 7 o'clock
precisely, and within ten minutes, accompanied by Lady Gipps, he entered
the crowded hall, and was enthusiastically received. Nothing equal to this
meeting has been seen in the colony; there was no array of government
officers to sustain a weak or doubtful cause, but a full attendance of every
class, spontaneously actuated to uphold Temperance, and to greet the
distinguished Patron of the Society. Most gratefully do we acknowledge
the presence of Lady Gipps; her kind and constant support of Temperance
is of vast importance; her Ladyship has the power to set fashion, and when
that fashion is set in the service of virtue, the influence thus employed
renders her a benefactress to the land. The number of ladies present,
afforded good proof that her Ladyship does not lack the sympathy and
support of her own class; who, in return were cheered and encouraged by
her Ladyship's attendance . . .

[Governor Gipps told the meeting:] In all times, and in all countries,
there will be men who push their principles further than others do. I am
myself a moderate man, moderate in most things, and therefore I am
satisfied with being a member of the Temperance Society: there are also
some few other things, in which I am satisfied with moderate well doing.
St Paul tells us that people do well, that is to say moderately well, who
marry; and I dare say most of you know that I am a married man: St Paul
goes on indeed to say, that men who do not marry do better; I do not at
all dispute it, but still it may perhaps be permitted to us humbly to doubt
whether the morality of the world would be much improved, if there were
none but such men in it. Now the moderate men, the men who marry, are
members of the Temperance Society; and this perhaps may be one of the
reasons why our meetings are always honoured with so large an attendance
of the ladies. The mention of the ladies warns me, that I have too long
delayed to notice them, and especially to thank them for their attendance
this evening. The cause which we are assembled here to promote, could
not indeed fail to prosper, if properly supported by those only of the fair
sex, whom I now have the pleasure to see before me: but then comes the
question, whether or not it is properly supported by you. In what degree,
or to what extent do you support it? Is it that of your heart, and that of
your soul, that of the earnestness that belongs to woman? Is it for that
purpose that you come here this night, or, is it that some amongst you at
least, may be led, by that frivolity or fickleness which alas! sometimes
belongs to woman too, to come here merely as they might go to the theatre,
for mere entertainment—to fill up the vacancy of an unoccupied hour, or
to gratify an idle curiosity? I exhorted you, I besought of you at our
last meeting that you would take this matter into your own hands; the

encouraging smiles which I then received from you were construed by me into promises, into assurances that you would do so. Was I wrong? If not, answer me, have you done it—Oh, that I could be assured that you had done so, or even that you would henceforth do it; then, indeed, could I safely and contentedly leave this great cause in your hands; Oh, that I could believe that the power, the influence, the soft persuasion of woman's eye, and of woman's tongue, would ever be exercised, as it most legitimately may be, to recall to the path of virtue, erring and simple men. The reverse of this is too painful for the mind to dwell on; that woman should renounce the tenderness of her nature, belie the softness of her sex, stoop from her high station, and condescend to be a minister to man, in his revelry—still worse, that she herself should be the victim of intemperance; that woman should herself be guilty of the bestiality of drunkenness; but this indeed could hardly be, for e'er it can arrive, the creature is unsexed, the soft and endearing name of woman shall no longer be applied to her; call her fiend—fury—Hecate or invent some new term of insult in the language; to designate a thing so fallen, and so vile. There is nothing in the whole catalogue of crime, so thoroughly revolting as drunkenness in a woman; there is no object of disgust or horror that offends the sight of God or man, so entirely loathsome as a drunken woman. It has been too much the practice of writers of fiction, and of poets to exhibit vice in an alluring or seductive aspect, but still I cannot call to mind a poet of any age or country who has pictured as an object of attraction a woman in a state of drunkenness. Ovid, the poet of love, the tender and gentle Ovid, keenly expresses the horror of it; the Anacreon, the poet of wine, as well as love, though he indeed, when stretched upon a bed of roses and of myrtles, call upon his mistress to bring him his cup of wine, even Anacreon himself does not, as far as I remember, invite his mistress to come and get drunk with him . . .

Document 2.2 A missionary despairs of converting the Aborigines

Missionary James Gunther's annual report for the year 1841 is an admission of failure. Earlier reports had presented the affairs of the mission at Wellington Valley in the best possible light. Any failure to convert was blamed on the corrupting influence of Europeans hostile to the mission. Gunther still bewails the impact of white society upon the Aborigines, but he acknowledges that the greatest barrier to their acceptance of Christianity is their adherence to their own culture, to the 'superstitions' of the old men of the tribe. In Gunther's very

masculine understanding, the giving of Aboriginal women in mar-
riage becomes central to a battle between missionaries and male
elders for the loyalty of the younger men. There is no suggestion here,
nor in earlier reports of European corruption, that the women might
claim some control over their own lives.[2]

Mission House, Wellington Valley,
7 January 1842.

ANNUAL REPORT OF THE MISSION TO THE ABORIGINES AT WELLLINGTON
VALLEY, NEW HOLLAND, FOR THE YEAR 1841.

Sir,

If the work of civilizing and christianizing a savage race was dependent
merely on human efforts, and if we were permitted to view it in a
calculative or speculative spirit, like common human pursuits, so as to
expect from a certain portion of time and labour devoted to it, certain
results; then, I candidly confess, I should be ready to despair of the
aboriginal inhabitants of this country ever being raised from their degraded
condition; since so little success has hitherto attended this mission, as well
as various similar attempts, in different parts of the country.

The hope warranted by the volume of inspiration, that the Church of
Christ will be extended to all nations, tribes, kindreds, and languages, is
the only ground that sustains me . . .

Amongst all those young men who for years past have been more or
less attached to the mission, there is only one who affords some satisfaction
and encouragement. Deep religious impressions have been made on his
mind, and we have reason to believe he is undergoing a change of
character. For more than two years, he has distinguished himself above
the rest by a desire for improvement, enquiry and reflection. He has
gradually shaken off the yoke and domination of the elderly men and
superstitious notions from his mind. But I am sorry to observe that this
young man is not likely to live much longer, so as to become useful to
his countrymen, he having for a considerable time shown strong symptoms
of a consumptive disease, and is, of late, quite unable to make any bodily
exertions.

As regards the others, I can give no very favourable account of their
conduct; during the past year several of those who used to stay at or
frequent the mission, resorted to their migratory habits . . . Even those
few who may be considered as still attached to the mission, only about
four, besides the one I have described, have too frequently, during the
year, made excursions into the bush; and when at home they evinced not

much desire for instruction and improvement . . . Their thoughtlessness, a spirit of independence, ingratitude, and want of sincere straight dealing, often try us in the extreme. One boy who continues with us receives more regular instruction, but advances slowly; he is very quick and handy for little errands. Two young women, who have never left during the year, are occasionally instructed, and attend regularly prayers. They have conducted themselves tolerably well as domestic servants, one in particular; the other, who was less steady when single, has improved since she has had a husband. But what I observed before applies to all; the best of them cause us much trouble to bring them into orderly and industrious habits, and at times grow quite insolent. Civilized habits, however much some may occasionally fancy them, or conform to them, will never, I feel convinced, become natural and easy to the present generation, unless a new principle be implanted in their mind, and a thorough change effected, by the influence of Christianity . . .

During the past year I have had particular opportunities to become acquainted with the nature of the absurd laws, the vile and superstitious practices of the aborigines, and the unbounded sway which the old men exercise over their people, to counteract every improvement. Those two young women alluded to were married, one in May, one in June last, partly through my influence, to what we considered suitable partners, that is to say, some of the young men more advanced in civilization. But according to some strange laws and practices of theirs, the particulars of which are too lengthy to be detailed here, these marriages were considered illegal, and the elderly men, perceiving that their strong hold was about to be shaken at its very foundation, were utterly enraged, and endeavoured to excite every aborigine against the mission, which for a time prevented even some of our young men to come near us; they even threatened the parties in question with death. Had I exercised no influence in the matter, these young women, who have for years been instructed at the mission, would in all probability have become the prey of very unsuitable men (for not one of our young men could in their opinion have legally married them), most likely elderly men, possessed perhaps already of more than one wife. Indeed the evils resulting from polygamy . . . are great and manifold. On the one hand, it causes constant strifes and fightings; on the other hand, the elderly or influential men, possessed of a plurality of wives, being in reality only the keepers of them, have it in their power to hold out certain allurements to the young, who cannot obtain wives, and by obliging the latter, as it is considered, the former can command or extort implicit obedience. This accounts in a great measure for the well known fact, that aboriginal males, however useful and steady they may have been among Europeans when boys, as soon as they grow up to manhood they fall back into their wandering unsettled habits.

I lament much that the difficulty to obtain aboriginal children for instruction has increased almost to an impossibility. In whatever direction I may go, even at a distance of 40 or 60 miles, the parents conceal their children as soon as they hear that a missionary approaches their camp; and when I come upon them by surprise, I have the grievance to observe these little ones running into the bushes, or into the bed of the river, with the utmost speed. This, as well of the dispersion of some young men, who were formerly here, is evidently owing to those unhappy disturbances and strange proceedings, which, as is generally known take place on the mission. Such things could not gain us the confidence of the aborigines, but must necessarily leave an unfavourable impression . . .

A considerable portion of my time, during the last year, has been taken up in travelling, not so much in behalf of the blacks, but more to administer religious ordinances to the white population, mostly at a considerable distance . . . In my journies I generally fall in with a few blacks, and if possible have conversation with them; but their stupor and carelessness are truly discouraging, and the sad European society in which I often find them, increases the difficulty. Drunkenness, I am sorry to observe, spreads more and more among them in every direction. We have seen the last year more of it on the mission than ever before . . . It is truly distressing to behold the wretched condition into which these poor savages have been placed, since civilized people have been settled among them. To see them on the one hand exterminated by violence, which I fear more frequently occurs in the interior than is publicly known; and on the other hand, gradually swept away by debauchery and other evils arising from their intermixture with Europeans; to observe their morals, if possible, more corrupted by those who ought to teach them better; to see rarely a good example set them, even by those from whom we might justly expect it . . . and yet to hear these corrupters of the savages declaim against them and missionary efforts, and to enveigh against the whole race without any feeling of compassion, when some commit an outrage; these are considerations which must prove deeply affecting and lamentable to every man of just and humane feeling, and to the Christian who is desirous to improve the spiritual and temporal condition of his fellow men. His prayer indeed must be, that God in mercy may open the eyes of those that sit in heathen darkness, and awaken those that have but the name to live, and are dead.

I have, etc,

(signed) James Gunther, Missionary

Document 2.3 A lady reformer finds a working man a wife

Caroline Chisholm (1808–1877) printed the following letter (probably with some editing) in the pamphlet advocating female immigration which she published in Sydney in 1842. She goes on to describe her response to this and to other letters from bushmen asking her to find them brides among the immigrant women under her care. Chisholm had set up her Immigrants' Home to protect newly arrived women from men's sexual demands; she had no doubt that unmarried and unprotected women in Sydney were in moral danger. Her solution was to find them work in respectable homes, ideally in the country, with the expectation that they would soon marry; she advocated low wages for women servants so that they would not be discouraged from marrying. Chisholm assumes here that the male passion endangering single women would be somehow tamed by marriage; that love would civilise men.[3]

c.1841

Reverend Madam,

I heard you are the best to send to for a servant, and I heard our police magistrate say, it was best to leave all to you; and so I'll do the same, as his honour says it's the best. I had a wife once, and so she was too good for me by the far, and it was God's will, ma'am; but I has a child, ma'am, that I wouldn't see a straw touch for all the world; the boy's only four yeare old: and I has a snug fifty-acre farm and a town 'lotment, and I has no debts in the world, and one teem and four bullocks; and I'se ten head oh cattle, and a share on eight hundred sheep, so I as a rite to a desent servant, that can wash and cook and make the place decant; and I don't mind what religion she bey; if she is sober and good, only I'se a Protestant myself; and the boy I have, I promised the mother on her death bed, should be a Catholic, and I wont, anyhow, have any interferance in this here matter. That I do like in writing nothing else, I wouldn't, mam, on any account in the world, be bound to marry; but I don't wish it altogether to be left out. I'll ge her fourteen wages, and if she don't like me, and I don't like her, I'll pay her back to Sydney. I want nothing in the world but what is honest, so make the agrement as you like, and I'll bide by it. I sends you all the papers, and you'l now I'm a man wot's to be trusted. I sends you five pounds; she may get wages first, for I know some of the gals, and the best on um, are not heavy we boxes; and supposing anything should happen, I would not like it to be said she come here in rags. I wants also, a man and his wife; he must be willing to learn to plough, if

he don't now how, and do a good fair day's work at any think: his wife
must be a milker, and ah dustrious woman; I'll give them as much as they
can eat and drink of tea and milk, and whatever wages you set my name
down for, I'll be bound to pay it. With all the honer in the world I'se
bound to remain your servant till death.

[Chisholm commented:] There was something in the character of this
honest bushman to admire; he had gained his freedom, sent money home
to his parents, and, during a long and tedious illness of twenty months,
he had tended his sick wife with patient care. Who would not get up an
hour earlier to serve such a man?—I did, for I knew that early in the
morning is the *best* time to choose a wife. I went first into the govern-
ess-room—all asleep; I unlocked the Home-door—some dressed, others
half-dressed, some too very cross: I have often remarked, that early in the
day is the best time to judge of a woman's temper; but I wish this to be
kept a secret. I remained half-an-hour in the Home; I then went through
the tents, could not suit myself, and returned. At the Home-door, I found
a girl at the wash-tub; she was at work with spirit; she was rather good
looking, very neat and tidy. I went into my office and ascertained that, on
board ship, her character was good. I desired the matron never to lose
sight of her conduct, and to report the same to me. Day after day passed,
and I was at last fully determined to place her within reach, that is, in a
respectable family, in his near neighbourhood; but I was able to arrange
better, for I found that, amongst the families, there was one related to her.
I immediately engaged them as his servants, they were a respectable
couple; the man was a very prudent person. I told them to take the girl
with them, and get her service near them, and on no account to let her
live with a bachelor. I gave the girl three letters to respectable ladies, and
she was engaged by one the fourth day after her arrival at—. About a
fortnight after, the bushman wrote to thank me, for sending him the
married couple; and concluded by saying, 'With regard to that *other* matter,
upon my word, you have suited me exactly; and, as soon as our month
is up, we is to be married'.

I received forty-one applications of this kind; but the above is the
only girl I ever sent into the country with a *direct* matrimonial intention.
That I take pleasure on hearing when a girl is married is a fact; and I also
like to see girls *placed* where they will have *a fair chance* of being well
married. With reference to the above applications, I may say petitions, so
urgent were the prayers of many, I usually said, I was sending good girls
into the country every day, and that I never sent a girl into the country
when I knew anything against her character.

Several men called on me, when they came into town with their drays; and I may remark, indeed, it is only *justice to them to do so*, that the men said, their only reason for troubling me was, that they should not be deceived in a girl's character. 'All I want, ma'am, is a decent *sober* girl, that will attend to her religion, and make my home happy: she need not work more than she likes.' Another said, 'I don't care if she has not a rag her own, if she has only a good character'. Another, 'I would like a woman that can talk to the children about being good: I know if I was to get a woman with a bad character I should end my days at Norfolk Island—character is all I care for; if she is pretty, well and good, but if she is not, if she is good, I shall love her'.

Document 2.4 A wife chronicles an unhappy marriage

Annie Baxter's biographer notes that her journals were 'Annie's self in words'. She composed them with the intention of showing them to very close friends, and in the expectation that her husband would read them uninvited. At the time when she wrote the entries below, Annie Baxter (1816–1905) was, as she said, 'a good wife' to her husband 'in all but the one instance'; she kept house for him, and looked after his business affairs, but after discovering him having sex with an Aboriginal woman she refused to have him in her bed. Annie in her turn had a brief affair with a government official. The extracts below begin at the point when the affair is over and Annie is planning to leave her husband and go back to England.

Annie Baxter reveals herself as very well-informed in sexual matters, and very confident. Other wives may well have believed, like Baxter's 'pretty little friend Mrs C.F.', that they had no power to avoid unwanted sexual relations with their husbands; families with ten or more children were not uncommon in the 1840s. But Annie Baxter knew better.[4]

Yesabba [northern New South Wales]
July 1843

I think I had written about thirty pages at the other end of this book, when one day my amiable consort tore them all out! Nothing could have more annoyed me altho' if he had asked me to read it, I would (notwithstanding a few pieces of abuse of him) have shown it to him—not so! He went while I was in the settlement and made a second key to my drawer, read my journal—and replaced it—in the meanest manner possible—This, he may see with all my heart—and I trust he will like it . . .

[When Annie Baxter returned to the farm, there] . . . commenced the most terrible disturbance I ever witnessed—Still I continued to plod on in the path of duty! Oh! If ever I had loved a man with my whole soul, I should have hated him after such an outbreak! How much worse so then when I entertain such thorough contempt for him!

Maria [her niece by marriage] came back again the following week—I was obliged to send for her Papa to take her home—I could not bear that a girl so young should hear the dreadful language that was made use of by her Uncle—He struck me several times and even threatened and attempted to cut my throat—Really I sometimes wish he had! for the torture of my mind is scarcely bearable at times—I know, that my old presentiment will be verified yet—I shall die wretchedly!

Captain Briggs [a neighbour] offered me a place in his house if I would go—but I knew how ill he could afford it—and therefore remained—I firmly believe that no woman of the *lowest* description ever had more abuse than I have—And yet positively he has the audacity to wish me to behave as a *wife* should! He told Captain Briggs that I had left his bed without rhyme, or reason—How well he knows to the contrary. I wrote to William [her brother] saying that my health required a change of air—and asked him to lodge my passage money in Mr Miller's hands but it will be nine months before that can be . . .

I am making my clothes to go—but I often think, I shall never wear them, for so happy a purpose! This may be from my low spirits—but I have strange ideas sometimes—At times Baxter says the day I go, will be his last! at others he wishes me to send him various things from England—And now he is continually annoying me to sleep with him again before I leave—Now this is a most *knavish* idea—He knows very well that after having had four miscarriages and not having for so long a time been in the way of having more—that I should naturally be enceinte [pregnant] immediately—He would then lay it to my conduct on board a ship going home—But I had advice from one older party than myself—on no account to humour him in this—There was no occasion for giving in—for I am not of a prostitute disposition—& this would be mere prostitution . . .

15th Friday

On Monday last, I received a note from Margaret, and some lollypops, too! Last week I had three books sent up—They were *The Bishop's Daughter*—*Emma de Lissan* and *Klopstock's Memoirs*—The latter work I admired excessively! I never heard of him previously, altho' he is the 'Milton' of Germany, but this is from being unacquainted with their language—His letters to his wife, and hers to him are very beautiful—How they loved each other, 'twas earthly, and Heavenly! Would to God mine could have been the same for my husband! What ecstasy such feeling must be! on dit [people say] that 'stolen sweets are sweetest'! I doubt it—I should prefer uninterrupted intercourse . . .

I was settling Mrs Johnson's account yesterday, & she was telling me that Mrs Rudder had told her to make haste back, as she expected her accouchement [going into labour] immediately! This is only the 13th! And the poor children have positively scarcely a mouthful to eat—this is tempting Providence indeed! *Why* do they have any more? I remember telling my pretty little friend Mrs C.F. that she must not have any more children—She answered quaintly, 'But how is it possible for married persons to avoid it?' Just as if the bare ceremony of matrimony was to be the cause of myriads starving!

Document 2.5 A wife perseveres in a grim marriage

Eliza Brown and her husband Thomas, the 'Mr Brown' of this letter, came from the same middle-class background as the Baxters (Document 2.4), but the impact of pioneering on their marriage was very different. Annie Baxter uses her journal as a stage to display her sensitivity and her husband's cruelty; Eliza Brown's letter to her father displays her support for her husband's gloomy authority. There is an element of special pleading here; living in poverty and isolation in Western Australia, the Browns cannot survive without financial support from Eliza's father, and Thomas Brown's management of the family's affairs (and his inability to pay his debts to his wife's family) has to be justified to his father-in-law. By contrast Eliza makes nothing in this letter of her own labours in making the family self-sufficient—note the bread, mutton, bacon, pork, butter, candles, eggs, poultry and so on. Nor does she mention that she is again pregnant. Further disasters were in store for the Brown family, and Eliza's children never received the gentlemanly education that she hoped for them.[5]

Grass Dale [Western Australia]
August 17 1844

Dearest Papa,
I am in possession of yours and Matilda's [her sister's] combined letter enclosed in a closely written envelope in which you acquaint Mr Brown of the state of affairs at Summertown, and it bears the several dates of Feby 15–19, March 1st and 6th. We received the letter on the evening of

the 10th. I had been most anxiously on the look out for tidings as report had brought out the intelligence that poor Mama was no more. Some passengers by the *Trusty* of the laboring class about two months ago told the Viveash's they had heard of her decease just before leaving Oxfordshire, and Charlotte Smith also in writing to her sister mentioned that there was such a report. It was so likely to have been founded on fact, considering her emaciated and melancholy state that I had no hope left that there would not be a confirmation of it.

You will have had several letters from me since that of September 8th 43 if they have safely reached their destination. I forget the dates of them but from this time think of taking an account of all letters sent as well as continuing to keep those we receive . . .

I have acknowledged in many instances receiving the case No. 4 . . . and hope you have had the satisfaction of hearing it long ere this. I have parted with £60 worth of the things and shall if necessary dispose of more, indeed with all except presents and what we cannot possibly do without of plain wearing apparel that the packages contained. Mr Brown intends reserving the child's carriage that has come in the case per *Unicorn*, but every thing else that is disposable will be converted into cash. Perhaps I may never see the contents for it is uncertain whether we shall have it brought over the Hills, this depends upon whether the contents will sell well in Perth. I long to see the letters that are enclosed in the box but must wait patiently until Mr Brown can afford me that pleasure. His engagements are so very pressing that he cannot go below just now.

We quitted Mr Hardey on the 1st of April and are now on our own and proper side of the water. Hardey is finally settled with both for rent and compensation for our giving up the farm. I told you what he asked for the latter, £210, the value of sheep at that time was £1 per head and we gave him 210 sheep for compensation.

Great progress has been made since we have been here in many things. Stock yards are put up in the same substantial manner as the garden fence I once described to you. Mr Brown has done all the ploughing with his own hands and an additional quantity of land has been cleared, also a portion of the walls of the house put up, but this work is at a stand still at the present, it being the season to plant, trench and manure the garden which is a matter of too great consequence to be neglected. A season passed of necessary work to be done there would put us back so much in one of the enjoyments of life, a well cultivated and fruit bearing garden. Besides we can have no wine until we produce it for ourselves, that article from necessity having long been done away with . . .

You perhaps wonder what we have done without a house the last five months, with a prospect of five months more passing away before we shall inhabit one. We live in one end of a thatched shed adjoining the stock yards where there is just room for a table, the sofa Mr Brown made, our boxes (some of which serve as seats for the children) and two beds. Our goods are stowed away in a compartment in the middle of the shed, and the plough box, we have a nook behind these; detached, we have a temporary kitchen and dairy made of boughs and split wood with loose straw thrown over the top. The fire is out of doors and when it is very cold we have a pan of hot embers brought into the shed. It was severely cold for several weeks in June and July, we had ice ½ an inch thick (with occasionally a greater thickness) morning after morning in the water buckets . . .

The children thrive in our gipsy mode of life as regards robustness of frame and activity of limbs, but the coming to this country has a great disadvantage for children in one respect, the dearth there is of good instruction. I had hoped and endeavoured to teach my children until they might be put into abler hands, but the increase of family diminished my opportunities and energies for keeping up sufficient discipline to be enabled to do much if any good with the elder ones. I believe that it is a generally received opinion that it is almost impossible for a mother to perform the office of governess to her own boys with any chance of a satisfactory result. I had hoped otherwise but experience tells in favor of that opinion. In any case I sometimes think I do more harm than good to them and that is by not possessing the necessary virtues for the vocation.

Our boys would be quick enough and good enough if ably super-intended, and our intention is (should not bad fortune baffle it) to have a youth in his first zeal from one of the Normal or Diocesan Schools either in England or Scotland to take the superintendance of the four boys both at their studies, at work in the vineyard and at play, with two other (the sons of gentlemen to be educated with them) which would defray the expense of salary. You do not know how my hopes rest on this. After two more years the promising Kenneth would be injured for want of mental culture, and in two years the others will be quite ready for a Master's firm hand. All four in fact might then be trained together and continue our pride and delight without bowing the spirit down in almost fruitless endeavours to teach them.

I am entirely out of brown holland and calico now for making into garments for the children so they will be but poorly clad soon if I cannot avail myself of anything that has come from England for their use. Shoes and boots they wear only on Sunday when they go to Church, and that is only the two eldest, the other two wild little colts never have been shod.

I shall leave a little room for Mr Brown to say a little . . .

> I remain Dearest Papa
> Your affectionate Daughter
> E. Brown

[Despite signing off Eliza Brown continued the letter:] Mr Brown declined to avail himself of the small space left to write in, having more to say than will fill it . . .

This letter has not been written all at once. I have dated it for post day, indeed I write with difficulty and but a little at a time, having a very bad thumb caused by a trifling cut. It gathered and is very slow to heal, the general consequence of a cut at this season of the year in this country.

We have encountered some frowns from Fortune in our Colonial enterprise which in my hopefulness I was slow to recognise. Mr Brown became the anxious man soon after we entered upon Hardey's farm, but continued perseveringly labouring from day to day, though without hope to cheer. He appears gradually to be losing the load of care now that incubus is done away with, as he now sees we shall prosper if supported by our English friends. After the house is finished our expenses will be very small, our settling them will be accomplished, and all its attendant inconveniences and expenses at an end. We shall then employ but one man except the herdsman and the shepherd, and do away with these even should it not be remunerative to retain them. All the substantial necessaries of life are produced from our own farm, bread, mutton, bacon, pork, butter, even candles made from sweet mutton suet, eggs, poultry etc. Tea and sugar which we have to purchase are only used now for the shepherd when he is stationed at the back of the grant, at home milk suffices except occasionally when a guest arrives or I who am privileged sometimes enjoy a cup of tea or coffee generally indulged in through Mr Brown's persuasion. Clothing for the family is nearly all we should find it necessary to purchase. £25 worth of goods sent from England yearly for sale in this Colony would put sufficient funds into our hands to meet passing wants and any more of our English income we do not intend to touch until our debts are paid in the Mother Country. Here we shall incur no further liabilities and become quite straight with the assistance from home that Mr Brown is about to seek.

I am warned by him that a wrong impression is conveyed in my letter as regards Hardey being settled with, it is true we have settled with him but are still liable ourselves for some portion of funds furnished which was done by drawing a bill. This Mr Brown would not have had recourse to could he have sold sheep, cattle or horses, but these he could not dispose of at any price, and Hardey was threatening law proceedings on the second day after the rent became due. It is true sheep were nominally £1 per head but there were no buyers. 200 of our wether lambs went to Hardey in part payment for rent at 10/- each.

This letter is spun out to a trying length, but I trust you will have patience with me,

Yours

E. Brown

Document 2.6 A Mechanics' Institute discussion class debates the inferiority of woman's intellect

In October 1853 the Swan River Mechanics' Institute in Perth spent five of their weekly meetings debating the topic 'whether Women do or would possess the same amount of Intellect as man if they had the same advantages'. It was the most popular topic for the year, and the most fiercely debated. The debaters—all, of course, men—drew their arguments and examples from history, literature, education, psychology, and especially the Bible. It was remarkable how often arguments about intellect became arguments about power; man's superior capacity for reason justified man's authority over women.

The debaters were mostly clerks, skilled tradesmen and small business men. They read eagerly on the topic but did not always express themselves clearly; nor did the members appointed as secretaries always understand the arguments that they were taking down. Mr Farrelly's (or Farelly?) opening address appears to question the concept of pure intellect, but one cannot be sure.

The account below begins on the fourth evening of the debate.[6]

24 Oct, 1853

THE LAST DISCUSSION RESUMED BY MR FARRELLY

The mind is one whole and indivisible. If the female at her sphere of life displays a superiority in each position she will be found to excell over the men. Mind is possessed of three distinct things. Memory Will and understanding each is distinct from the other . . . Memory calls back circumstances against the intention or desire of the Will. Rebuts the idea of becoming a Materialist. The understanding is not matured at the same time with the Will. Woman occupies the highest position in Society and the greatest degree of intellectuality.

Mr Chester Senior

It does not require much intellect to govern, a Female of 18 is capable of governing or if she is not capable she does not govern. Woman in another world is equal to man. Then why not in this? Fools must and often do govern if born in line for the purpose and without reference of intellect so that taking the admitted popular view of it it matters but little whether the party possesses it.

Mr Lazenby

Any man of understanding should see that intellect is requisite for governing Wisely etc. If Women had been borne Poets they would have distinguished themselves as such. In any branch either Cooking or any other they do not excell over the men. Women have not sense equal to men altho witty lively etc.

Mr Johnston

Mr Farelly does not believe that women are superior to men in creation. Is sorry to hear Mr Chester's description of Governors as Fools and Brutes. Intellect is required to govern. Enquires Whether a Fool or a man of Intellect and good sense was most capable of Governing the Channell Fleet or Acting as Secretary of State as Members of the House of Commons etc. etc.

The size of the brain does not shew amount of intellect or the Whale would be most useful for that purpose. Catherine of Russia was a Brute in her Government and also several others. Delights in the fact that visionary governments have failed while intellectual ones have succeeded. Men of Genius have failed in intellectual reasoning in their governing capacity when placed in the House of Commons instanced Isaac Newton Addison etc etc. While Channing, Pitt Huskisson Wellington and other wise men possessed of intellectual powers succeeded. Man has from Creation held the power of Governing. Women are superior in their own domestic affairs and feelings and management of their children.

Women have not succeeded in excelling in anything nor have the upholders adduced any individuals in support.

Mr Smith

Admits that Women are not possessed of the same amount of Intellect as men because they have not had the chance of education but if they had then they would excel. St Paul states that he was to be recommended to the Women that helped him in the Gospel. Scriptures bear out that they have taught the Gospel.

Mr Fox

Men have a superior power of Intellect to Woman. Woman have a refined Intellect. Man has a Masculine Mind each use it according to their sphere. Mr Smith did not understand Mr Johnston's remarks and therefore did not know how to refer to them and argue against them. Women are so constituted that they never have and if they had double the advantages either in education or in any other sense whatever their advantages might be they will never excell over the man.

Mr Allmond

Cannot supply the intellect required by Mr Fox. proposed an Ammendment to Mr Lazenby's proposition that the Women not having received an education equal to their men as the reason they have not excelled but that when they have the same chance of Education there they will excell.

There must be a difference between the Intellect of Males and Females. Intellect can be expanded in the female sex. Colleges are established to expand Woman's Intellect. It has taken 6000 years to expand man's intellect but the Colleges for females have taken but 20 years.

Mr Darcy

Girls are more perceptive in their ideas than boys. Women in America have petitioned for their rights. When Men accrue to a great name as Vocalists they are unworthy of the name. English Law says that Woman at 18 are capable of managing but Men not so until 21.

Dr Gray

Women are not equal to man in Intellect or sound sense. they are satisfied and have been for ages past with their condition in Society in England and elsewhere. They are incapable of equalling the man and taking the reins of Government into their own hands and of ruling over the man— domestically or otherwise. Advises all who are of a different opinion to give their wives the ruling governing powers in all their affairs and they will find it so . . .

31 Oct 1853

. . . THE LAST DISCUSSION RESUMED

T. Mews

Thinks if Women had the same advantages as men they would equal them in intellect.

A. Gray

Is of opinion that Women is not intended to rule over men but that from Creation to the end of time the Almighty determined that man should rule not only every living creature but over Women also. Consequently Women have not an equal power in intellect as men and although education would much improve their reasoning faculties yet they never have and never can equal the man in sense or power or reasoning or in any particular wherein it is required.

B. Smith

The Protestant Bible states that Women helped Paul to Preach the Gospel 4 Chap Phillipians 1, 2 and 3 verses. Man and Woman are made alike in Intellect.

Fox

If Woman had more advantages than men they never will equal or pass them quoted St. Paul's remarks Ist Tim 3 Chap Verse 16 where he commanded Women not to Preach altho every Minister's Wife is supposed and always should help her husband.

Chester I. Senr

If Mr Johnston were to look thro any history he would find that numbers of Brutes have governed referred to Edward 1st Henry 8th Richard 3rd and others and to the wars between Scotland and England. Duke of Wellington wished that all poor men should become soldiers under him. Questions whether females have a right to govern or whether they should do so. A difference exists between the minds of men and Women but in their own way—equally strong sometimes stronger and Women really do govern from their Infancy.

O'Reilly

Women have not the same strength of mind as man and never would if they had the opportunity for Education.

Powell Snr.

From the time of the Creation woman was not superior to man and Physically they never can be so. Admits that Women are capable of stating their views in Public as to Religion but never has heard a Woman capable of explaining Scriptures in any way equal to man.

Lazenby

Has not heard a single argument against his proposition worthy of an answer altho much twaddle has passed; has noted and brought before the Meeting all the Women he could who have distinguished themselves. Scriptures do not prove that women were ever intended to Govern. Kingly power is known to be hereditary. Intellectual power is not so. Has instanced several men with a power of Intellect who in their sphere without

Education in their various branches shown a power of Intellect and Genius which Women have not. Scriptures do not prove that Women should be public preachers altho they do labour in the Gospel and be helpers therein with their husbands advice.

Women never have had and never can have the same amount of Intellect and no one among us considers his wife is superior in Intellect to himself or superior in Governing powers, the Almighty gave Adam or man wisdom to give names to the Brute creation he did not give it to the Woman. Women never will to the end of time give the same evidence of their superiority of Intellect or commonsense.

The Chairman then put the question to the Meeting
Whether Woman do or would possess the same amount of Intellect as man if they had the same advantages. Carried that they would not.

The above Minutes approved on behalf of the Meeting.

G. Lazenby
Chairman

Document 2.7 A husband asks his wife to join him in the colonies

Francis Mapleson, a plasterer and moulder by trade, joined the rush to the Victorian goldfields but found, as he said, that the rapidly growing city of Melbourne was the 'Surest Diggings' for him. In his absence, his wife Susannah supported herself and the children by keeping a shop in London. When Frank wrote, asking her to join him, he did so fully aware that she might not 'agree to his proposals'; the £50 he sent for her passage money was hers 'to do the best you can with whether you come or not'. What he offered was not romantic love, but a more familial kind—'I cannot Live without you and my Boys'—plus a partnership in a business enterprise. And both Frank's letter and those that follow it here show that other family members were expected to be part of that same enterprise.[7]

Melbourne.
March 15, 1854

My Dearly Beloved Wife, Children and Friends,
With much pleasure I now address you—with a more Favourable account of this Colony. It is much better than ever I expected, as any one else that comes here. Person are getting settled here, and Building Fine Substantial Houses with ornaments, and gardens Set out with Fountains etc. The worst

is to obtain competent men for the work. It a lucky stroke for me—as money is no object here, I have this last six weeks been modelling, Moulding and Casting Trusses &c.—And have now commenced a very Beautifully Designed Fountain for Carlton Gardens at Abbotsford near Melbourne It is Sullivan's job, But I am working it. My Dear Wife I never saw my way so clear towards Independence as I do now. I want you here, and my Moulds Models and Castings, To make our start in this wonderful Improving Town. If we should fail, I can at any time get a job at Common Plastering and bring home my ten guineas at 4 o'clock on Saturday afternoon for a weeks work, at any rate we could save Something out of that, not to be grinned at. Take my advice, Dearest, and Pack up what clothes you and our Dear little Boys have got and what small things that is necessary such as Linen China ornaments Books not Forgetting my Illistrated Exhibitory. Do not buy any new thing if you have enough for the voyage—no matter what you wear on the voyage, So Don't throw away any old clothes. Sail From the London Docks not come to Liverpool as I did although it made very little Difference to me, But it has to Familys which I know for a Fact, they thinking to gain a Cheaper Passage. Perhaps they did, But payed through the nose For every thing else besides being Detained. If my Brother Charles and Mary-ann Likes to come with you I have every reason to believe that they will Bless the day—when they started for Melbourne If Charly likes to get a good Supply of Ceiling Enrichments, Centre Flowers, wax made up, Models of Small Figures, and geletine, for moulding the said groups, also any thing else necessary For Carrying on Business, And Pay Part of the Freightage per Ton And be Partners, And work together with Honesty and live as Brothers should, For this Most Florishing Colony My Dear Susan, I will send you an Order on the Colonial Bank for Fifty Pounds, as I promised in my Last Letters, To Do the best you can with whether you come or not, God forbid I should advice you or any one else wrongfully, I never did yet. And it would be unnatural For me now—I should like you Brother Henry Sister Elizabeth To join you the reason I wish it is because Henry would do as well as myself, Davis and Caroline would do very well in the Bush as farm Servants I cannot hear of anything Favorable in his Trade here, I don't know any thing about Sidney, respecting the Boot tree and last making.

My Dear wife, Brothers and Sisters if agreed to my Proposals, Find Some owner or Agent, of not Less than a 500 ton Ship, to bring the whole of you at a Considerable reduced Price, For Intermediate or Second Cabin, with Beds Bedding Usetensals &c, if Possible, if not you must go a Cheap way of getting them they are all very cheap if Properly Managed, you want a hook Pot wash Bowl plate Drinking For each made of Tin, Also 2 or 3 Slop Pails Knifes and forks Table and Tea Spoons And a few Articles of Crockery ware, Stow away Some Bacon Eggs Pickles, little Flour, in case you should not have a Sufficient allowed you, Bring Carbonate of Soda to make Bread with if there is a Chance, Have the above mentioned Provisions in a Cask, with a lid and Padlock, My Dear, you will find it very miserable aboard Ship, Unless you have netting or needle work I dare say you can Find Plenty to do for our Dear Boys, for the Colony, Bless there little Hearts, there is not a day, But I think of you and them, And very often Dream at night, I am as true to you My Dear now, as Ever I was, Since we were married And I cannot Live without you and my Boys. There is splendid whether here for weeks and weeks now and then a Hot winds which makes the dust Blow, Smothers every thing, But what matters if we are doing First rate and saving an Independence than we can return to old England and live a life of Comfort, We know not how long our lives are to last, So its as well to prepare as soon as we can, The diggings is Favourable, But I am for Stopping here, it is the Surest Diggings For me, Tell Charley to Send or Bring Some Small tools. and Large gageing Trowels I bought three Small tools for 2/6 each and could sell at 4 times that price I am in hopes of haveing a Considerable Sum of Money by the time you arrive here to Start Business, Plaster and Cement.

Believe me my Dear Wife
I remain your Affectionate Husband
Francis Mapleson.

30 Charlton Street,
St. Pancris. London.
July 3rd, 1854.

My Dear Brother,
I hope this will find quite well I have writen this to tell you about your Poor Wife. She is very ill wich no dout you will know By your Brothers Letter before you received this. She was taken ill six weeks ago on Saturday last she was taken ill with the Bilous feaver it then turned to Brain feaver and for a month she was considered to be in the Greatest of danger we was up all Night and day with her thinking every hour would be her last her head was shaved and some Leaches a plied and 4 or five Blisters on her and her head im Beded ice for weeks together she did not know any one not even the Dear children but now I am happy to say that she is considered out of danger and been this last fortnight but still in that weak state she can not Rise herself in Bed no moore than a new Born Baby I sincerely hope with cair and nurishing things that she will soon

be restored to her Dear Children. Mrs. Day told me that its nothing will make her happy until you meet again the worry that she hase had have been to much for any woman to bare up against. Mrs. Burjis and myself have managed to keep the Business in the Shop together but there have been a great out Lay altho we have not had strangers in to asist us but you know how expensive illness is Mrs. Day say that as soon as she is able to be mooved she must go in the Country for a few weeks as much for change of scene as for change of air so we think of sending her down to Wimborne as soon as she can take the journey. Henry came up to see her a live when he left her he have invited very kindly for her to come down to Wimbourne we are expecting to hear from you by the next Mail that comes in. Susan very much hope that you will come home if you do not I hope you will send for her you will know by this time wether you can get a better Living there than you can at home and Pray do write often. She must have something to chear her up. Your mother and Sisters are all well but your Uncle William is dead and Buried this fortnight past and your brother and his sc . . . ue [shrew?] of a Wife is still at Sidham they never had the kindness to take the Poor Children a way from home for a week or two when we had got the Feaver in the house nor yet to sit up for one hour to relive us that could hardly drag one Leg after the other, all they was looking out for was gain all they did was write to you and that they might have left alone untill the danger was over its not like where you can write now contridict the next say it what I call unnesery truble altho if I had got you hear I would not spare you I can tell you I would for old and New, You must excuse moor at present but be shure to write soon I must tell you your Dear Boys are quite well they often talk about there father that is in the ship they are two nice children.

Good by may God bless you I am most affectionate Sister
Caraline Davis

I wish kind care to you I hope I shall have better news for you next time.

London.
Oct. 8th, 1854

My Dear Husband,
I received your very kind letter this last week and it has put me in such good spirits to think that the time is not far distant when I hope to meet you and to bring our Dear Boys to see ther father the Children are quite well and I am much better but still very weak my Dear Frank I have only just heard that the over Land Mail leaves London this Evening and I have only a few minutes to write but I now that you would be anxious to hear

from me and to know that I received your money order quite safe and of corse I do [not?] Hesetate in making up my mind to come.

I can only say that I will again tell you all particulars we are all well my Dear Husband and hope to meet you soon

from your ever affectionate wife
Susan Mapleson
good by God bless you

Document 2.8 A middle-class sister and brother consider their career options

Catherine Spence's first novel, Clara Morison, *was published in 1854 when its author was twenty-eight years old and looking for respectable employment—a difficult quest for a woman. She places the two heroines of her novel, Clara and Margaret, in different versions of the same dilemma. The conversation reproduced here from the novel shows the very different possibilities open to educated men and women in the developing colonial democracies.*[8]

'Gilbert', Margaret answered, 'I have a great deal to say to you . . . surely there need be no half-hints or beating about the bush between brother and sister; particularly between such a brother and sister as we are. I have always thought that such a family as ours forms a valuable element in colonial society; we came here not to make our fortunes and leave the colony forthwith, but to grow up and settle in it; we have all rather more than average abilities; we have had good principles instilled in us from early youth; we have all a deep feeling of our accountability to God for both our private and public conduct; we have all, I think, a love for the country of our adoption, and a wish to serve it; and we are not eager about money—we do not care to make haste to be rich, at least we used to show moderation on this point, though lately I have been grieved to see this passion growing upon you.'

'It is not love of money, Margaret,' said Gilbert, eagerly; 'it is because wealth is the only lever by which we can move our little world. It is money that brings distinction, influence, and authority, and because nothing else can do so. We have no patronage in the colonies; even supposing I became a first-rate lawyer, as I could if I tried, should I ever have a chance of rising to the bench, or even of being advocate-general? . . . Every office is filled by some needy hanger-on of Downing Street; by some second or third-rate middle-aged men, who would never understand our wants, and never learn to care for our interests . . . '

'But before you are a first-rate lawyer, I expect that things will be changed here. I think that the discovery of these gold-fields will throw us at once into a more advanced state; I do not mean of morals, but it will bring us improvements in arts and sciences; we shall have steam and railways; towns will grow suddenly into cities; population will increase at an unexampled rate; and not only diggers and speculators will come to our shores, but men of intellect and enterprise . . . And, Gilbert, we shall soon be an important nation; you must get into council by-and-bye, and help to clear away the cumbrous and expensive trappings of justice . . . If you can make any improvements in our criminal law—if you can make our prison discipline reformatory—if you can do something towards raising our moral standard of education, so that we may not sink in the scale of nations through having been deluged with thieves and pickpockets—you will have lived to a great and useful purpose. Yes, Gilbert, you must get into council, and I must live to see it.'

'As a delegate!' exclaimed Gilbert, scornfully. 'Shall it be mine to implore the most sweet voices of the lieges, with bowing and cringing? to represent all men as naturally equal? and—reckoning the most ignorant mechanics or day-labourers as wise as myself—humbly beg them to accept of me as their mouth-piece, and return to my constituents every session for instructions what to say, and how to vote?'

'No, you must be a representative, not a delegate,' Margaret answered; 'you need not cringe to the people, but, on the other hand, you must not despise them. They certainly have a right to some courtesy and consideration. You must speak the truth, and deal honestly, and I believe you will inspire confidence . . . '

'If I were to go to the diggings, would you stay contentedly with George?' Gilbert asked.

'No; I have thought of opening a school in the most populous part of the town. I suppose I might expect a grant from government, and that even our liberal legislators would not prevent me from teaching religion, as far as a human teacher can instil it. I can afford to teach for very low fees, if I had not a high rent to pay for my school-room, for my wants are very few. The very poorest children I would teach for nothing, for you know, Gilbert, that there is a great lack of labourers in this harvest, and girls are tempted by the high wages offered them, to go to service before they can read their Bibles, and before they have any distinct principles of right and wrong to guide them through life. They are exposed to many dangers and temptations, cast amongst strangers with empty minds and uncultivated consciences; they marry young, and often imprudently; and when children come, they do not know how to teach them anything.

"Religion can be taught only at the mother's knee", say our liberal members; but if the mothers know nothing of it, what is to become of the children; I suppose it is better that they should perish for lack of knowledge, than that the government should lift its finger to save them. But so long as the same government will let me work on sufferance in a cause which it disowns, I suppose I may do so.'

'But you do not like teaching, Margaret,' said Gilbert.

'I can't help my likings or dislikings, Gilbert,' she replied.

'But do you think you will ever make a good teacher, without some natural taste for the occupation? It is dreadful drudgery to teach such ignorant and tiresome children as you propose to instruct. You will meet with nothing but ingratitude from your pupils and their parents, and you will perhaps hear the inspector say, that Miss Elliot is in great want of training, and that she has apparently taken up the business for a livelihood, as she has neither the acquired skill nor the natural talent requisite for success. To think that *you*, who have never been found fault with in your life—*you*, who are so admired and honoured in your own family, should be subjected to such remarks! The man might recommend you to go to a normal school!' [for training teachers]

Margaret's colour had changed several times during her brother's speech. She put her hand to her heart, as she answered—'Perhaps the best thing I could do would be to go to a normal school, but there is none within reach. I must do something more interesting than washing dishes and sweeping floors—very good occupations in their way, but not enough to fill my mind. I have been grieved at my distaste to teaching, and that at twenty-five I am not as pliant as I was at eighteen; but . . . I must bend myself to the only career now open to me, and undertake a sort of ragged school.'

Document 2.9 A young lady seeks economic independence

Menie Parkes was eighteen years old when she wrote the following letters to her father, Henry Parkes, then the editor of The Empire *newspaper and a Member of Parliament. His reply does not survive, but it appears that he answered her plan for economic independence—opening a school—by suggesting a more radical movement into the public sphere. Parkes seems to have offered to employ his daughter as a kind of parliamentary secretary. Menie's response is also reproduced here. In the event, neither plan came to anything.[9]*

April 24th [1858]

My dear Father,

I have for some time felt that I should prefer earning my own living, to being dependent on you, as I now am, and have formed a project which I think must meet with your approbation.

I will study pretty closely, during the next twelve months, the common course of an English education, the rudiments of the French Language and Theory of music; I would then, open an infant School under 12 years of age undertaking to prepare them thoroughly for a higher school, and to teach the elder children the stepping stones to Music, French, and Drawing (things I know are very little attended to in other schools, because the children must practice and so no time is left for theory, but which is nevertheless very important).

I would charge for each pupil, 2 Guineas per quarter and supposing I only had 4 pupils; this would amount to 32 Guineas the year, sufficient to clothe myself and one of the children [her sisters] but, it is not improbable that I should have 12 or 15.

If my plan succeeded, in a short time I might engage teachers for accomplishments, which would further add to my own gains.

The school hours would commence at ½ past 9 and close at 4, as others do, allowing me plenty of time to rest, beside the periodical holidays, so that, you see, I should not be overworked, but find a pleasant occupation profitable.

If I gained enough I might be able to pay for Music Lessons for myself and Mary and of course I should continue to teach her as before.

Do not throw this aside as a foolish, girlish idea for really I am in earnest and should feel very, very much happier if I saw any prospect of rendering myself independant, and do not think it would be any sacrifice on my part for I shall feel much gratified if you consent to my plan.

I shall be in my 20th year at the time I mention

I remain My dear father
Your affectionate daughter
Menie

May 5th 1858

My dear Father,

Your letter disarranged all my thoughts, and certainly very much surprised me; I had just reconciled myself to the idea that you did not think mine worth notice when I received it.

You warn me, dear Father, not to indulge in morbid feelings; I think I can safely say that you can not count up one half the reasons for thankfullness and joy that I find in my life, it is very seldom my thoughts are other than joyous, and if they are sad, they are sweeter even than the glad. This sounds rather romantic, but it is true and as I cannot explain myself better I will even let it be as it is.

I cannot think that all things should be held subordinate to the purpose of fitting myself for married life, when I may die at any hour, or if living, may never marry:—ought I not rather, to fit myself to pass through the world unaided? And then, if God rule that I shall become so far happy as to be a wife and mother, surely His guidance and my own love for the dear beings with whom I should pass through life would teach me far better than all forethought how to do my duty womanfully towards them.

For *your* plan now—my reasons for it are—*First* that I feel more than ever the desire to have some definate and from day-to-day-continuing aim in life.

Second I do not think it right that I, if I have the ability to help myself should be doing nothing but hanging a burden upon you.

Third It is a dear wish of mine to be independent of any one at all.

Fourth I think the intellect is brightened by being used, and mine wants rubbing up a little.

Fifth I should like to spend more of my time with you.

Sixth I do really like your plan better than my own.

And now against it.

First I doubt my ability to undertake what you propose. Summaries of news, or anything that is merely collecting, classifying, or condensing events or the works of other men's brains I think I am equal to, but no further.

Second Your arrangement about coming up and down in the steamers seems to me very expensive, the least it would cost would be £1 in the week.

Third I am afraid that if at any time I should fail, you would become angry and as sure as you did, what little intellect I have would become confused at once I am certain.

Fourth Mamma does not like the plan at all; she says that it would perfectly unfit me for womanly life that I should become estranged from her, that I should often get wet through going down and so risk my health and she thinks the steamer plan decidedly too expensive.

Now dear Father, if you say 'Yes', I say Yes willing, if you say 'No' I say No too.

What do you think I want with £2 or £3 a week about 10 shillings is enough to clothe me and I do not want any more.

If you decide that I shall remain where I am I hope you will allow me to look forward a year hence, when we leave Helenie it is possible

some other plan may be made for my assisting you and in the meantime,
this preparation for so doing would be a point for me to aim at.

Your affectionate child
Menie Parkes

Document 2.10 A woman asks for the vote for women

*Manhood suffrage—the right of all men to vote—was achieved in
South Australia, New South Wales and Victoria during the last years
of the 1850s. The inclusion of women in what was sometimes called
'universal' suffrage was never seriously considered by legislators at
the time. Women made almost no public protest about their exclusion
from political citizenship. The letter following is one of only four
discovered in the major colonial papers of the period. The author is
very much at home in the language of the very same male democracy
that excludes her. We know her only by her signature here, 'H'.*[10]

Sydney Morning Herald, 2 July 1858

Sir,—May I beg your insertion of the few following remarks, upon a
question deeply interesting to a large proportion of your readers, and one
which will well bear ventilation just now. I refer to the claims of women
to participation in the elective franchise.

That the elective franchise is not a natural or inherent right in any
class of the community is sufficiently proved by the history of the
representative principle. The franchise is a privilege conferred by the
commonwealth itself, upon certain classes of its members. The question
then is: are there any valid reasons for refusing this privilege to women,
who, but for their sex—the accident of birth—would, by the present laws,
be entitled to it? I opine that numerous positive evils result to women,
and through women to society at large, in consequence of that policy
which restricts the franchise to male persons only; and that there are no
objections to a more equitable distribution of civil rights, which will bear
the test of calm, impartial, scrutiny.

In the first place, Sir, it seems to me that this restrictive policy
introduces a principle into our polity as, to my thinking, erroneous. It
applies a physical condition as a test of moral fitness. A man possessing
a certain fixed property qualification is presumed to have that degree of
intelligence necessary to a right exercise of this civil privilege; but a
woman—although she have tenfold more discretion, talent, virtue, knowledge, genius, or property—shall never under any circumstances be
admitted to participate. Because she is a woman—and for no other reason,

she is, and so long as the present system lasts—she will be disenfranchised. I confess I do not see the justice of this, while women are competing with men now in many a walk of life, and with quite as much success upon the whole as the more favoured sex can boast of. Did the mischief stop at this, Sir, I could perhaps be better content, though even then the injustice to that large class of women who are and always must be independent of husband or brother would not be the less: but it does not. It leads to the habitual depreciation of women. While every possible inducement to active exertion is held out to a man, women are forbidden to obtrude beyond the precincts of home. Men are well educated, but women are neglected. Having no political power in a free commonwealth, the wisest woman must in a sense be of less value than the ignorant, but qualified male. Society feels this, and acts on it too, most painfully to our feelings at some times. It degrades us in our own eyes, encourages frivolity of mind and habit, for it makes us think our time and talents are of less importance to the State than those of the other sex. It lowers our self-respect, and so offers a field for the intrusion of seriously vicious influences. It brings women into general contempt. They were saved from this when the feudal practices answered to the feudal principles. When the strong arm and ready hand were really the most needful matters to public policy, women were not contemned because they were women. They could not bring that to the public service which was most necessary. It is otherwise now. While women are as well able to be wise and pay taxes as men are, they are debarred the correlative privileges of men; and men, forgetting their own injustice, contemn women now because while the old feudal inabilities have passed away, the old feudal disenfranchisements remain. Disenfranchisement . . . limits our social importance, confines our ambitions to the becoming of wife and mother . . . I used to wonder, when I heard of women ascribing much of the sex's immorality . . . to the operation of our laws, shutting us out from political privileges, conferring numberless privileges in respect not only of the elective franchise, but of property and other things upon men, but I do so no longer. Much of the general misunderstanding of and about women is most clearly traceable to our political *non status* . . .

There are no unanswerable objections to this extension of the franchise; at least none have yet met me. It is useless to say that a woman's possession of the franchise would provoke dissensions in married life. Married people who could seriously quarrel upon such matters must be those alone whose homes are already made unhappy from some other cause. I have little fear that the wife would not as readily and certainly respect her husband then as she does now. Nay, if I know anything of the sex, deserving husbands would find themselves the stronger for the woman's greater power. It is equally useless to urge the impropriety of women being mixed up with election bustle and riot. It is quite fair in answer to such an argument to ask whether if women were invested with the franchise, elections would not be more orderly? Which is most feasible, that men should reduce women to participation in the practices of which they are themselves ashamed, or women induce men to conduct themselves at such times with the greater propriety? Equally futile is the objection that women are ignorant of public life and public characters. The same argument has been urged against every extension of the franchise, and with equal justice. Nor does the universality of the custom of excluding the suffrages of women afford any sufficient reason for refusing the privilege I claim. The world has all been barbarous. Hitherto class by class of men has uprisen and broken through the toils in which that early barbarism had involved them. There is scarcely a single one among the classes now most powerful whose suffrages were not at one time universally excluded. The argument has not held good in any one such case. Why should it more apply to women than to men? The question is whether while the race has always been unjust to men, it has always dealt justly with women? Were men alone oppressed by barbarous politics? Were women always free? Sir I maintain that it is not because justice has never been done to women, that therefore it never should be done. Let it be shewn that women have no claim—that because of a physical inferiority . . . they ought for ever to be classed politically with idiots, lunatics, traitors, and felons, all of whom are alike incapable of the franchise, and I abandon myself to contented darning for all time to come . . .

Sir, I do hope that the Legislature will at least concede a partial reform. There are many women here possessing property, sustaining such social positions too, as if they were men would perforce confer the franchise. They have not disqualification but the accident of their sex. Surely to them, at least, may be conceded so much as a share in the election of tax-making members, while they themselves are taxpayers.

Your obedient servant,
H.

Document 2.11 A wife advises her husband on raising sheep

During the 1840s and 1850s, Charlotte Bussell worked alongside her husband John to establish their Western Australian farm. In 1858 they were planning to concentrate on wool production, and Charlotte paid a visit to her brother John's property in New South Wales, to see

how they did it over there. Her letter to her husband suggests a woman
who knows her own worth.[11]

Terragong, N.S.W.,
September 1st, 1858.

My dearest John,

The spring has commenced and so has the lambing. I rode out to one of
the stations 2½ miles off the other evening to see them. They were looking
so well and healthy. The weather is mild and lovely, such a contrast to
our lambing season.

The fold was on the side of a hill, and formed into three compartments
. . . I was amazed with the odd terms they have for distinguishing the
inmates of the different compartments. There were 'the full-bellied mob',
'the strong mob', and 'the green mob'. The first and largest are those that
have not yet dropped their lambs, but are expected to do daily. The second
are those that are about a week or ten days old, and the third those that
have been born within the last day or two. They are all kept distinct, that
they may be driven as far as the strength of each respective mob will
enable it to go, and no further. The entrances . . . are all at different sides,
so that they go off in different directions. The *green mob* keep nearly in
sight of the fold all day, but the shepherds with their long boughs in their
hands are perpetually moving about, disturbing the lambs gently, that they
may not sleep too long, which I suppose enables their mothers to give
them food. As soon as the green mob are about a week old, and considered
strong enough, they are drafted into the *strong mob*, and walked to a
greater distance. Of an evening, the shepherds shut up the green and the
strong mobs first. Then all hands go off to assist the shepherd who has
charge of *the full-bellied mob*. Here they find a great number of lambs
that have been dropped during the day, or perhaps within the last hour or
two, so that they require to be carried home . . . In this flock John took
me to see, there are about twelve to fourteen hundred ewes, and not one
lamb has he lost yet, so much does care and a proper system effect. He
rides out every morning after breakfast to see how they are going, and
generally again in the evening, and you and I will do the same, dearest,
when I come back again. This time next year, I hope ours will be lambing.
In April you must put the rams into the fold and not before, and you must
allow two rams for every hundred ewes. If you have a less number a great
many of the ewes will not lamb. Some consider three rams necessary for
every hundred, so, dearest, you must increase your number forthwith, if
you have not already done so. In selecting, observe that the wool is very
close, and apparently ribbed. The more wool upon it, the more valuable

the ram is; it should be down to its feet—over its head, so that it can but just see out of its eyes, and its body completely covered underneath as well as on the back. John called me out to the yard the other evening to see one he had given ten guineas for, and had since been offered 20 guineas, but he would not part with it until he had obtained young stock from it. He pointed out to me the peculiar merits which were the quantity and fineness of its fleece . . .

Tomorrow I am going to ride out with John, to his mountain station, where I have not been yet. It is about five miles off. The flock we have at the homestead is a wether flock, with rams included, altogether about 1,200. You would be surprised to see how the wealthy squatters in this country keep branching out and forming new stations. They think nothing of distance and difficulties. The greater the difficulty the more pleasure they seem to have in contending with and overcoming it . . . They are very fond of asking me questions about Western Australia, and seem astonished at the small way in which we go on, after being there so many years. 'The Swan River settlers, Mrs Bussell, appear to have no grasp of mind. Their views are too narrow, too confined. They should come here and learn a lesson. We never allow anything to daunt us. We don't believe in impossibilities.'

You say, or at least the girls do, that Mr Wright is very fond of this expression. I suppose he acquired it here. I hope, my own darling, you will use it when you think of fetching me from King George's Sound, and not let the difficulty of the undertaking annoy you. As to the funds, something will be sure to turn up, but you must not delay—for the present arrangement for steam communication is only promised until the 11th of December. After that the Home Government are going to make another arrangement with the Cunard Company; so that if I do not leave Sydney by the December mail of the 11th, no one can say how long I may have to wait . . .

Document 2.12 Parliamentarians approve a divorce bill

Unlike British legislators, who tended to see divorce legislation as a means of freeing men from adulterous wives, the colonial law-makers who supported divorce legislation did so for the sake of industrious women tied to absent or violent husbands. In the South Australian Legislative Council (a very middle-class body), this chivalrous attitude extended to a general reluctance to pass that clause of the bill which allowed men divorce on the grounds of simple adultery by their wives, but required wives to prove aggravated adultery; the debate is repro-duced here. The members of the democratically elected House of

Assembly were much less chivalrous; a small minority wanted to amend the relevant clause to include equal grounds for husbands and wives, but others wanted to delete the clause altogether, allowing only judicial separation and not divorce. In the end the bill passed both Houses unamended.[12]

Tuesday, September 7, 1858

LEGISLATIVE COUNCIL DIVORCE AND MATRIMONIAL CAUSES

The Chief Secretary, in accordance with the notice which he had given, asked leave to introduce a Bill intituled 'an Act to amend the laws relating to Divorce and Matrimonial cases in South Australia'. The purposes which the Bill sought to attain had been the subject of grave consideration by the Imperial Parliament. The subject had been debated in both Houses of Legislature, and the result had been the framing and passing of an Act nearly a literal transcript of which he now proposed to introduce to the notice of that House. He would endeavour briefly to apprise hon. members of the novel features which were enunciated by this measure. It proposed to give powers to the Supreme Court of this colony to grant divorces in cases of adultery, or cruelty, or desertion for a period of two years upwards. That was, it proposed to give the Court power to pronounce a judicial separation—such a judicial separation as would have an exactly similar effect to a divorce *a mensa et thoro*, as pronounced by the Ecclesiastical Courts at home. The operation would sever the tie between husband and wife as effectually as if though they had never been united; but neither would have the power to marry again. There was a further provision in the Bill, by which a wife, who had been deserted by her husband, might at any time make application to a stipendiary magistrate, or a Judge of the Supreme Court, and obtain protection of any property which she had accumulated during her desertion, such protection operating, not only against her husband, but against her husband's creditors. The Bill also authorised a Judge of the Supreme Court, in such cases as detailed in Clause 12, to decree an entire dissolution of the matrimonial tie. It also gave power to the Judge to decree an order for alimony, after such dissolution had taken place, and provide the best means of education and taking care of the children by the marriage . . . The Bill was very nearly a transcript of that which has been introduced in the Imperial Parliament, being merely altered to adapt it to the judicial system in South Australia . . . With respect to the merits of the principles contained in the Bill, he thought the House would agree with him, that there should be some law of the kind in South Australia, for he thought there were few hon. members

who had not, in their own individual experience, witnessed the social evils
arising from husbands deserting their families, and afterwards returning,
and sweeping away the hard earnings of an industrious wife. (Hear, hear.)
Under the existing law a worthless husband might do so again and again,
till the poor woman at last, in all probability, became spirit-broken, or her
moral courage gave way, and she was driven to an immoral course, and
her children became members of the Destitute Asylum, and a permanent
burden on the country. He was confident that hon. members would agree
with him that social evils of that kind should be remedied with as little
delay as possible. (Hear, hear.) As to the absolute dissolution of the
marriage tie, which the Bill also provided for. Extreme cases occasionally
arose in every class of society, such as were indicated in Clause 12. Under
the existing law, he was aware of no remedy, but the injured party was
obliged to pass his or her life in misery and torment, and their earthly
career was probably terminated by some act of brutal violence. The only
course of procedure under the present state of things, was to apply to
Parliament by petition for a private Bill, and this Bill, after passing through
the usual formalities, and going through both Houses of the Legislature,
could not be assented to by the Governor, but must obtain the assent of
the Queen before it could become of any value. He thought the House
would agree with him that it was the duty of Parliament to give the same
facilities in all matters of legislation to the poor as to the rich, which the
present Bill proposed . . .

Tuesday September 21

. . . The 12th clause ['On adultery of the wife, or incestuous adultery etc.
of the husband, petition for dissolution of marriage may be presented.']
was recommitted.

The Hon. Captain Hall thought it was a one-sided clause. He thought
there should be no partialities. What was wrong in one sex must be so
also in the other. They should not make one law for the man and one for
the woman. The commandment made no difference. Certainly the enlightened Legislature of another country had passed a law similar to that before
the Council, but they might strike out a course for themselves, and by
maintaining the 'rights of women' they would not be retrograding in the
scale of civilization.

The Hon. Captain Scott proposed to insert the word 'adultery' before
'incestuous adultery' [which would have had the effect of making the
grounds for divorce the same for men and women].

The Hon. the Chief Secretary read a passage from a recent dispatch,
to prove that if there were any material alteration made in the Bill, as not

being in harmony with the English Act, it would have the effect of invalidating it.

The Hon. Mr Forster, on moral grounds, approved of the suggested alteration. But rather than the Bill should be jeopardized, he would like the clause to be postponed. The social effect of adultery in a wife was also greater than it would be in a husband . . . .

The Hon. Mr Morphett hoped the Council would take the same view as he did, and oppose the alteration of the clause. It was precisely the same as that passed by the English Parliament. The only fear was that they might be looking to make divorce too easy if they agreed to the amendment proposed. The object of the Bill was to bring the matter out of the Ecclesiastical Court into the Civil Court . . .

The Hon. A. Scott said the clause as it stood was an instance of the stronger party against the weaker. It intimated that the wife could do no wrong, but that the husband should be allowed greater indulgence. (A laugh.) A slight laxity of morals would be all. The hon. gentleman concluded with the hope that the clause would be remodelled.

The Hon. Mr Ayers said that morally, the duties of husband and wife were the same; but the present question was whether they should pass an Act similar to the English Act or not. There was so much jealousy maintained at home with regard to any alteration in our Marriage Act, that he thought it would be only putting the Act in jeopardy to amend the clause as it stood . . .

The Hon. Capt Hall said some of the speakers seemed to think that half a loaf was better than no bread. Rather than lose the benefit of the Bill he should withdraw his opposition.

After some further discussion the clause was passed as printed.

Document 2.13 A young lady finds that men are vile

Blanche Mitchell's diary has something of the self-dramatising quality of Annie Baxter's (Document 2.3). However, it was not intended for anyone else to read, and was more of a confessional for its young author. As the daughter of an important government official, Blanche mixed socially with members of the wealthiest and most powerful families in Sydney, but financial difficulties made her position insecure, and she was prone to depression.

At the time of this extract Blanche, aged sixteen, had only recently begun attending the kind of balls and parties where she would meet young men to whom she had not previously been introduced. Few Sydney-born bachelors were considered sufficiently eligible as marriage partners by families like the Mitchells, and Blanche and her friends were steered into the company of visiting gentlemen, often military and naval officers. But not all the visitors behaved like gentlemen.[13]

Thursday 18th August, 1859.

. . . At six began to dress, for some of the *Pelorus'* [the officers from a visiting warship] are coming over. Soon a good many ladies came who were to form some of the party, and when the room was full of girls all dressed in white and all standing in a row, only two of the *Pelorus'* officers came, the Chaplain and the 1st Lieutenant. Of course we were very much astonished to see so few and Mrs Mann [the hostess] told Mr Kelly, one of the two, to go over and fetch some more, which was agreed to after a great deal of laughter. Mr Kelly left and we all waited for the others. After some time four more came and we commenced dancing which did not cease till two in the morning. But oh! I dislike all the officers, they are not gentlemen. One of them, a Mr Jay, a young fellow who I danced very much with, kept perpetually giving me a gentle squeeze now and then and taking hold of my hand and squeezing it and then placing it on his heart. I, oh I am so dreadfully foolish, so silly and weak. I am too young to go out! I am at present in a great rage, how shall I write what one of the officers did to me, to *me* the daughter of Sir T. Mitchell and superior to them all, to *me* as if I were a barmaid or a servant of any description! To be insulted, and I like a fool never got indignant at the time, never shewed any anger, but I will here write the fact. One of them, Dr Bowen, who at first I thought a very nice fellow, asked me to walk out in the verandah with him, and I foolishly went. As soon as we came to a dark part of the verandah he took my hand and commenced pressing it gently and then more, and at last took my whole hand and kept it close in his. I got dreadfully frightened, felt as if I would faint. He then asked me if I would go to another part of the verandah with him which was farther away, but I refused and said I would rather go in. Still he kept my hand and seeing that I did not draw it away, he put his arm round my waist and kept it there and I, why did I not then move his arm away and say peremptorily to go in? No, although I repeatedly said it I did not move because I was afraid of offending him. I felt inclined to faint and could hardly breathe. He went on talking I do not know what about nor what I answered, I only knew it was very wrong and that I ought to behave more firmly. But these reflections were of no use for I never moved and finally he put his head closer to mine and kissed me and instead of springing up and rushing away I just quietly knocked my head away and said, 'Oh we had better go in', and instantly went in when, shame to me, I mentioned nothing about it but danced with him the following dance and then again later a quadrille and laughed and talked with him. I could not have taken notice of it, for I was so thunderstruck, so ashamed and indignant that I could make no mention of it though of course I ought to have done so. So dreadfully miserable about it, did not know what to do, but pretended to be quite cheerful and gay. At last they went and we, after eating supper, retired to bed. Another thing, too, Dr Bowen said I was asking him what was good for chilblains and he told me a cure if I would try it. We all said we most certainly would and then he said essence of tulip which is pronounced 'too-lip'. We thought it was tulip that he meant and said to-morrow we would get some. After they had gone Miss Rogers told us it meant two lips to kiss, that it was a common saying. That was such a horrid thing to say. Went to sleep in high indignation at that horrid Dr Bowen.

Friday 19th August

This morning told Minnie in strict injunctions of secrecy of that horrid Dr Bowen, felt melancholy all the morning about it and how carelessly and badly, in fact with what levity I had behaved. She was equally shocked at me. Came away about twelve. Told Milly and Alice about it who were perfectly surprised and scolded me very much. Oh, what shall I do? If the world hears of it I shall lose all my character and be considered so light. Why did I not run away from him! Oh have I done wrong? I was too inexperienced to know better but my own sense should have guided me. When I look at other girls I fancy now how different they are to me, they have not suffered such a degradation. Oh, what shall I do? Cried all day, could do nothing, reading had no interest for me. Milly says she shall tell Mrs Mann and then how badly they will think of me. Received comfort from Mamma, who consoled me and told me to think no more about it, that I had only acted wrongly in dancing with him again, etc. Felt comforted. Oh, in how many cases of sorrow has Mamma eased me from trouble and how do I requite her! Felt almost ashamed to look anyone in the face. Mr Dauncey bantering and laughing at me. Went to bed early . . .

Part 3
Frontiers—rural and urban 1860–1885

In the 25 years from 1860 to the mid-1880s many white women shared with white men the prosperity that came from a booming economy. New mining possibilities attracted men into Queensland and the north. Squatters also pushed the frontiers of white settlement further north and west, repeating the destruction of Aboriginal lives and lands of earlier invasions. The Selection Acts enabled aspiring farmers to acquire small allotments carved from squatters' runs. Some succeeded in gaining a comfortable living and some failed; others eked out a mere subsistence only by the hard work of all family members, including women and older children. Compared with even the poorest of white female settlers, however, Aboriginal women suffered desperate privation in areas where their traditional lands had been usurped by whites. The creation of separate missions and reserves, intended for their protection, often subjected Aboriginal women and men to further oppression from white officials and missionaries, whose record in this period of Australian history ranges from the insensitive to the disgraceful.

These years also saw the remarkable growth of colonial cities and towns, foremost among them Melbourne and Sydney, founded on the wealth and increase in migration generated by the gold rushes. White women in cities, as in rural areas, had very different prospects, depending on their own or their male relatives' income and occupation. Factories were built, and shops and offices proliferated, offering white women opportunities for paid work other than the usual domestic service. But the work could be hard, hours long, and the financial rewards meagre. Male trade unions were small and craft-based, their members concerned more with protecting a 'social wage' that would support their dependent wives and children than with fighting for justice for women workers. The tailoresses of Melbourne who formed a union and staged a notable strike in 1882 had unusual, but short-lived, success. Amid the affluence of colonial cities, slums, overcrowding and poverty developed in parallel with the tree-lined avenues of the suburbs and the neat cottages of better-off working-class people.

In the suburbs married women in comfortable circumstances could enjoy the material privileges of their domestic existence and, if their marriages were amicable, found their own ways to exert influence over their husbands. Women with servants at their command had the time to exert their abilities in such activities as involvement in benevolent societies which were crucial in mediating between colonial governments and impoverished, ill or abandoned women and children. For many middle-class single women this was scarcely sufficient labour, and unremunerated at that. As the campaign to provide secondary education for girls took hold, some aimed at university degrees and professional work. New and radical liberal voices were raised, advocating civil rights for women, the reform of marriage laws on divorce and property and the right of women to vote for colonial legislatures. One woman, Henrietta Dugdale, wrote of a utopia where women would be men's equals, and the supposed womanly qualities of nurturance, good sense and peace would predominate over the supposed masculine qualities of aggression and power.

Document 3.1 A white Queensland girl observes Aborigines

Rosa Praed (1851–1935), who later became a prolific novelist, spent her early years on her father's station, 'Naraigin', in rural Queensland. In 1902, in London, she wrote an autobiography, My Australian Girlhood, *and sketched with some nostalgia her memories of station life in the late 1850s and early 1860s. Rosa Praed is an exception among the many Europeans who left Aborigines out of their narratives of colonial life. As a child she had played with Aboriginal children and observed local Aboriginal life with intense curiosity. Nevertheless her recollections are imbued with the patronising racial attitudes prevalent in white society, and in the final paragraph of this passage she echoes, albeit with more sympathy than many whites showed, the common opinion that the Aborigines were a 'dying race'. Certainly, the Aboriginal population had been severely reduced by European diseases and by the cruel consequences of dispossession, but the view that the indigenous population of Australia would disappear was more a case of wishful thinking than a demographic fact.*[1]

c. 1860

The lagoon was another great feature in that childlife, and also the Blacks' camp beside it, where Billabong Jenny, our black nurse, used to take us, when mother had things to do or went out riding on the run with the gentlemen and left us in Jenny's charge. The dogs would rush out barking as we approached, and the blackfellows sprawling on the 'possum rugs by their fires, with their dirty bits of cooked bandicoot or snake or iguana beside them—I can smell the burnt flesh now—would slap at the dogs, calling 'Eoogh! Eoogh!' which in the camp means that there's nothing to get into a fuss about . . . .

The gins and the picaninnies were always in the lagoon, which facilitated our intercourse. They used to dive under the blue water-lilies and pluck up the roots, that were like small yams. When roasted in the ashes, these bulbs became yellow and powdery, and were as dear to our semi-civilised palates as they were to the stomachs of our savage companions the picaninnies. Gastronomically speaking, I learned a good deal from the Blacks, particularly from a certain half-caste boy called Ringo, who was the first object of my youthful affections. Indeed, there was serious thought of an elopement to the scrub with Ringo, but upon going into the question of the marriage laws of the race, we discovered that he, being a Cuppi, was bound to wed with a Dongai, or undergo the penalty of excommunication, and perhaps death. So reflecting that as I was not a Dongai, though living near the Donga Creek, we should probably both be knocked on the head with a nulla-nulla and then eaten after a corroboree, we thought better of the elopement. Ringo taught me also to find and appreciate a fat, white grub, the native name of which I forget, though I should like to recommend it to European and Australian epicures. I also made acquaintance, under Ringo's auspices, with the flesh of the iguana and that especial delicacy, the eggs of the black snake. I learned, too, at the camp to plait dilly-bags, to chop sugar-bags (otherwise hives of native bees) out of trees, to make drinking vessels from gourds, and to play the jew's-harp; but English life is not adapted to the display of these accomplishments.

The camp Blacks were not considered domesticated, and were migratory, coming and going about the stations, and just staying as long as they found themselves comfortable. They were only pressed into service when shepherds were scarce, or 'rung' trees—that is, gums which had been barked and allowed to wither—required felling. But we had several blackboys in regular employment, and these lived in a hut, wore clothes, and had adopted, as far as possible, the customs of the white men. These were Bean-Tree Dick, Freddy, and Tombo. They would not do anything except stock-keeping work, but used to ride among the cattle, looked for lost sheep, and brought up the horses. Their moleskins were always white; they wore Crimean shirts, with coloured handkerchiefs knotted above one shoulder and under the other, and sang songs in their own language set to operatic airs—they had learned them from a musical officer in the Native Police of the district . . .

Poor Tombo! In after years he forsook the paths of virtue, rejoined his tribe, met a missionary, and became demoralised in a township. He caused one of his child playfellows considerable embarrassment once in Brisbane, on occasion of a foundation-stone being laid by the Governor, or something of the sort. The child was a grown young lady then, and very proud of herself, as in the wake of a political personage she marched towards the dais for privileged spectators. But lo! from beneath the sawn wood erection, a blackfellow rushed forth, scantily clad, the tattoo-marks visible, extremely tipsy, and with a clay pipe thrust through his woolly locks. He took her hand; his greeting was effusive.

'Hallo! Budgery you! Sister belonging to me. Tsh! ts. ch!' making the Blacks' click of tongue and teeth expressive of admiration. 'My word! Ba'al you been wear-im frock like-it that long-a Naraigin! You pidney? (understand). What for you no glad to see Tombo? Plenty mine been brother belonging to you. Plenty mine been show you crack-im stockwhip. Plenty mine been carry you over creek,' and so on, through a list of humiliating reminiscences.

Our camp Blacks at Naraigin never stayed with us long, but would move on up or down the river, as soon as they were tired of us or we of them.

They had gradually got into intercourse with the Whites through bringing fish from the creek and things from the bush to the stockmen's huts, and had learned to love the stray presents they got, such as a pinch of flour, or sugar, or tobacco, the remains of any carcases of beasts that were killed at the yards, or a 'White Mary's' cast-off petticoat. Very often

they would be at variance with the tribe—perhaps for having transgressed
the strict marriage laws, which prohibit union within certain degrees of
relationship—and then they would come and put themselves under white
protection. Billabong Jenny and her husband Mundo were outcasts of this
kind, he being a Hippi, and she a Cuppi or Combo—I forget how it exactly
works out—and forbidden to wed. Anyhow, they took the law into their
own hands and escaped from the tribe . . .

Several years after that, White Massa sent messages and tried to
persuade the chiefs to forgive Mundo and Billabong Jenny, and to admit
them again into the tribe. He thought that he had succeeded; but the law
of the Blacks is not lightly to be set aside, and in due course there came
a command to Mundo to attend a great corroboree. Then Mundo was
afraid, though he still felt that a white medicine man who could pialla
[talk to] Debil-debil in a dream might have power with the native elders.
He was begged to disobey the order, but Mundo only shook his head.

'Ba'al you pidney, Massa,' he said. (You don't understand, Master.)
'Blackfellow not like-it white man. Suppose altogether Black chief say
come to corroboree—when like-it that, blackfellow must go.'

So he went sorrowful; and there came shortly afterwards a message
for Billabong Jenny telling her that Mundo was dead. Then arose a howling
from the camp such as had never been heard. The next day when we went
down to the Lagoon, Billabong Jenny was seated under a gum-tree alone
uttering dismal cries, and gashing herself with a knife, so that blood
mingled with her tears. After that, she lay in her gunyah, her head bound
up with dirty rags, her face hidden as she crouched with it against the
earth. She would not speak when we spoke to her, nor did she break
silence for many days till the time of her mourning was ended.

Oh yes, in the Blacks' camp, as in the squatters' humpey, there are
the human affections and the common emotions which men and women,
and even the beasts, share. There, too, the gins mourn their mates, and
the mothers love their babies. On the Burnett, though in summer the sun
scorches, and parching winds bring sandy blight, and flies torture, and
drought is a terror; yet in winter the same wind pierces chill to the marrow
of unclad creatures, and there are autumn rains which stream through into
the Blacks' gunyahs. Bad it is for the gin who has no 'possum rug, and
is burdened perhaps with a puling hybrid picaninny—a reproach to her
among the men of her tribe, so that she is desired of none of them. There
was Nunaina at our camp, who had a sickly yellow baby. She had come
from a tribe on the Milungera side, and she had lived in a Chinese
shepherd's hut, and had learned to speak English. She was a very pretty

gin, with smooth hair and large, soft eyes and lissome limbs, but she had fretted herself thin because the child was ailing. It had rained; after the rains came a cold wind, and food was scarce, and Nunaina shivered, and the baby cried, tugging at empty breasts. That was when the lagoon overflowed and joined the creek and the men crossed in tubs to take rations to the shepherds on the other side . . . It was when the waters went down that a little procession came out of the camp, following Nunaina and the child, which they laid under a gum-tree to die. Nunaina's face brightened as the little thing seemed to revive with the weak spirit and water that was poured down its throat, but she was bitter and very sad. 'How I make that fellow warm?' she said. 'Ba'al me got plenty blanket.' Then there was a great wail, and an old gin picked up the dead child. Nunaina threw herself upon the ground and put dust upon her head, and the other gins went back to the camp weeping. In the evening they made a hole for the little picaninny under the gum-trees, and then they shifted camp, for Blacks will not stay where one of them has been buried, believing that the spirit of the dead haunts the spot. A few days afterwards Nunaina came back, worn almost to a skeleton with grief; and she dug up the child's body and wrapped it in her blanket, and carried it away up along the Donga to bury it in the country of her own tribe.

But who cares now about the joys and sorrows, rights and wrongs of savages who cumber the earth no more! There has been no one to write the Blacks' epic; not many have said words in their defence; and this is but a poor little plea that I lay down for my old friends.

Document 3.2 A lady reformer on the tensions of city life

In the early 1860s Caroline Chisholm sustained her lively interest in colonial affairs. Unusually for a woman in this period, she was in great demand as a public speaker, and depended on it for her income. Always a protagonist for women, albeit within her own definition of their best interests, Chisholm here decries the squalor of much working-class housing, and criticises the behaviour of men who sought leisure away from the domestic hearth. She supported closer settlement of rural areas and emphasised the cottage, surrounded by garden, as the ideal location for family life. This was in line with her earlier advocacy of settling the interior of the country with small farmers, who, married to respectable young women and raising families, would have a 'civilising' influence on what she saw as the rough, male culture of the squatters whose sheep occupied large tracts of the countryside.

The Sydney Morning Herald *reported the following speeches.*[2]

February 1861

ST. BENEDICT'S YOUNG MEN'S SOCIETY—LECTURE BY MRS. CHISHOLM

The first lecture of the season in connection with this society, was delivered by Mrs. Caroline Chisholm, in the Society's Room, Abercrombie Street, yesterday evening. There was a very large attendance, the capacious room being full to excess. The Rev. Mr. Corish occupied the chair, and introduced Mrs. Chisholm, who proceeded to deliver a lecture on the early closing movement. After a few preliminary remarks, Mrs. Chisholm proceeded to touch upon the matter of the speeches recently delivered in the Temperance Hall . . . She complained that the speakers at the meeting referred to condemned the ladies as being the sole causes of late shopping. She admitted that the ladies did shop late, but she was quite certain it was the primary fault of the gentlemen. Why did not the legislators of Macquarie-street set an example by closing early? (Cheers.) She always considered that the morning was the proper time for business, and therefore she would like to see the business of the country done in the morning. (Cheers.) She proceeded to argue that the gentlemen were the primary cause of the late shopping system in this way—The gentlemen-husbands—instead of doing much of the work at their homes—work that the husbands alone ought to do—they left it at an early hour for their business, and spent their evening hours in other places than their homes, and consequently the time of the wives was taken up in doing the work referred to. Consequently they had to defer shopping till the evening. Or perhaps the husband, though wealthy, would allow only a certain amount as wages for servants, and consequently the wife could only keep two instead of three servants, and she therefore had to assist till late in the day, and hence again the necessity on that account of late shopping . . . Mrs. Chisholm proceeded to speak of a variety of topics—such as the conduct of husbands to their wives, domestic life in Sydney, and the desirability of having husbands returning home early and of remaining there. In order to accomplish this latter, Mrs. Chisholm advised all the ladies present to take in a newspaper. In the course of her experience she had known many instances where husbands had been induced to stay at home, and where eventually they educated themselves through having a daily newspaper taken. As there was a preponderance of ladies present she recommended them to note well the names of those drapers who closed their establishments at six o'clock. She then took occasion to combat a statement frequently put forth, namely that the squatters were the pioneers of civilisation in the colony, and of the settlement of the interior. She spoke at some length on the part she had taken in bringing people to the colony, and of getting them settled in the interior, and maintained that she was as much a pioneer of the settlement of the interior as any person in the colony. This statement was greeted with enthusiastic cheering . . .

June 1861

MRS. CHISHOLM'S LECTURE AT THE TEMPERANCE HALL

Last night, Mrs. Caroline Chisholm delivered a lecture at the Temperance Hall in Pitt-street, on the subject of 'Our Home Life', to a very crowded and attentive audience, consisting of not less than 600 persons . . .

What was a home? There was not perhaps a single person present who had not, each one of them, his or her own idea of what a 'home' actually was. Generally, however, the prevalent idea of a home appeared to be that of a small cottage and garden, for seldom or ever was a mansion the ideal home of those minds who eagerly and longingly looked forward to it. In one of her walks she had seen and spoken with a man who was waiting, as he told her, to know whether the home that he had already designed for his future wife was likely to be his home in reality;—whether the Land Bill, of which they had heard so much, was to be a great reality or a great sham. The man had deliberately planned the snug little cottage which he some day hoped to be able to build, and had mentally arranged its minutest detail in anticipation of the time when the young woman to whom he was engaged (and whom he had left behind him in England) should be enabled to come out to the colony and become his wife. Home was not merely a place of shelter but a place where the door might be open for everybody—except, indeed, the landlord coming for his rent. She spoke feelingly in saying this, having herself to pay a high rent for a house in which she lived, the rooms of which were so small that she could not walk in them with comfort . . .

After alluding to the melancholy fact that but too many houses had been broken up by the discovery of the gold-fields, and their inmates left in Sydney to penury and ruin, the lecturer proceeded to quote largely from the evidence taken before the select committee of the Legislative Assembly appointed to enquire into the state of the residences of the working classes. The facts made public in these documents were such as disclosed a very sad state of things. But too many in this city were compelled to live crowded together in small, ill-ventilated, and filthy domiciles which were not homes. One result of the miserable nature of the house accommodation afforded was this, that when those who came to New South Wales to find gold or to get money, did obtain what they sought for, they left the colony as soon as ever they could. No effort was made to retain those who had here enriched themselves. They liked the country and the climate—but yet they left, because here they had no home. Let them look at the number of children that were so constantly dying in this city. Why was no effort made to save these? All these poor innocents wanted was fresh air, plenty of room in the father's own cottage, and plenty of fresh milk. Mrs. Chisholm then illustrated her conception of what a home was by reference to the splendid surburban mansion of a distinguished bachelor, and to the Australian Club in Bent-street. Neither of these two places came up to her idea of a home. Nothing, she felt bound to say, was more destructive to the happiness of a home than those clubs, where bachelors lived and married men resided apart from their wives. They could not expect to leave a race of fine men and beautiful women if they allowed so large a proportion of the people to continue to exist in the miserable, cramped-up places which were provided for them . . . The lecturer then proceeded to speak of cases of female seduction, and expressed her hope that some protection might, ere long, be provided by the law for the victims, and direct punishment for the seducers. She adverted to those cases, because they were difficulties and causes of sorrow which but too often clung round many a poor man's cottage.

. . . Mrs. Chisholm would allow none to impugn her loyalty to the Queen; who was the pattern of those domestic virtues which adorn a home. Still it was, in her opinion, only right to say that there was no stability to the throne where cottage homes were not to be found. It was cottages that made a man love his country. What they wanted was these cottage homes, with arm chairs for their aged parents, and with cradles for their young children.

The lecturer was frequently interrupted by loud applause, and received a unanimous vote of thanks.

Document 3.3 A widow persists in asking for charity

The nineteenth-century concentration of women in the home left them especially vulnerable. The illness, death or desertion of a breadwinner could plunge even moderately comfortable families into poverty, and for the many already on the subsistence line destitution was often immediate. Women struggling to support families with poorly paid domestic labour found times of economic recession particularly hazardous. In the following documents the widow Honor Scattergood

attempts to keep her family afloat. She petitions the Western Australian
Governor for monetary assistance and to have her children admitted
to the Perth Poor House, a government institution for those not able
to support themselves. The unwillingness of the government to grant
assistance is especially notable, as is the authorities' preoccupation
with the morality of those granted relief.[3]

Fremantle, W. Australia
1st July, 1862

sent to His Excellency the Governor

THE PETITION OF HONOR SCATTERGOOD HUMBLY SHEWETH

That your Petitioner's Husband died after a long sickness (9 months) on
the 23rd April 1862 leaving Me with 5 young children the eldest only 9
years of age. When My husband was a patient in Perth Hospital, I applied
for relief to enable Me to support the children and 1/- was kindly granted
to me which I received during March and April but unfortunately it was
taken from me in May. The object of My present Petition is that something
may be done for my children as I am unable to support them. I have now
sold all the wearing apparell left by my poor Husband in order to get
them food and I can struggle no longer without assistance. If they could
be admitted to the Home at Perth or if the former relief could again be
allowed me with that little I can earn myself I think I can manage to keep
them and myself without farther trouble. My Youngest child is only 7
weeks old, and I humbly hope and trust that this petition will meet with
your Excellency's favourable Consideration

and your Petitioner Will ever pray
Her X Mark
Honor Scattergood

Forwarded to [Resident Magistrate] Fremantle
Fred Barlee

3/7/62 To be returned

This Woman has now been two months without assistance—Sufficient
punishment for getting '*drunk*', she is in great poverty. I think she should
now be allowed the 1/- per diem from the 1 of July or be admitted with
her children into the Poor House

J. Brown J.P.

Inform Mr. Brown that 1/- per diem may be paid to this woman till the

end of the current month, when she and the children may be forwarded
to the Poor House,

Fred P. Barlee

*In September 1862, Honor Scattergood was in trouble again, but was
briefly victorious over officialdom.*

Fremantle, Western Australia
4th September 1862

Honoured Sir,
I take the liberty of Writing You a few lines and hope you will be so kind
as excuse Me for so doing as my reasons are very urgent, I came up to
Perth yesterday and had an order from Thomas Brown Esq. to admit me
and family into the Home and was desired by Him to present it to Mr.
Wakeford and Wait for further instructions. When I got up to Perth with
the Children unfortunately Mr. Wakeford was out of Town after a deal of
demur two of my children Were admitted and I returned to Fremantle.

If Your Honour Would be so kind as to allow the one shilling per
day, which with my own exertions I could provide a decent home for
myself and the remainder as my eldest daughter could mind the infant
sister when I was at Work if this cannot be granted I have no resource
but the Home for which I am very thankful but would rather remain outside
where I might have opportunity of bettering myself and not be all My life
a dependent on the Public.

Her Mark X
Honor Scattergood

The Honourable The Colonial Secretary
On the 3rd instant, during my absence at Fremantle Mrs. Scattergood
presented herself at the Poor House with an infant and two children. The
Matron informed her that she could not admit anyone without an order—
whereupon Mrs. Scattergood produced a paper signed by Mr. T. Brown, but
not addressed, dated Fremantle Sept. 2/62, as follows 'Have the goodness to
receive into the Perth Poor House Mrs. Scattergood and children in accordance with instructions given by the Hon. the Colonial Surgeon July 5th
1862.' The Matron then received Mrs. Scattergood and infant and two
children, a boy aged 9 and a girl aged 3½, but Mrs. S. left immediately with
the infant stating that she was going back to Fremantle to fetch the other two
children which she has not yet done. No intimation whatever of any
intention to receive the Scattergood family into the Poor House has reached
me and I had consequently given redirections to the rations with reference to
them. Under these circumstances I trust His Excellency will acquit the

Matron of same in allowing the two children to remain without their mother. Mrs. Scattergood is a woman of notoriously bad character and on the 25th June last the Rev. R. Martelli personally requested me to receive some of the children into the Poor House stating that their mother had been deprived of the money relief from the Govt. on account of her profligate life. I declined to recommend that any of the children should be received into the Poor House on the ground that to do so would be merely to leave the mother more free to lead a life of vice—I still think that two of the children should not be kept in the Poor House and I would therefore recommend that they should be sent back to their mother at Fremantle. If Mrs Scattergood were admitted into the Poor House with the whole of her family the cost would far exceed the 1/- per diem, to say nothing of the fact that there is not accommodation just at present for such an addition to the inmates. If Mrs. Scattergood and her eldest daughter were so disposed I think they might possibly be able to contribute largely, though perhaps not sufficiently, to the support of the whole family—I would under all the circumstances suggest that the only government relief given to Mrs. Scattergood should be 1/- per diem but with a distinct understanding that it would be withheld or renewed from time to time by the Resident Magistrate according to her conduct.

Henry Wakeford, Police Magistrate 9/9/62

And again in 1863 . . .

Resident's Office
Fremantle, April 1, 1863

The Hon The Col Secretary Perth
Sir,
At the risk of appearing importunate—I am compelled once again to bring before the notice of the Government the case of Honor Scattergood and her young family.

I had the honor of informing you in my last communication that this woman was about to ejected from her present residence.

Mr. Barker of the firm of Albert & Barker has this morning appealed to me in her behalf. He lives near her and has reason to know that both she and her children are literally starving. He heard the children crying for bread last night and on their applying to his wife for a little meal—he kindly supplies them with tea and sugar—and 2 loaves of bread. This casual relief cannot of course be continued—nor can we see a widow and her young family starving before our eyes.

I beg strongly to press this urgent case on the notice of the Government—and to recommend that I may be authorised to allow this woman at the rate of 1/- per day—not paying her the money—but paying her credit on a storekeeper for that amount in rations.

> I have the honor to be Sir
> Yr Very Obed^{nt} Serv^{nt}
> Thomas Symmons
> Resident

Document 3.4 A sister keeps house in Queensland

Most unmarried middle-class women in the nineteenth century lived with relatives. Rachel Henning (1826–1914) came to Australia to join her brother Biddulph and sister Annie, and in the early 1860s they were living on Biddulph's property, 'Exmoor', in north Queensland. Their material situation was comfortable and Rachel Henning relished the much greater freedom that many white, middle-class women could enjoy in colonial society. In these letters to her sister Etta back in England she discusses, among other issues, what employers often called 'the servant problem'. She took for granted those who worked to make her own life easier, as she did the Aborigines whose land she and her family had appropriated, and this thoughtlessness makes her condescension all the more striking.[4]

> Exmoor,
> September 17th 1864.

My Dearest Etta,

Biddulph brought up the English letters with him. We were so delighted to see him back, for we were getting quite uneasy about him and began to fancy all sort of things which might have happened on the road.

. . .

Biddulph seems greatly to have enjoyed his visit to Sydney, for though his mornings were all taken up by business, he used to spend his afternoons in driving out the young ladies of his acquaintance and his evenings in visiting. His business prospered, too, for he got his licences for the new Flinders run without any difficulty, and is formally installed in possession.

. . .

I should be sorry to leave Exmoor on many accounts, but I do not dislike the idea of further rambles and journeys in this wild country, and a settlement on the broad prairies of the Flinders. We may never go, but, as I said before, it is possible.

How I should like to be with you sometimes, but I think it will be a long time first, especially if we go out to the Flinders, as in that case Biddulph will not very likely marry for a long time, unless he were to fall in love before he goes, if go he does.

I do not think I am likely to return to England unless Biddulph were to marry, much as I wish to see you all again; and, fond as I am of home, I do greatly enjoy the lovely climate, good health and free outdoor life that we have here, and, though I like Aunt Vizard and love her, she would be a poor exchange for Biddulph, who is the very kindest of brothers and the pleasantest person in the world to live with.

I can be of some use to him, too. Annie keeps house and cooks, etc., but I keep all his books and accounts, copy his letters and invoices and am generally his clerk, and it is a department I much prefer to making puddings.

I was amused at Aunt's idea, in her last letter, that we should feel like Nodenic the Goth at the 'unaccustomed face of man', the fact being that I never in my life saw so many strangers, and that, too, from all parts of the world—some fresh from England, some from Sydney, Adelaide, the Far North, and all parts of Australia. A Mr Steward, who was lately here, had spent half his life in Madagascar; another had just come from India, another from California, etc., etc. We have had quite a houseful lately.

. . .

Your affectionate sister,

Rachel Henning

Exmoor,
January 23rd 1865

My Dearest Etta,

We have no servants just at present, as Tom and his wife are to leave by the first opportunity, and we have not yet replaced them. It seldom answers to have servants back when you have once parted with them. Emma was a good servant when she was here before, but since her return her principal occupation has been quarrelling with Tom.

We have just been edified by the sounds of a war of words, and what appears to be missiles flying in the kitchen; then I saw through the back window of the parlour Emma rushing out of the kitchen discharging some missile—I think a saucepan lid—at Tom as she went, and rushing up to the men's huts at the top of the paddock with a tomahawk in her hand. Then we heard Tom bewailing himself in the kitchen, and saying if his poor old father could have known, etc.

Next Biddy, the black girl, made her appearance in the parlour grinning very much, and tomahawk in hand. She said, 'That fellow [meaning Emma] been running away with tomahawk, and mine been running after and took away tomahawk, that fellow no good.' A sentiment in which we heartily concurred. These quarrels are a source of great delight to the blacks, who stand in front of their camp and hold up their hands and roll about with laughter. But they are very disagreeable, and I shall be glad when the happy couple take their departure.

. . .

I have had some nice rides lately. There is a flock of sheep now at the Eight Mile, and we go out there with Biddulph when he takes the rations and counts the sheep. It is a beautiful ride there. The road is pretty the whole way, and then you turn off and cross the Bowen, and go through a little patch of thick wood till you come out on the plain where the station is. Such a pretty place. The little hut stands out against the dark forest, and in front are beautiful green downs, where the sheep feed.

It is rather hot going there, as we have to start pretty early and walk our horses the whole eight miles, or nearly so, as otherwise the packhorse would make a pudding of the flour, tea and sugar, and break the bottles of vinegar and lime juice. We generally leave the station about sundown, and the canter home in the cool twilight and starlight is delightful.

. . .

I liked to hear about the children's garments very much. It must have been a great undertaking to turn a whole suit of tailor's clothes for Leighton, and you were very clever to succeed in it. I know nothing about tailoring. Annie's face would be a sight at any interference with Biddulph's clothes, but I have learned a good deal of dressmaking since I came out here, and no doubt the tailoring could be also acquired when necessary.

I wonder if you wear those very small hats, which they depict in the London news, and which Emily sent up to us as eligible articles for the bush. We wanted some new hats very much, and were rather grieved when we unpacked things that look like a good-sized saucer on the top of your head. I mended up my old one, and left the new one undisturbed in the box ever since. Annie wears hers on Sundays, but as her face is still longer than mine, I cannot be complimentary as to her appearance in it. For the rest, we are well off for clothes this summer and could even hold on through another winter if necessary, but I suppose we shall go to Sydney in the autumn.

Ever your affectionate sister,

Rachel Henning

Exmoor,
April 18th 1865

My Dearest Etta,

. . .

Old Mrs Lack is staying with us now. She is the mother of Mr Lack, who owns Blenheim, the next station to this. She was here for two or three days last year; now she has been here about a fortnight, and will stay a week longer. She is rather a nice old lady, very gentle and lady-like, though slightly meandering; but when you have lived a long time in the bush you get lazy, and do not like the trouble of entertaining anybody. Gentlemen visitors are different, as they entertain themselves or you.

Mrs Lack rode on horseback the first five miles of the way, and we drove over with Biddulph in the buggy and met her about eight miles from here, and I rode the horse home, as we thought she would be tired. She goes home next Friday, I believe. Mr Lack is coming over on Thursday evening to slay beef for us, and takes his mother back next day.

. . .

I have been telling Aunt that the first grave has been made at Exmoor, an event in the history of the station. A family travelling with two drays and horse-teams passed the house and camped over the creek one evening a few weeks ago, and a man came up after dark to ask for some medicine, etc., for his little girl who had been ill a fortnight—of diphtheria, I should think from his description. We gave him some milk and promised to come and see the child next day, but at daylight next morning he came over and told Biddulph the child had died in the night, and asked for some old cases to make a coffin.

Biddulph offered to have one made and send it over, but he preferred doing it himself. We asked if his wife would like us to come and see her, but he said she would rather not, which I did not wonder at. Biddulph also offered to come over and read the service when they buried the child, but he said he did not care about it, so we could do nothing for them.

He had three children; this was the eldest, a little girl of five. There were several men with the drays, and they buried her in the morning, and then harnessed their horses and went on their way.

I went across the creek in the evening to where they had camped. It was very sorrowful to stand by the little lonely nameless grave among the gum-trees, and think what it must have been to the poor mother to drive away that morning and leave her little child among strangers. We did not even know their names. The grave is in a beautiful spot on a high bank shaded by trees, and the creek flowing beneath. It is fenced in most

securely with whole trunks of trees so that it can never be disturbed. That
is the first grave. I thought, who can tell whose the next will be?

The mailman is just come in, so I must not write any more now.
Your ever affectionate sister,

Rachel Henning

Document 3.5 A politician with a radical view of women's rights

From the time of the publication of British liberal John Stuart Mill's
The Subjection of Women *(1869), like-minded thinkers took up the
cause of women's political emancipation. George Higinbotham
(1826–1892), a lawyer and journalist who first entered the Victorian
Legislative Assembly in 1861, promoted a number of liberal causes,
including the spread of democracy, the opening up of the land to
small farmers, and secular education. Higinbotham was a staunch
supporter of extending the principle of political equality to women.
In 1870 he had piloted through the Victorian Parliament legislation
that gave married women the right to control their own property and
in 1873, when female ratepayers were granted the right to vote in
local elections, he proposed that all Victorian women should be given
suffrage and be allowed to elect members to parliament. In spite of
the substantial minority of politicians (16 out of 40) who supported
him, his proposal was defeated and it was not until 1908 that women
were at last permitted to cast their votes in Victorian elections.*[5]

1873

ELECTORAL ACT AMENDMENT BILL

Mr. Higinbotham proposed the following as a new clause:

'The words "male person" in the 4th and 8th sections of the principal
Act importing the masculine gender, and the words "male persons" and
"person" in this Act, shall respectively mean and include and relate to
females as well as males.'

. . . At the same time he believed that the present was a not unsuitable
occasion to bring forward a proposal for the enfranchisement of women,
and to record the opinion of the House thereon. He was aware that the
subject was one somewhat difficult to handle in an assembly of this kind.
When it was last before the committee some honorable members treated
it in the same way as the proposition to give the right of voting to females
was treated in the House of Commons, namely in a spirit of polite

jocularity, which appeared to them to be the fittest tone in which to deal with the question. He confessed that while he disagreed with those honorable members, he felt that the proposal itself was one which necessarily assumed, from its novelty, an abstract character which almost unfitted it to receive due consideration and attention from a deliberative body. At the same time he wished to bring forward and explain briefly the reasons which commended themselves to his mind as being those which would support it. It was only recently that a proposition of this kind was brought before the world at all. Not till quite lately, in Europe and America, was the claim of women to political rights so much as heard of, and certainly it still appeared that it would be a very considerable time before it was recognised. Nevertheless it had been asserted on behalf of women, that they ought to have equal political rights with men, and although the demand was nearly wholly a novel one, it seemed to him to be one which it was very hard indeed to find reasons for resisting. He had heard it said that nature had made women different from men, and that was alleged as a reason why they should not have given them the same political rights as men. The observation was no doubt a perfectly just and true one, but the conclusion drawn from it appeared to him absolutely and wholly irrelevant and futile. The same argument was frequently used in reference to the claims of all men to equal political rights. Over and over again had it been offered as a reason why equal political rights should not be given to different classes of men that they were differently constituted by nature, by habit, and by circumstance. That different men possessed different natural capacities, and different degrees of culture was repeatedly urged as a good cause why different degrees of political power should be allowed them. In regard to men, however, people were beginning to find little difficulty in disposing of arguments of that sort. They were beginning to see that natural differences constituted no ground whatever for artificial inequalities, and that to impose political inequalities upon various classes of men, because nature had made them different, was to mistake altogether the character of, and to distort those natural differences, which, because they were natural, were healthy and sound. And if the argument was found to be an unsound one in respect to men, he believed it would be discovered to be equally unsound with regard to women. He was satisfied that, as soon as women demanded, as he believed they would, equal political rights and equal rights of citizenship with men, it would be found impossible to rely upon that argument or any other as sufficient reason for refusing to recognise the claim. For himself, being unable to perceive any plea upon which it could be resisted, he was willing at once frankly to recognise it. He avowed that the chief and principal ground on which he made his present proposal was that he believed its adoption would be one step, and an important step, towards that general and complete political equality, which it appeared to be the chief purpose of this age to effect. It was said that this was an age chiefly distinguished by the destruction of monopolies, and this monopoly of political rights by men was one that did not become at all more venerable by being aged. It was very old and thoroughly well established, and he was not at all surprised to find that several conservatives were opposed to its abolition. He did not accept the fact that it was aged as any argument whatever in its favour. The chief reason why he proposed to do away with it was because it was an inequality that could not be defended upon any rational principle which had yet been urged. It was argued that if this claim were allowed, certain serious evils would arise; and, when this subject was last discussed by the committee, some honorable members speculated on the particular effects which would probably follow the extension of political rights to women. Such speculations did not, however, very much commend themselves to his judgment, because he regarded them as very uncertain in their character and difficult to pursue to a satisfactory end. At the same time, he might say that, so far as he could speculate on the probable results of the political enfranchisement of women, he believed they would not be at all injurious, but, on the contrary, highly beneficial. With respect to women themselves, what consequences were to be expected from the adoption of a measure of this kind? He apprehended that so long as women did not set a very high value on political rights they would not be disposed to avail themselves very largely of their possession; and he was, therefore, free to confess that, until they became sensible of their value, it was not at all to be desired that they should extensively use them. At the same time there were, no doubt, very many women who were without scope in which to pursue their natural and particular tendencies of character and thought, and who were inclined and anxious to take a more active part than was now permitted them in the political affairs of the world. If such women were allowed a sphere of political action, he believed nothing but benefit would arise to them and others.

With regard to political life and action generally, it seemed to him that the effect of women taking part in politics was likely to become purely beneficial. Certainly he must say that politics and political life, as managed and dealt with by men, appeared to be taking a by no means satisfactory turn in the present history of the world. It seemed to him, that, at the present day, politics and politicians were gradually becoming more and more separated from the social and civil life of communities than they were in former times . . . If true political questions—not party questions, or those connected with the success of particular factions in the Legislature—intimately connected with the improvement of the conditions of society, could be brought within the scope of every family in the community, and be made household words, that would do much to elevate the character of political pursuits and redeem that of politicians. He should hope that giving political power to females would have a strong tendency in that direction, assuming of course that females were gradually brought to value and exercise the right of legislation conferred upon them. That condition of things would come in time, although slowly; and just in proportion as the right was valued and exercised would more humane, just, and liberal views of politics be entertained throughout the length and breadth of the land. He confessed that he speculated with very good distrust upon the effects of any change of this kind. He greatly preferred to rest himself upon the principle that seemed to him the most safe, rational, and indisputable, namely, that inasmuch as nature made no inequality—although it had created a difference—between the two sexes, art ought not to establish one; and inasmuch as there were some females in the world, at the present time, who claimed for their sex the same right as men to engage in political affairs, he was prepared, on the ground of the apparent justice of the demand, to concede it. With that view, and chiefly and principally for that reason, he asked the committee to consider his proposition. As he had said already, he did not expect it to be carried, but he believed that if the subject were brought forward on a suitable occasion—and he trusted this would be regarded in that light—it might be not unprofitably discussed, for it would tend to promote thought, and extend the boundaries of the political system of the colony with advantage to the Legislature and the community.

. . .

The committee divided on the question that the clause be added to the Bill—

Ayes 16
Noes 40
Majority against the clause 24

Document 3.6 A woman remembers selectors living in poverty

Mary Gilmore (1865–1962), who later became a respected poet, writer and activist, grew up in the Riverina area of New South Wales. From the comparative comfort of her tradesman father's home, she observed

*women and men struggling with few material resources behind them,
to keep their farms going. She wrote about her childhood in a book
of recollections,* Old Days: Old Ways, *first published in 1934.*

*The Selection Acts of the 1860s gave families small blocks of land
carved from squatters' holdings, in return for fixed, theoretically
affordable payments. This process contributed to the dispossession of
Aborigines from their land, but their white successors nevertheless
faced considerable hardships as they strove, in the harsh climate, to
yield European crops from often unsuitable terrain.*[6]

c. 1870s

Mrs Rickly, of Rickly's Farm, had twelve children, six boys and six girls,
and she made hats of grass for all her boys. Wheat and stock being at
their beginnings, straw had to be saved for cattle-chaff and house-thatch.
Patiently each summer she went out and picked the stems of the fine
Riverina grass, and (this being her only time of rest) in the early dusk of
winter, or at daylight in summer, she sat and sewed, sewed, sewed them
into hats.

In the early morning as she bent to her stitching, her Bible lay open
beside her. She had just light enough to read, and her eye would catch a
word and memory supply the rest as she worked. In the evening when
the dusk did not allow of reading she verbally taught the family the texts
and the lessons she herself had learned. There was no reading at night, as
there were no candles. They had a few wooden matches—the old sulphur-
headed matches—and when they had used the last of these they had to
go out to the fire for a light when one was needed in the night, as was
the case once when one of the children was ill. My father finding it out
gave them a box of vestas—wax vestas as the new wax match was called.

In the night the sick child had waked up crying, and just as Mrs
Rickly sat up to get out of bed she heard a snake in the room. There was
no way of getting light except by the father shouting to the eldest boy,
outside, to bring a fire-stick. The boy was a heavy sleeper and they called
long before he woke . . .

When I first knew the Ricklys in the early seventies their house was
a house of stubs with a thatched roof. And as they could not afford much
thatch the top was sodded over with earth, to weight the straw and to
keep out the rain. The boys slept under bags, a tree their shelter; the father
and mother had a possum-rug; the girls had patchwork. One quilt had
been made by Mrs Rickly's great grandmother, one by her own mother.
Both had been given her for her wedding. What beautiful everlasting
sewing, and what slender starry patterns they both had! More than ances-

tral, they were racial. Now they are lost to us here, though revived in Europe and the Old Country as a result of a new world's search, first in ancient chateaux in France, and then across the Channel.

The girls, as soon as they could hold a needle, were set to work on new patchwork. But the new was not the old. We, in Australia, had not the patterns in prints that would make them. So the square, the triangle, and the diamond had to be used, with the colours set out as best one could arrange them. My mother, taking over a bag of patches, they were gone through; the woollens where big enough were set aside to make patch-hats and caps for the use of the little boys; the muslins were of no use for quilts, and the cambric and prints had the wrong colours. Still they would be used. The muslin trimmed the girls' hats; cambric pieced-up, made handkerchiefs; the print and other odd pieces were sewn together for petticoats. Being unseen their patterns did not matter.

The family so far had never gone to school. There was no school within six miles it is true, and the days of compulsory education had not begun. Nor had free education. We paid a shilling a week then. But in any case there was too much for the Rickly children to do to spare time for school. Almost with bare hands the farm had to be made. There was no money for more than the annual free-selection payments to make the property freehold. English, the family had the land-hunger of the land-starved English farm-labourer. They had seen that ownership gave standing and stability, and ownership they must have. Indeed they told us this themselves; and they were but one case among many. So everywhere families paid the price of land in premature ageing through overwork after birth, and through parental overwork before they were born.

Parents having survived by sheer tenacity of life in the homeland where they had meat only at Christmas (or at most on Sundays, and only otherwise as a charity when sick) throve and added strength to strength on the lean red meats of Australia—possums, kangaroo, and wallaby. As it was with others so it was with these of whom I write. Their meat was possum. No possum was allowed to be killed for sport in any of the trees near the house.

When I best remember the Ricklys, they had a cow and a calf, an old horse, a pig, and a few fowls. Before they had the cow they had had a couple of goats. When they killed a spare billy kid they had a change from possum meat. They could not afford shot, so any game that could not be caught in a gamekeeper's rabbit-snare, knocked down with a stick like a possum, or caught in a covered crow-pit, was beyond their reach. It was said that they ate the crows they caught. With the cruelty of the times people called them 'crow-eaters', and they were despised accordingly by those who lived in the altitudes of 'killed meat'.

When they got the cow—an old one given them by a neighbour kinder than most—as soon as she was milking the whole yield was set for butter to sell. The family ate none of the butter; and most of the skim milk when skimmed went to nourish the growing pig. Only the girls, the mother, and the very little boys, had milk when they had tea, and it was only on Sundays that they all had tea. Perhaps indeed it was only when strangers came that they had milk; for I remember (and now with what grief) how little went into the girls' tea, and how much went into ours when we visited there.

For the first slender handful of wheat sowed the earth was turned up for it with a spade, a heavy home-made wooden spade, the man himself being his only working animal.

I think it was my father gave the horse that followed. I know my father made the first plough, which was of wood. The next year my grandfather, Hugh Beattie, buying a new one, gave his old share to go in place of the iron-bark or boree point my father had made. So the following year the family made money; it had a bag of wheat to sell. But it was the man and the woman who, as horses, had pulled the harrow over the seed when it had been sown. They had gone out in the dusk to do it; but a neighbour somewhere near had seen them and deridingly told it. Yet we all knew that they had to do it because the horse was old and must be spared; and we all knew they waited till late dusk hoping to be unobserved.

Still this harrowing was not wholly unusual. When land was everything, money hard to get (some full men's wages were only five shillings a week) and when horses had not multiplied, or had been killed off as brumbies by in-coming frontier settlement, in the first wheat plantings in Riverina, many harrows were hand-pulled, and sometimes, as in the present case, women had to do it.

Document 3.7 A man puts the case for women's higher education

Charles Pearson (1830–1892), a liberal reformer like Higinbotham, became the first principal of the Presbyterian Ladies' College in Melbourne in 1875. In his lecture, 'The Higher Culture of Women', delivered at the school's opening ceremony, he sets out his arguments for women's education. An essential component of this, he said, was sound academic schooling at secondary level, at a more rigorous standard than was usually considered suitable for girls. This view was especially important in the context of arguments for women's entry into tertiary education, which were gathering strength in Australia, influenced by debates in Britain and the United States, and which bore fruit in the graduation of the first woman from an Australian university when Bella Guerin gained her Bachelor of Arts degree from the University of Melbourne in 1883.

How to argue the case with parents, many of them with traditional aspirations for their daughters? Here is one mode of persuasion.[7]

11 February 1875

. . . But, speaking generally, our schools and colleges, our courses of public lectures and institutes, are all so many protests against the theory, that to keep a woman out of mischief you must give her the occupation and tasks of a cook, a housekeeper, or a sempstress. None the less, opinions differ, and will no doubt long continue to differ, on several questions that go to the very root of female education. It is still doubted, for instance, whether any but a superficial and low culture will not interfere with the most obvious vocation of women as wives and mothers; whether, assuming them to be highly educated, we ought to allow them to go on and compete with men in what are known as the learned professions; and even whether they can hold their own if they are admitted to such a competition. A witty American has summed up these controversies in the epigram, 'Ought women to learn the alphabet?' Like most epigrams, it is a little unfair to the views actually held by the opposite side. But I take it, it indicates the direction in which we are to look for an answer to these questions. Our theories, after all, are of little account when they come into conflict with circumstances; and there are changes going on in the world which are practically settling this question of woman's education . . .

So far, I hope I have carried you along with me to accept two propositions: (1) That circumstances from time to time make a change in the education of women necessary, and (2) That so far the change has been in favour of teaching more, not of teaching less, of making the training more intellectual, not more industrial; that the growth of wealth has relieved whole classes from the obligation to much drudgery, and that the place of women in a sober society is higher than it was in a drunken one. These statements are not I think very extravagant.

The questions I next have to consider will be, (1) Is not the intellectual training a little overdone at present, so as to be injurious to health? (2) Would it not be well to teach practical household work rather than Latin and algebra? And (3) Does it not unfit women for society if you make

pedants of them? . . . so far as I can judge, the general results of the
controversy may be summed up in three or four conclusions.

I. I think we may fairly believe that in America, where the cry of
alarm has first been raised, the danger to health is a little greater than in
England or Australia. The ordinary life of American women has special
causes of disease. They pass the long and severe winter in rooms heated
to excess by stoves; they are suffered from youth upward to indulge in
unhealthy food; they take little exercise, walking or riding; and they enter
upon society at an early age. Put girls under these disadvantages, and even
though they be quite innocent of book-learning and of the higher culture,
I take it they will contrast unfavourably with the mass of those who have
grown up as English girls generally do, breathing fresh air, eating simple
food, taking healthy exercise, and remaining in the school-room till they
are young women.

II. Excess in study is not more dangerous than excess in dissipation.
For one girl who ruins her health over Euclid and the Latin Grammar, is
it too much to say that fifty are permanently the worse for a thousand
forms of fashionable idleness and excitement, for novel-reading and
theatre-going, for balls and picnics, and for the consuming *ennui* of a life
wasted upon trifles?

III. The danger from over-study is not confined to girls. Every year
has its little roll of boys and young men, who have broken down in school
and college in working for an examination; who are thrown back for years,
if they are not wrecked altogether. Nevertheless no one argues from
the failures for withdrawing boys from school, or forbidding them to
compete . . .

The result of our inquiry so far, if I have carried you along with me,
I think goes to prove that women have more spare time for intellectual
work than they had; and that they can work to a fair amount without
injury to health, so long as they are not over-stimulated by competition,
or distracted by occupations and fatigues of another kind. The question
will still remain whether it is desirable to give the growing generation of
girls a higher culture. May we not end by making them 'over-educated
for their intellects', to borrow the Duke of Wellington's definition of a
statesman of his party . . .

What are the careers for which it is thought that women will be
unfitted by a higher education than they receive at present? No one will
question that those who have to live by their work, as governesses, as
teachers in schools, or as writers for the press, ought to receive a thorough
training for their work. Few, again, will doubt that unmarried women may
healthily spend much of their leisure time in study, if it be but to save

themselves from some *ennui* and at least some frivolity. The doubt I suppose is whether, when four out of five women have to be wives and mothers, it is worth while to give them more than the most superficial acquaintance with the names of things; whether they will be better companions to their husbands, better housewives, better mothers, for having learned the Latin grammar, and attended lectures on history or physical science?

Unquestionably they will be better companions; more intelligent, more vivacious, with more character and self-respect. The world's recorded experience hitherto is not favourable to the effects of intellectual idleness on women's character . . .

However, we take broader ground than this. If knowledge did not fit women specially for their special duties, so long as it did not unfit them we ought to give it. Dismiss all theories about the admission of women to political rights. Assume that the married will remain as in England, barely able to own property in exceptional cases where the law interferes to protect them, though this of course is no longer true of Victoria. Still women exercise, and to all time will exercise, a most tremendous indirect influence over children, husbands, lovers. Is it desirable, at least in Protestant and constitutional countries, that this influence should be unintelligent, formed perhaps by the clergy, or by the habits and opinions of a narrow home circle, and never corrected by reading or instruction? . . .

I have purposely abstained from touching the question of professions for women. It is more important in England than in a new country. Still I do not think we can doubt that, as population increases, there will be a larger class wanting to supplement their incomes by work of some kind, and a growing feeling that it is as absurd to keep women out of professions, for which we may think them unsuited, as to legislate in any other way how natural forces are to work. 'Allah,' says the Turk engineer, 'has made his rivers crooked: we will not be wiser than Allah,' and he doubles the length of his canal by cutting it circuitously. 'Nature,' says the conservative theorist, 'has intended women to stay at home and manage their houses, and we will not recognise the fact that a certain considerable percentage of women must for ever remain without houses to manage. They may be teachers, but they shall not have that training and those tests, which make the teaching of men efficient. They may be nurses, but they shall not acquire that medical knowledge without which tenderness and care may sometimes be the most dangerous of allies. It is unfeminine, improper, indelicate, that they should lecture to public audiences, or argue in courts of law; but reason and custom permit that they should amass large fortunes by singing and acting on the public stage.' I cannot believe that these grotesque anomalies of opinion will be allowed to keep women many years longer from the career open to talents. Sooner or later, they will be allowed to try freely in what fields they can contend with men.

Document 3.8 A journalist reports on prostitutes and charity workers

John Stanley James (1843–1896) was a journalist who wrote vivid sketches of Melbourne life under the pseudonym 'The Vagabond'. He had a sharp curiosity about the less conventional aspects of colonial social conditions. In this extract, published in The Vagabond Papers *in 1877, he visits the Protestant Female Refuge situated in what is now Swanston Street. His ambivalent attitude towards the prostitutes he meets is reflected in the mixture of chivalry and condemnation with which he describes them. His view of the ideal woman as a frail creature convinces him that factory life is too strenuous for young women and yet he also condemns the prostitutes for their 'choice' of an 'idle' life. His attitudes reflect the common, masculinist assumption that the men who use prostitutes are the innocent party in the encounter.*

Prostitution flourished in colonies where men predominated and women faced limited, low-paid employment. Middle-class women provided a pool of charity workers in colonial towns and cities; a few were prepared to help 'fallen women', provided they were penitent and docile.[8]

1877

THE PROTESTANT FEMALE REFUGE

. . . The 'social evil' is an outcome of civilization which has been, is, and, I am afraid, ever will be, and which flourishes as a protest against many of the restrictions which society binds around the sexes. But all evils, necessary or inevitable—and I class this amongst the latter—may be curtailed. It is an unfortunate fact that this vice flourishes here in Melbourne in most undue proportions. The ranks of the fallen ones are full, and new recruits are always on hand. Taken *en masse*, the rising generation of young women, who should be the mothers of the Australian of the future, are neither physically nor morally adapted for the position they should naturally fill. And studying the status of the working girls of Melbourne, I cannot but think that it would have been better both for their minds and bodies if Elias Howe had not invented the sewing-machine, which seems a Juggernaut, crushing much youthful innocence beneath its evil sway. The life of a factory girl is, physically, almost as unnatural as that of the harlot. At present, however, we care little about this; we reck not of the injurious social influences working all around us; we refuse to see the Upas plant of 'larrikinism' and female vice springing up, which may yet bear deadly fruit in the future . . .

In this country it appears to me that the influences of religion do not extend much beyond the churches. Private philanthropy or volunteer missionary work is also, I am afraid, of small avail in dealing with the 'social evil'. I say so, as lately, since I was reformed by my visit to Abbotsford, I have, disguised as a Scripture reader, been doing a little missionary business amongst the fallen women of Melbourne. I am bound to admit that my success is about *nil*. The members of the aristocracy of the *demi-monde*, who so freely bleed our gilded or woolly youth (serve them right for their folly), laughed at me. 'Do you think I'm a fool?' said one girl, who has, until you look between the lines, a face like a vestal [virgin], and a heart like the daughter of the horse-leech [who cried 'give, give'—Proverbs 30:15]. 'It's better to be as I am when you make lots of money at it. What have I got to repent of? I'm bad! All right! It pays, don't it? You bet I make them pay. They say I've got no heart or feeling. What feeling did any man ever have for me? It's the way we are treated at first that makes us what we are at last.' There was a good deal of truth in this. A woman's heart will get early hardened by the faithlessness or bad treatment of her first lovers, and the successors have to suffer for it. This girl clothed in silk and jewels, glorying in her beauty and iniquity, was certainly in better case than if scrubbing floors or running a sewing machine. I was forced to admit to myself that it was a folly to talk to her now of the virtues of chastity, poverty, and hard work . . .

. . . Thus this handsome and vicious young party, one of the many who glory in their life, and whom it is useless attempting to reform. If, however, they will keep out of the theatres, and not flaunt their saffron to the temptation of poor working girls, I don't know that they do much positive harm; and, although they help to ruin the ignorant and callow heirs to countless bullocks and sheep, they have some good qualities in being charitable to their poorer sisters . . .

All, however, who strut in the bravery of sin, satin, and furs, are not hardened. There are many who repent, and would abandon their life if they could. But the millstone of debt is round most of them . . . 'Do you think I like this life?' said a girl to me. 'I hate it, and would leave tomorrow if I could; but I'm always in debt. I owe over a hundred pounds.' 'Why should that stop you?' I asked. 'Well, I owe the money, and it would not be honourable to cut away without paying. Besides, if I got a respectable situation, I should be sure to be found out, and "given away" by some of them' . . .

Another also expressed a dislike for her present mode of existence. 'But what can I do—I can't do hard work. I might get a barmaid's place, perhaps, but in many houses that isn't much better than this, unless it was in a respectable house, and I couldn't get in there, known as I am.' 'No,' said I, austerely; 'you, none of you want to work. You prefer idleness, and fine dress, and the indulgence of your passions, following out your natural instincts, and going to perdition wilfully. The devil's tail, which seems to be particularly long in Australia, is coiled around you. But if you have no sense of religion, nor fear of your future state, think what you will be in a few years. Your beauty will be gone, old before your time, disease and drink will do their work, and you will become like many of these "low women" you now despise, who pass their lives between Little Bourke-street, the police court, and the gaol. Some of you who now flaunt about so gaily will return to the gutters from which you sprang.' 'I would die before I would come to that,' said one. 'Don't think I'm as bad as that,' said the second girl, who had large Juno eyes, and a lazy, imperious manner, but who looked too good for her trade; 'you don't know how I came here. When I had my little baby, I had nowhere to go after coming out of the Lying-in [maternity] Hospital. I must keep it, and I had to take to this. If there had been anywhere I could have gone with my baby I would not have been here,' and the woman shed soft tears for the memory of her dead child. The maternal instinct is generally strong even in these 'fallen ones', and their love for children the one touch of nature which makes them akin to all womanhood . . .

The other morning, reading *The Argus* whilst lying in bed, as is my wont, I perused a sub-leader advocating the claims of the Protestant Female Refuge . . . I took cab thither, and was landed at the top of Madeline-street, where an irregular block of ground is fenced off from the inspection of the curious, the only outward sign being a blank cottage wall and a doorway, bearing above it in plain letters, 'The Refuge'. After ringing, the door was opened by a good-natured-looking young woman, who admitted me on my claiming to have business with the matron . . .

. . . Mrs. Hurry [the Matron] kindly volunteered to show me everything, not, apparently, being afraid of any evil consequences likely to accrue from my sudden and unexpected inroad . . .

Opening a door we were in the ironing-room, where some twenty-five girls were at work, their voices ringing out cheerfully above the clattering of the irons. 'Hush!' said Mrs. Hurry, reprovingly. 'You see they are not used to visitors, sir.' 'I like to hear it; let them sing, by all means; it shows they are happy,' said I. I was surprised at the youth of most of the inmates. They were nearly all between the ages of fifteen and twenty. There was no stamp of vice nor degradation on any of them. In their neat linseys and tweeds they presented all the attractions of youth, good looks, cleanliness, and content. One of the sub-matrons bossed this room, where all hands were working, it being the end of the week's ironing. Adjoining is the washing-room, which, if not so well-appointed as that at Abbotsford or Kew Asylum, still contains every requisite for getting through work. In another room the 'sorting' takes place. We then inspected the drying ground, from which a good view of Kew, Hawthorn, and the ranges is obtained. 'Now,' said Mrs. Hurry, 'we'll go and see the babies.' An old cottage is used as the day nursery; and, in the verandah of this, eleven infants, from two to twelve months old, were lying in cradles and on cushions and pillows. They crowed merrily and lustily, happily unconscious of the stigma which society has placed upon their birth. One of the inmates was in charge of the nursery, but whilst I was there the dinner hour occurred, and I was pleased to see the mothers rushing for their babes, and, clasping them lovingly to their breasts, bear them off triumphantly to the day-room . . .

. . . Then I interviewed Mrs. Hurry as to the objects, working, and success of the Refuge . . . The Refuge principally lays itself out for taking young girls after the birth of their first illegitimate child, before they are hardened or demoralized. Many of them come from the Lying-in Hospital, on leaving which they have, as I have before shown, too often no resource but the streets. A great number are graduates of the Industrial Schools; when they go out into the world, either the revulsion against their former seclusion, or the abnormally strong passions of Australian youth leading them crooked.

On entering the Refuge, they have to give a promise to stop twelve months—a term of probation which it is considered will ensure the breaking-off of all old connexions. During this time they have careful training and supervision, and are generally turned out capable of doing all domestic work. It is a gratifying fact that a very large proportion of those who have left the Refuge are known to be doing well, and Mrs. Hurry speaks in high terms of the conduct of the girls now in the house. Although the regulations are not hard, a residence of twelve months in the Refuge certainly requires patience, endurance, and self-denial. The inmates rise in the morning at six o'clock, work till eight, when there is a cessation for breakfast of tea and bread and butter. At eleven the same refection is given for lunch. At one, there is dinner of soup, meat, vegetables, and often pudding. Tea at six, same as breakfast, and from thence, until ten o'clock, when they have all to be in bed, the inmates can make their clothes, read, chat, or listen to some of the ladies of the committee, who come and read and talk to them. Morning and evening prayer is read by the matron; and on Sundays, a chance Church of England or Presbyterian clergyman may come and perform the service. Besides reading, the only recreation the inmates have is keeping the little plots of garden ground, which are divided out to each; but I can't say much for the results I saw, the grounds of the Refuge being generally in a very dreary condition.

Although there are many things in the report which I might cavil at, still, on the whole, I am pleased with the Refuge, and think it is doing a very good work.

Document 3.9   A woman speaks out on women's rights

Catherine Helen Spence (1825–1910), writer and reformer, came to South Australia from Scotland with her family in 1839. She took a keen interest in the public life of her new country and used her pen both to earn a living and to champion numerous causes, many of which involved the rights of women and children. This piece on marriage and divorce was originally published in The Register *in Adelaide in 1878. Divorce was a key issue for those concerned about women's lack of power in the legal system inherited from Brtitish law. (Document 2.8 is an extract from Spence's novel,* Clara Morison.*)*[9]

July 1878

In taking up an old-fashioned novel—one of Richardson's, for example—and reading it in the light of modern ideas, nothing strikes the reader more forcibly than its exaggerated view of marital and parental rights as over and against the rights of wives and children, and the very low idea which even good people then entertained of the responsibilities of the stronger and the rights of the weaker to justice and consideration. Modern opinions reverse the view, and the wider the knowledge and the greater the power the more they are held to be a trust for the benefit and protection of the ignorant and the feeble. But although this is the prevailing tone of the best literature and of the most cultivated society, such a view takes a long time to reach that stratum of society where it is most needed. It takes a long time even to give force to law, which is one of the most efficacious means of educating public opinion; and the Statute-book and the police courts still show that offences by the weaker against the stronger are considered aggravated, while those by the stronger against the weaker are taken with extenuating circumstances.

Public opinion in England as expressed in the law is yet considerably behind the educated intelligence of the age with regard to marriage rights and marriage wrongs. Any offence or crime committed by a wife against her husband is still looked on as a sort of petty treason, and so late as 1760 the murder of a husband by his wife was punished by the severe sentence of burning, while any offence or violence committed by the husband against a wife is reckoned as so much less heinous than any similar crime against any other person, because she is regarded as somehow his property. A wife is liable to the heaviest punishment for transgressions which on the husband's part would be expiated by a fine. There can be no question that adultery is a greater offence in a wife than in a husband, but taking the cases otherwise on their own merits it will be found that owing to the difference in physical strength between the sexes the woman who injures her husband does it by deceit and guile. If she takes life, it is by poison; if she is unfaithful, she tries to keep it secret. Her only open weapon is her tongue, and though it is provoking enough it makes no visible wound; whereas in the incomparably more numerous cases among the poorer classes of injury by men towards their wives the strong hand and violent blow and loud curse have a remarkable frankness about them. There is comparatively little secret made of the existence of the rival on whom the family earnings are squandered; there is little delicacy or subterfuge as to language, or gesture, or blow, or kick. Work may be done or let alone; the wages may be spent in every form of vicious indulgence; the earnings of wife or children may be all at the command of the head of the household; but there is little sense of shame on his part for doing what he likes with his own, and he has a consciousness that if his wife cannot stand this, and brings him up before the police court, the punishment awarded will cost her as dear as himself, and that he can pay her out when he returns to the bosom of his family with all his marital and parental rights in full force.

Again and again has flogging been recommended for brutal assaults on women and children as being summary, cheap, and essentially retributive, and as injuring as little as possible the family of the culprit; but although the evidence of judges, magistrates, and recorders has been overwhelming as to its being advisable nothing has been done . . . But there is another point of view to which attention may fairly be directed. Will the flogged husband return to his home and his duties in a better frame of mind than the fined and imprisoned one? And will wives not dread the immediate return even more than the delayed one to such an extent as to prevent them even more than at present from bringing the offenders to justice? This is one of the greatest difficulties in dealing with this class of crimes, for often lingering affection, and still oftener fear, makes the wife weaken her case, and keep back the worst wrongs she has endured. Such cruelty as is often brought before the police courts would in a higher rank of life be considered sufficient ground for judicial separation, and often for absolute divorce; but there is at present no adequate means within the reach of a woman of protecting her person or even her earnings against her husband's claims. If affection still lingers—if for the sake of the children she wishes to give him another chance—she will probably not apply for such separation; but if it is only fear, such a Bill . . . would allow the same court which sentences the husband to give the injured wife a protection-order for her earnings and the custody of her children, and also enforce an order for the husband to pay his wife such weekly sums for her own and her children's maintenance as the court sees fit. Magistrates are already empowered to give the wife protection for her earnings in the case of desertion, which is a minor offence. In many of the cases of wife-beating there is adultery as well as cruelty on the part of the husband, which should give the wife a claim for an absolute divorce. Cruelty, even of the most aggravated kind, without proved adultery is not at present held to authorize divorce, but it is well worthy of consideration whether in the interest of public morals where the offence has been great and deep, not repented of on one side, or condoned on the other, the release from marriage bonds should not be made complete after the lapse of a reasonable time from the judicial separation, the sum which the first husband is bound to pay being diminished if the wife makes a new marriage. The difficulty in enforcing the payment of a weekly amount is felt in England, and an order would be still more easily evaded here. Wife-desertion is a question which affects all the colonies, each one complaining that wives and families are deserted by their natural head and are made burdensome to the state. An intercolonial union might give increased energy to the search for the defaulters . . .

Document 3.10 Aboriginal women describe living conditions on a reserve

As the white invasion spread and Aborigines were unable to sustain livelihoods on their own land, colonial governments legislated to establish reserves and mission stations to offer them some minimal protection and subsistence. Those who ran these establishments were often dictatorial, carrying out policies that ranged from the insensitive to the cruel. Coranderrk, near Healesville, north of Melbourne, was formed in 1863. Reports of mismanagement and allegations against the Rev. F.P. Strickland led to a parliamentary inquiry which reported to the Victorian legislature in 1883. In these excerpts Aboriginal women take an all too rare opportunity to voice their concerns.

In the parliamentary report, the women are described as 'aboriginal' with a lower-case 'a', which is a general European term for the indigenous inhabitants of any region. Now, when we refer to the original inhabitants of this country, we spell it with a capital 'A' as a mark of respect. Today, of course, many Aborigines prefer terms from their own culture to describe themselves—Koori, Murri, and so on—which do away with the colonising words imposed by Europeans.[10]

1882–3

MRS. ANNIE HAMILTON, ABORIGINAL, EXAMINED

2796. How old are you?—I do not know. I came in Mr. Ogilvie's time.

2797. Where did you come from?—Euston.

2798. Where were you married?—Here.

2799. What part does your husband belong to?—Kilmore.

2800. Have you any children?—Three girls and one boy.

2801. Are they healthy?—Two of them were sick, when they said it was fever.

2802. When they said it was scarlet fever?—Yes.

2803. Do you think it was scarlet fever?—I do not think it. He had a sort of scab.

2804. What does your husband do?—Work in the paddock.

2805. Do you get enough clothing?—One pair of boots a year.

2806. Do you get enough to keep you warm?—No, two flannel petticoats.

2807. Flannel jackets?—No, I used to wear them but I had to knock it off.

2808. Do you get flannel to make shirts for your husband?—No, we have to buy them.

2809. Do you get enough rations?—No, we are out before the week is out.

2810. How do you manage?—From my friends, who have more than I have.

2811. Do you pay it back?—Yes, when I get my rations.

2812. That will make you short the next week?—Yes.

2813. Do you ever have enough to last you the week?—No, the children eat it and run me out of rations.

2814. How old are they?—One four, the other three, and a baby one year old.

2815. How much do you get for them?—Half a ration for the four-year old and the three-year old until they are full grown.

2816. What kind of rations do you run out of—everything?—Yes; sugar and flour and tea.

2817. Do you get any meat at all except what you buy?—No.

2818. Do you pay for it?—I pay when my husband gets paid. We go in debt. Perhaps we get it on Friday, and not then till Tuesday. Sometimes he goes fishing to make the bill less.

2819. Do you get plenty of blankets to make you warm?—Only one a year for the children and all. Do you wear them out before the end of the year?—Yes, when we wash them they get worn out.

2820. Have you a good bed and bedstead?—I bought an iron bedstead.

2821. Have you got a mattress?—Yes. We had to get the straw; we were not allowed to get straw one year, so I cut some rushes from the hill.

2822. Have you a good hut?—Yes.

2823. Is it warm?—Not lined. The wind comes in. We had to line my bedroom with bags.

2824. Do you get good health yourself?—Not always. I am sometimes sick.

2825. Do you get any medicine when you are sick?—Not medicine to cure me. Sometimes I have to go without. The medicine I get is nothing but water almost.

2826. Does it taste of brandy or wine?—No, no taste at all.

2827. Have you to buy your own candles?—Yes, and kerosene.

2828. Do you get any currants?—No, except at Christmas day.

2829. How much do you get?—A pannican or so.

2830. Does your husband ever go to stations to work?—No, only to Wappan.

2831. When your husband has been in the habit of going to Wappan did you ever go with him?—No, I was at home.

2832. When you are sick what do you complain of?—A pain in my side and a cough.

2833. Does your husband go shearing?—No, he was milkman at Wappan.

2834. He always brought home a cheque for you?—Yes.

. . .

MRS. CAROLINE MORGAN, ABORIGINAL, EXAMINED

2840. Have you been long here?—Seventeen years I think I am.

2841. You came here immediately the station was formed?—Yes.

2842. Where do you come from?—The Loddon.

2843. Were you married then?—No.

2844. You got married here?—Yes.

2845. Where does your husband come from?—My first husband came from Kilmore, my second from Echuca.

2846. How long have you been married this time?—Six years.

2847. Have you any children?—Yes.

2848. Any by the first husband?—None now. My last one died lately.

2849. Where?—Here.

2850. How many by the present husband?—Three living now.

2851. What is the age of the oldest?—Six now. He would be seven on the 14th of January.

2852. Do you have good health or are you sick?—I was always a sickly woman. I was never very healthy.

2853. Were you healthy where you were before you came here?—I do not remember.

2854. You have always been sickly here?—Yes.

. . .

2927. Say anything you have to say—do not be frightened?—[The witness handed in a paper.]

2928. Who wrote this?—Tommy Dunolly wrote this.—[The Chairman read the same as follows:]

This is my evidence. Coranderrk, November 16th 1881. I have asked Mrs. Strickland for a pair of blankets for my sick boy. She told me that she must write to Captain Page first. Then I told her, must my little boy be perishing with the cold till you get a letter from Mr. Captain Page? She told me she had orders only to give a pair of blankets for every hut. Then I told her, what must I do then, I have three beds? Then she told me that she did not know. I then told her that we always got blankets for the children before she came here. Another time I asked her for three pannicans. She also said that Captain Page never gave her orders to give them out to the huts. I told her that we got knives and forks and pannicans before she came here. She said she would write to Captain Page about these things; but I never heard nothing more about them since until I saw one of Annie Hamilton's girls coming up with a pannican from Mr. Strickland. So I went down and asked her if there were any pannicans came lately. She never said yes or no, but just turned around and said,

'How many do you want?' I said 'Three, if you please.' So she gave them to me, so I thanked her for them, and then I came away home. My husband also asked Mr. Strickland for a pair of boots for my poor sick boy, Marcus, and Mr. Strickland said there was none; so he said he would send in for a pair to Healesville; so he sent in for a pair and I got them. So when pay-day came, Mr. Strickland took 10s. of my husband's wages to pay for the boots. We thought that Mr. Captain Page was to stand responsible for those boots, but it seems we had to pay for them. When my poor sick boy was very bad he was longing for eggs; so my husband tried in the neighborhood and could not get any; so my sick boy was dying. He asked Mr. Strickland to send to Mr. Captain Page for some eggs; so Mr. Strickland said he would see. So when Mr. Strickland came up and visited him, the sick boy asked him again about the eggs, and Mr. Strickland said, 'Well, my boy, if I send to Captain Page he would laugh at me for the idea of sending for eggs to town from up country.' So I told Mr. Strickland that my husband tried round about the neighborhood for some eggs and could not get any. Milk I get very little; I get from half of a cup to a cupfull—never more than that. So anything we ask for we get very little of it.

Caroline Morgan+

MISS EDA BRANGY, ABORIGINAL, EXAMINED

'Sir,—I am now about to bring my complaints before you. When we used to have our meals in the big room, we used to be locked up, and if we wanted anything it was given through the wires, just like we were prisoners. We never got any blankets since Mrs. Strickland has been on this station; the only two that got blankets were Bella Lee and Lizzie Edmonds; the blankets that I have got are from Mr. Green's and Mr. Halliday's time. Mrs. Strickland gave Tommy Dunolly a blanket, because his wife was ill, and said that Tommy Dunolly was to return it. And beside, Mrs. Strickland used our blankets on her own bed and on her daughters' beds too. And about the washing, I used to do for Mrs. Strickland and receiving no wages for it: I once asked Mrs. Strickland why did not she pay me for washing for her. So she said that she was not going to pay us orphans. Bella Lee and Mary Ann are doing Mrs. Strickland's washing, and they don't receive any wages. Mr. Strickland came home from Healesville one afternoon, and what do you think we saw? A bottle in his pocket containing liquor, because we could smell it as soon as he came near to us. I got three witnesses—Tommy Dick, Alick Briggs, and Joseph Hunter. Mrs. Strickland is supposed to be the matron, but we find it very different indeed. Instead of Mrs. Strickland giving out the orders, the Miss

Stricklands give out the orders. What we have to do? Mrs. Green never sends her daughters out to order us about like the Miss Stricklands do. When Mrs. Strickland is inside she would send out one of her daughters to watch us, like a cat watching for a mouse; not so with Mrs. Green. I think we have reason to complain about the treatment we get here. And when we are out of bread we are obliged to send up to Tommy Dunolly, and beside bake damper; and beside Mrs. Strickland keeps back some of the loafs until the baker came, and then she would give us the stale loafs, and take a new loaf for her table. And, again, Mrs. Strickland never came into our bedrooms to see if they are all right; but if she knew that any visitors were coming up to see this station, she would be on the look-out to see that all was clean, and also the big room, and the little children would be made to put on their best dresses; but if anybody didn't come, there would be the difference. The only food we get for breakfast is bread and treacle and sometimes steak. Not so with Mrs. Green; we would get everything we wanted. There were two men here, named Mr. Wilkie and Major Bell. They used to eat the Government rations, and also the Miss Stricklands used to send down milk every morning, and that is the reason that sometimes we used to get short of bread. But if Mrs. Green was back we would be satisfied. Miss Strickland teaches the boys in Sunday school. When they were reading, Miss Strickland says to David Banfield, 'You and your father are leading the people astray, instead of telling them of God.'—Sir, I am yours truly, Eda Brangy.

Document 3.11 Working women take industrial action

Until the early 1880s unions had been very much the concern of men in the skilled trades. Sewing and tailoring, an area of skilled work where women were concentrated, was carried out in workshops, and in the home as part of an exploitative system of sweated labour (i.e. middlemen took work to women who had to stay at home with their families and paid them less than the going rate.) At this period women's wages were fixed at a rate one-third to one-half of men's. In 1882, when the Melbourne clothing firm of Beath, Schiess & Co. cut seamstresses' meagre wages and other employers looked eager to follow, the women came out on strike and formed a union. As these extracts show, The Age *took up the fight on behalf of the strikers.*[11]

December 1882

STRIKE AMONG WOMEN IN A FACTORY

A considerable amount of excitement prevails amongst the people employed in the various soft-goods factories, owing to a strike which has taken place at the factory of Messrs. Beath, Schiess and Co., Flinders-lane. It appears that material reductions in the prices paid to coat, vest and trouser makers have been made from time to time during the past twelve months. Last week it was proposed to make a further reduction, when the hands concerned, who are principally women and girls, struck work. The number affected is between 200 and 300, and they declare that the proposed reduction will bring their wages down to starving point. With the exception of about 20, who have resumed work, the remainder continue on strike, and profess themselves determined to remain so if they can be backed up by public opinion, which they maintain they have a right to demand in a democratic colony like Victoria. The strike is of still greater interest from the fact that two other firms engaged in a similar business are waiting the issue between Messrs. Beath, Schiess and Co. and their *employées* to decide what steps they will take. It is known that if those on strike give way, and return to work on the terms proposed, these firms will immediately follow the action of Beath, Schiess and Co. Hence the attitude of those on strike is watched with a considerable amount of anxiety, as a principle is involved which affects the future of the girls engaged in factories in the colony. We learn that they are firm and determined in their aspect, and have quietly resolved not to submit to the terms which have been proposed. A man who buys a ready made sac suit of clothes, and pays £2 10s. for it, will be surprised to learn that the girl who made his coat received before the reductions alluded to were made only 2s. 8d. for her work; that the maker of his vest received only 11d., and that the trouser hands received a correspondingly low price. We are informed that some twelve months ago the vest hands were paid 11d. for men's vests. This amount was subsequently reduced to 10d., then to 9d., then to 8d., and the *employées* bore these reductions patiently; but when they heard there was to be a further reduction to 7d., they resisted. Three months ago it is stated that coat hands were paid 2s. 8d. per coat; this amount was reduced to 2s. 5d., and last Tuesday it was intimated that there would be a further reduction to 2s., which they also opposed. The trouser hands also struck against the lowering of their small earnings, and, as stated before, none but a few coat hands have resumed work. Most of these have been compelled to do so from family circumstances. Despite the reductions we have mentioned, the price paid to what are known as 'buttonhole hands' in coats has been reduced to the extent of 1s. in paget coats and to 8d. in sac coats. We are informed that under the reductions two of the smartest girls in the factory were unable last week to earn more than 15s., though they worked hard for fourteen hours a day. Girls who used to get 10d. each for children's holland coats are now expected to make them for 6d., and it is claimed, as a whole, that girls cannot honestly make a living at the prices proposed by Messrs. Beath, Schiess and Co.

THE WORKWOMEN'S STRIKE

The chief topic of conversation among the working classes yesterday was the strike of the workwomen employed by Messrs. Beath, Schiess and Co., clothing manufacturers, of Flinders-lane, and steps have already been taken by several of the trades to assist their sisters in the field of labor in the action they have taken by resisting a manifest injustice. A meeting of the *employés* of the Langlands Foundry Company was held during the dinner hour yesterday, when it was unanimously resolved to assist the factory hands, and a committee, consisting of Messrs. Greig, Warner and Bennett, was appointed to confer with those on strike. They will meet at the Trades' Hall at half-past six o'clock this evening for that purpose, and are desirous that a committee of Beath, Schiess and Co.'s *employés* should be appointed to join them. They will also be glad to see representatives from other trades and workshops who may be willing to co-operate in rendering practical assistance to the workwomen. Several members of the French polishing trade have also intimated to us their desire to assist in any movement that may be originated to protect the factory women and girls from the, what one of them termed, 'greedy propensities of the employers'. We are further informed that special meetings of several trade unions are to be called to consider the matter if, in the meantime, the firm does not re-instate all those who have been compelled to strike. We have made most careful inquiries, and the more evidence we receive the more are we convinced that Messrs. Beath, Schiess and Co. are in the wrong and that public opinion will be against them. A letter from a sympathiser with the women and girls in the action they have taken has been sent to us, with half a crown enclosed, as the foundation of a fund to recoup any losses they may sustain through the strike, and from conversations which have been reported to us the fund is likely to receive a considerable amount. Small though the strike is—merely between 200 and 300 women and girls—it has assumed a serious aspect from the fact that the girls are helpless. Men under similar circumstances can hold indignation meetings, and publicly make known their grievances; women cannot. They can only depend upon friends to champion their cause, and in this case their dependence, as they say, rests entirely on the press, to whom they appeal to ventilate their grievances. In addition to the particulars which appeared in yesterday's issue we may mention the following facts . . . [A] coat hand says: 'I used to make from 18s. to 20s. per week; under the new prices I could not make more than 14s. or 15s. I have to pay 11s. per week for my board, as I have no father or mother, and how can I live respectably on that?' Another hand states: 'I have been engaged on first class work, and have averaged 24s. per week. The reduction will bring me down to 18s. or £1 at the most, working from half-past eight in the morning to half-past five in the afternoon with half a hour's interval for lunch and three or four hours' work in the evening at home.' Another coat hand declares:—'I am considered a good hand, and under the proposed reduction I could not earn more than 15s. a week, working fourteen hours a day. I have parents, but of course I cannot expect them to keep me, I pay them 10s. a week for my board, the same as I would have to pay anywhere else, which leaves me only 5s. a week to keep myself in clothes and boots.' Two sisters, acknowledged smart hands, state they averaged 12s. 6d. per week each. Under the reduction they could not earn more than 10s. a week, but that was only in cases of emergency by taking work home after being employed in the factory from half-past eight in the morning to half-past five in the afternoon . . . The prices paid to machinists have also been lowered. A machinist—a most intelligent young girl, says: 'Six weeks ago I got 5½d. for sac coats, a halfpenny was then taken off, and on Tuesday last the firm wanted to take off another half-penny, which meant that we should make a man's sac coat for 4½d., for pagets we got 7d., and they proposed that we should do them for 6½d. For first class pagets we got 7½d., and they now propose to give us only 7d. For this we struck work. To do the work at this price would be simple slavery; it was hard enough before.' Another machinist states: 'I cannot earn more than 13s. per week under the reduced prices, working from half-past eight a.m. to half-past five p.m., with half-an-hour to lunch.' Another machinist states: 'We used to get 2½d. per vest; then they reduced it to 2¼d., and now they want to knock off the other farthing, so we *struck*. I used to make 18s. per week, but at the last mentioned price I could only make 12s. or 13s. at the outside, and I have to pay 11s. a week for my board.' Another vest machinist says:—'I used to earn from 18s. to £1 per week; under the present arrangements I can only make from 15s. to 16s., and I have a sick mother and two little sisters to support.' A further complaint made against the firm is that from time to time when new hands are taken on, the best work—that is to say, the work which produces the most money—is given to them, while the old hands are given what is termed the 'rubbish'.

Document 3.12 A woman imagines a feminist utopia

Henrietta Dugdale (1826–1918) was one of the first in the colony of Victoria to voice public concern about the social position of women. She was the first president of the Victorian Women's Suffrage Society, formed in 1884, and notable for her espousal of dress reform, birth control and secularism. In 1883 she published a booklet, A Few Hours in a Far-Off Age, *in which she developed a vision of Australia in the twenty-first century. Her ideal future was a society in which emancipated women could live in harmony with men and on equal terms. In these extracts she describes three inhabitants of the future, a woman and her two children, who look back on the horrors of the twenty-first century (and earlier) and make comparisons with their feminist present.*[12]

1883

I stand in the doorway of an immense building, which appears to be devoted to the display of antiquities. Many people are entering, although the morning is young. A magnificent scene is before me.

At last I see a city in which are combined grandeur, cleanliness, order and picturesque loveliness. Between this one and those of the nineteenth century exists a difference as great, if not greater, than between the latter and the loathsome lairs of our cannibal progenitors reeking with refuse of human remains . . .

. . . No smoke-disfigured architecture. No stream of poisonous filth, running with ferocious delight on its deathly errand. No besotted-looking creatures offending passers-by with debasing language. No jails. No knots of babbling men standing around entrances to public-houses, vieing with each other for destruction of intelligence. Indeed, such things so pitiable could not be, for here are no such houses. No ill-fed, barefooted, unclean children, learning the probationary steps to scoundrelism. No suffering animals, urged by cruelty to overtax their strength. No decrepitude in age. No careworn faces. All are lovely with the light of knowledge—knowledge not in the capabilities of our lower natures, but towards which we are surely tending.

I know these graceful beings are humans—yet how they differ from my own poor self, and all others of our era. They appear *luminous* with integrity and benevolence. Both sexes are bewitchingly graceful. Women are rather taller than the generality of the present generation, but the men are not such fine animals as those of my century, though far nobler looking.

Their ambition has evidently been to attain efficiency in intellect and benignity in preference to the retention of tiger muscle. Another link to the brute fast disappearing . . .

Here are three mounting the stairs. A lady about fifty years of age with her only children—a daughter between eighteen and nineteen, and son perhaps two years younger. It is very fortunate they are unable to see the staring habits of our century, for they are all so beautiful in form and mind I cannot remove my eyes from them. Every trace of wild-beast treachery and cruelty obliterated. Grand creatures are these! Benevolent, courageous and intelligent as only very numerous generations of truth-loving ancestors could make them.

No, sceptics, 'distance' has not 'lent' this enchantment—that is, in the sense you imply—for I am near enough to hear the elder lady say:

'My darlings, this morning we will glance at some of the relics of what was once called the "Christian Era", subsequently designated by historians as "The Age of Blood and Malevolence", but which is, nevertheless, always of importance in the world's library from its having been the first link in the long unbroken chain of eras of civilization. If time will permit, we will take from the twenty-first century to the fifteenth' . . .

They have turned into a very long gallery, over the entrance to which is written: 'Christian Era, or Age of Blood to the Twenty-first Century'.
. . .

'Though,' continues this lady, 'you must naturally expect to find the brute still more unpleasantly prominent than you have yet seen.'

'*More* prominent!' echoes the boy. 'Then, mother, I think evolution most degrading if it proves that we came from beings lower than those we examined last Sunday and Monday.'

'My Frederick, I am not at all surprised at your opinion. Youth in the individual, as youth in a world, cannot judge accurately on subjects where accuracy is all-important. When the world was much younger, and the vanity of unthinking beings was, of course, very strong, most men thought as you do. When you are older you will not give so positive an opinion on any subject without reflection, or judge by the *portion* only of an argument. You will, more wisely, await the whole.'

'Yes, dear and generous-minded mother, you are right, as you always are. I ought not to have spoken so hastily, but I was thinking of that twenty-first century's mode of insulting woman by placing women members of the Senate in a third chamber to debate by themselves.'

Smiling, the lady replies: 'Oh! my true-hearted *chevalier des dames*, it is not known whether that arrangement originated in men's comical vanity, or from a wish by the women to secure quiet in their debates, the men being notorious in those days for their silly quarrels and irrelevant chatter . . . Grasp that, and you will not be surprised to learn that the males of these primitive people held their own sex in such veneration that quite young ones—puny in intellect, and without education—were, by act of senate, qualified to elect senators, enter upon the government of the world, and occupy the highest offices to the exclusion of the Infinite Intelligence, where possessed by women. So those poor vain creatures, with much assumption of wisdom, though still very apelike in various ways, made laws affecting women's liberty, property, and even her children, without consulting her, her happiness, or any higher feeling than their own self-love, comfort and aboriginal greed. In short, the women up to past the nineteenth century were really slaves in all but the name. It is known that men long retained much of brute strength, gained in the still earlier ages by fierce combats for possession of women to toil for them; and they sedulously preserved all they could of that great muscular power, because they imagined it to be a proof of superiority. By use of it they were enabled, during all the low ages, to keep women in a very subjective state, which you will find the more degrading the nearer we descend to the brute period. Little wonder then should we feel that when men commenced forms of religion they framed them with doctrines for continuing the humiliation of women. In all their so-called religious exercises they dinned in her ears old men's tales of how she had been the primary cause of every wrong-doing, for which she had been doomed to suffer cruel punishment, and be subservient to man through all earthly life. Some even went so far in their self-exaltation as to rear woman in the belief that she had no soul—no existence beyond the debasing one allotted to her by those near cousins of apes and tigers. The "religious" ceremony of marriage in use by the ancestors of our own race was characteristic of the very small place conscientiousness then held in the world's mind. Men trained to the profession of goodness—called "clergymen" or "ministers of God"—administered the sacred oaths, knowing they thereby assisted in the perpetration of a crime; for the husband—so the man was named, and meant master—vowed to the Infinite that he would endow his wife— old name for slave—with all his "wordly goods", and that he would "cherish" and "love" her. Except in very rare cases, the endowment not only ended in nothing, but he annexed everything valuable that belonged to her, under the miserable pretext similar to others they used in all their acts of unjust dealing with women—that woman's brain was inadequate to the care of her own property; and, with the same ape logic, they asserted that her strength was insufficient for the various light situations monopolized by man. So she generally performed the menial work, which was very severe in those days of crude appliances and badly constructed dwellings—so severe that she frequently died from the effects—lamed, and hands distorted in her heroic efforts to fulfil duties imposed upon her by the apish cunning of the males. The husband frequently proved his superior intellect by the rapidity with which he squandered his wife's property, and reduced her to hardships she never would have known had his sense or conscientiousness equalled hers. As to the loving and cherishing—alas!'

She is silent. Her kind eyes appear to be looking sadly and compassionately through the mighty past into the aching hearts of my century.

Document 3.13 Wives are told how to achieve marital bliss

An interesting household manual, The Australian Housewives' Manual *appeared in the 1880s describing in prosaic detail the ways in which housewives of modest means could stretch their husbands' income to keep up the semblance of middle-class standards.*

What was the wives' chief goal? Keeping their husbands well-fed and happy. In this, apparently, lay their own best chance for a satisfying life. The writer was known only as 'An Old Housekeeper'—not for her the reforming agenda of a Henrietta Dugdale. What was required of wives, according to this manual, was enormous self-denial and altruism to manipulate men in the domestic arena, activities Dugdale would have classed as part of the barbarous behaviour expected of women in the nineteenth century.[13]

1883

If you will bear these maxims in mind, you will have no difficulty in keeping your home in perfect order. You may often find some emergency for which I have been unable to provide in this book, but I venture to say that you will not find any wherein the consideration of these general principles will not bear you through. If your cookery seems to be troublesome, reflect that, at the cost of a few pence, you are preparing delicacies for your husband which a purse three times as long as that he possesses would not enable him to pay for. Every time you turn out a dinner for a shilling, by means of your skill, which would cost him five or six shillings if you both went to a restaurant, remember that you have practically made him a present of four or five shillings by adding the value of your labour, and still more of your intelligence, to the money he has furnished you with. If this reflection does not reconcile you to the pleasant task of preparing delicacies for his refreshment you must have very little love for him, or he must have a very thankless nature. In either case you are much to be pitied, but in either case your duty is the same, and that is to keep on in the right course, and trust to time to develop a proper appreciation of each other.

As a matter of fact, it is unlikely that you will ever be troubled in this way. On the contrary, you will find that your husband's appreciation of your skill will grow greater every time you exercise it. His home will become more charming to him with every succeeding week, and you more valued as its presiding genius. You will be so delighted every time you see a look of pleased surprise on his face that you will never tire of devising means to gratify him, and he will be so touched by your devotion as to look eagerly forward to the time he spends with you.

Think for a moment how easy it is for you to make him comfortable if you will but try.

It is a hot-wind day, we will say, and about half-past five o'clock, just as the sun gives its fiercest glare before going down, a wearied, perspiring, irritated man walks up to his own door. Every stitch he has upon him is sticking to him, and he has more dust in his eyes and whiskers than it is quite nice to have on one's boots. He is just in that frame of mind when the smallest demand upon his system would make him as fierce as a hungry bear. You, on the other hand, have—that is, if you have been guided by my advice—finished your light housework at least three hours before. Your house has been shut up on three sides, with the blinds down, the whole day, and in front of the south side, where no wind blows or sun shines, you have had an open window or two guarded by wet clothes, so that what air there is in the house is cool. You have had three clear hours of rest, so that you are cool, too, and are lightly clad in some pleasant, cool-looking stuff, so that your very presence, as you open the door, shows him something comforting and nice. You don't say much, because he is too much irritated to be talked to, and you are not too demonstrative because he does not want to be touched in his sticky, uncomfortable condition. But he passes into his bedroom, and there he finds a clean, dry suit of clothes, perfectly complete down to the smallest article of under wear, and quite ready to put on. Beside them are a couple of clean, large, white, bath towels, his sponge, flesh gloves, and anything else he uses for his bath. This is a sign that the bath-room is ready for him, and off he goes. Ten minutes' splashing, and five minutes' towelling, five minutes more for dressing, and ten for that adornment so dear to every man, and a very different husband comes out of the bedroom. He has on a loose, home jacket and pantaloons, in which he can lie and loll at his ease, a shirt made roomy at the neck, so that he does not feel the collar, cool socks, and easy slippers. He casts himself on the sofa in your little sitting-room, and a dish of cold meat, a potato, salad, a fruit tart, also cold, a crisp lettuce, a dish of cold fish, with cold, clear filtered water, a jug of cool ale, and perhaps a pot of hot tea, very refreshing even on a hot-wind day, if everything else be cold, meet his eyes. You still forbear to make much fuss during the meal, and you wisely take it away without any great clatter, reserving your washing up for the cool of the next morning. You go back to your sitting-room and find that, with heat and fatigue, he is half asleep, perhaps entirely so. You noiselessly sit down to your knitting, answering gently if he speak, but not speaking first, and he sleeps for half an hour. No woman worthy the name lives who will not enjoy herself more truly in that half hour, in the knowledge that she has charmed away her husband's pain and discomfort, than she would if he were subduing his weariness to attend to her whims and fancies.

But he wakes long before you think he does, and through his eyelashes sees you, careful, patient, striving for him, anxious for his comfort, and successful in securing it. The subdued light glances on your smooth hair and busy fingers; your face, in its quiet repose, takes back the charm of girlhood, and it is a refreshed, rejuvenated lover that startles you back into the world with a kiss, and with whom you enjoy that blissful evening's chat before your early bed-time.

Is there anything in this home picture out of the reach of any working man's wife in Australia? What does it want to realise it? A very little forethought, a very little self-control, a very little self-denial, the exact qualities which every woman who loves rejoices in exercising for the benefit of those whom she loves. Take the companion picture, and see what these same qualities may do for your husband on a blusterous, rainy night, when he has had a wet tramp from his work, and comes home chilled, muddy, and perhaps with the least taste of a cough in his throat, for a great many of our handsome, stalwart Australians are apt to be a little touched at the chest.

This time there is a cheerful light in your passage, a bright fire in your sitting-room, and another in your bedroom. You may not have the means of putting a warm bath in your bathroom, very likely have not, but you have set your largest foot-bath on a square of oilcloth in your bedroom, and you have poured a boiler full of boiling water into it. A large can of cold water stands by its side, and the bath towels and other paraphernalia are displayed invitingly over a chair close to it. Such clothes as he is most likely to want, warm, dry, and comfortable, hang over another chair by the fire or lie on the bed, and a kettle of boiling water simmers in the chimney, so that he may use it if he pleases. There is nothing like hot water to charm the chill out of cold feet and cramped limbs; nothing like warm, dry clothing to put new life into a drenched, half-frozen specimen of humanity. Again, in half an hour or less, your husband emerges from his bedroom. You are clad in a dress of purple or claret coloured stuff, relieved at the throat and wrists with white linen or lace. Your homely little dinner is on the table, and, as it is wintry weather, you have chosen wintry dishes. You have a nice savoury stewed steak, or a dish of haricot mutton, with potatoes baked in their jackets, a dish of baked apples, and some toasted cheese to follow, a bottle of stout, and, of course the inevitable tea-pot. The hungry man falls to, and once more you let him take forty winks in peace on the sofa while you remove the dinner things, and set them carefully away for the morning's cleaning up. He wakes to find his pipe and tobacco ready to his side on a little table, with the beer jug handy likewise, if he be given to that form of refreshment, and sees you neat, smiling, cheerful, opposite to him, ready either to go on with your knitting in silence, while he smokes and thinks, or to chatter to him as much as he will.

How do you think the evening will go? My dear, I am an old housekeeper, and I know men well, and women, too. Believe me, if you treat your husband like that, his inmost thoughts will be yours, his home will be his sure haven of rest, his paradise, the pride and joy of his life, and you will be what, thank heaven, many, very many women are—the one central point upon which everything turns, upon which his hopes and aspirations will be fixed, on which his faith will be so firmly planted that not the testimony of the whole world shall shake one iota of his confidence in you.

'But what a lot of trouble,' you say, thoughtlessly. 'Why should a woman do all this? Who is to look after her when she is cold or hot?' My dear, who is it that does in effect look after you at those times by giving up his days to labour and his nights to thought in order that he may find you the material to work with. There is no comfort you provide for him that you do not share. The home, which is his paradise, is your handiwork, your refuge, your pride, your castle, your very, very own, your actual self, a part of you inseparable. It is your heart and brain translated into the arrangement of daily life, and you need not fear but that it will be duly valued for its own sake and for yours, and that you will be honoured in proportion to the skill you bestow on it.

. . .

The one way for a wife to ensure her own happiness is by devoting herself entirely to secure that of her husband. No man is insensible to devotion, providing it be unaccompanied with display, and pure devotion is necessarily devoid of that very objectionable element. The wife who proves her devotion to her husband by quietly studying his tastes, deferring to his wishes, providing for his comfort, and making herself and his home attractive, will inevitably reap the reward of his utter and entire confidence, respect, affection, and esteem.

The secret of success is self-denial, and self-denial for the sake of those we love is the sweetest of all exercises—the one that brings the readiest and fullest reward. How often have you not, before your marriage, felt that you could willingly make any sacrifice, endure any deprivation, submit even to personal pain, if you could but add to his happiness. Yet, after marriage, there is too often a languid feeling of security, a lazy idea that nothing more need be done, a foolish conclusion that no further trouble is necessary, and that a husband who really loves his wife will not mind what he puts up with. Under these mistaken ideas married women neglect their personal appearance, forget their accomplishments, and are careless of their homes. 'What is the use of dressing to see nobody but him?' 'What is the use of singing or playing to one's husband?' 'Why should I make such a fuss to have the table attractive when there is no one here but ourselves?' These are the questions foolish women ask themselves, only to be defeated by all competitors as the practical reply.

Document 3.14 A journalist observes the white Australian girl

Richard Twopeny (1857–1915) was notable among the many writers whose observations of colonial life attempted to define the distinctiveness of Australian social behaviour. In Town Life in Australia *(1883) Twopeny attempts a task so many male observers ignored: the representation of the characteristic qualities of women, as well as of men, in this new country. Here he contributes to the fashioning of the young Australian woman, attributing to her (though in feminine terms) the independence, vigour, good humour and other characteristics that were ascribed to the colonial white male.*[14]

1883

Hitherto I have been writing of the properties and adjuncts of Australian life. It is high time to say something of the colonists themselves. And here I shall describe the types which the colony has produced and is producing, rather than such modifications as colonists born and bred in England have undergone during their subsequent residence in Australia—colonials as distinct from colonists.

. . .

When it gets into petticoats or breeches, the child must be treated of according to sex. And here *place aux demoiselles*, for from this time upwards they are a decided improvement upon their brothers. The Australian schoolgirl, with all her free-and-easy manner, and what the Misses Prunes and Prisms would call want of maidenly reserve, could teach your bread-and-butter miss a good many things which would be to her advantage. It is true that neither schoolmistresses nor governesses could often pass a Cambridge examination, nor have they any very great desire for intellectual improvement. But the colonial girl is sharper at picking up what her mistress does know than the English one, and she has more of the boy's emulation. Whatever her station in life, she is bound to strum the piano; but in no country is a good pianoforte player more rare, or do you hear greater trash strummed in a drawing-room. Languages and the other accomplishments are either neglected or slurred over; but, on the other hand, nearly every colonial girl learns something of household work, and can cook some sort of a dinner, yea, and often cut out and make herself a dress. She is handy with her fingers, frank, but by no means necessarily fast in manner, good-natured and fond of every species of fun. If her accomplishments are not many, she sets little value on those she possesses, and never feels the want of, or wastes a regret, on any others.

Almost all girls go to school, but the home-training leads to little obedience or respect for their teachers, and the parental authority is constantly interposed to prevent well-deserved punishments. Accustomed to form judgments early and fearlessly, each girl measures her mistress by her own standard; and if she comes up to that standard, an *entente cordiale* is established, the basis whereof is the equality which each feels to subsist independent of their temporary relations.

At seventeen my lady comes out, though for the last two, if not three or four, years she has been attending grown-up dances at the houses of friends, so that the edge of her pleasure has long been dulled. School once left behind, she looks upon marriage as the end and object of life; but it must not be supposed from this that she makes any attempt to catch a husband. Young men are plentiful enough, and she does not care when her turn comes. That it is bound to come she takes for granted, and accordingly is always on the look-out for it. The *camaraderie* which exists between her and some half-a-dozen men may lead to something with one of them; and meanwhile she has time to ascertain their dispositions and turn their qualities over and over in her mind till some one's attentions become marked, and she makes up her mind that she is suited or the reverse. She has danced too much before she came out to care much for it now; but in a warm climate, where verandas and gardens lend themselves so readily to flirtation, she retains a due appreciation of balls and parties, and gets a far larger number of them than an English girl of the middle class.

On the average, colonial girls possess more than their share of good looks; but 'beauties' are rare, and the sun plays the deuce with complexions. The commonest type is the jolly girl who, though she has large hands and feet, no features and no figure, yet has a taking little face, which makes you say: 'By Jove, she is not half bad-looking!' Brunettes are, of course, in the majority; and every third or fourth girl has beautiful brown eyes and an abundance of coarsish hair—which, by the way, she probably dresses in an untidy knob, all corners and no rotundity.

Her manners have lost the boisterousness of schooldays, but still often want toning down according to English ideas. Her frankness and good-fellowship are captivating, and you feel that all her faults spring from the head, and not from the heart. She is rarely affected, and is singularly free from 'notions', though by no means wanting in ideas and in conversation of a not particularly cultured description. With a keen idea of the value of money and the benefits to be derived from its possession, she never takes it into consideration in choosing her husband: her ideal of whom is above all things 'manly'—the type that used to be known under the description of 'muscular Christians'.

In religion her views are not pronounced. She attends church pretty regularly, but is entirely free from superstition, though not always from intolerance. Adoration of the priesthood is not at all in her line. For politics she cares nothing, except in Victoria, where naturally she espouses her father's side warmly, but in an irrational, almost stupid, way. Art is a dead letter to her, and so is literature, unless an unceasing and untiring devotion to three-volume novels be counted under that head. To music, according to her lights, she professes, and often feels, a strong leaning.

There is one thing about her that strikes you disagreeably in society. It is her want of conversation with ladies and married people. To a bachelor, to whom she has just been introduced, she will chatter away nineteen to the dozen; but, even in her own house, she has no idea of the social duties. Marriage, in her opinion, is a Rubicon, which, once crossed, if it does not altogether debar from the pleasures of maiden and bachelorhood, at least makes it necessary for married folk to shift for themselves. To talk or dance with a married man would be a terrible waste of time; and as for married women, she expects to join that holy army of martyrs in the course of time, and will then be quite contented with the same treatment as she has meted out to others. The politeness which springs from a sense of duty to others is little known to the Australian girl. If she likes you, she will make herself very pleasant; but if you are not worth wasting powder and shot on, you must expect to realize that disagreeable truth in all its nakedness.

In many things a child, she often looks forward to her wedding for the mere festivity of the occasion, and thinks how jolly it will be to have six bridesmaids, how nice she will look in her bridal dress, and how the other fellows will envy her chosen one. Generally marrying two or three years younger than the English girl, she would consider herself an 'old maid' at twenty-three; and for old maids she entertains the very minimum of respect, in spite of their rarity in the colonies. Once married, she gives up to a large extent, if not entirely, the pomps and vanities of which she has had her full during spinsterhood, and devotes herself to her household, children, and husband. She usually has a large family, and in them pays for all the sins of her youth. She has had her fling, and for the rest of her life she lives but to serve her children and make them happy, recognising that in the antipodes 'juniores priores' is the adopted motto.

Document 3.15 A novelist remembers women's power in the family

Reformers were beginning to construct a path for women's empowerment with legal and political emancipation, but many understood, too, that in certain circumstances women could and did gain considerable power in the family. Here, in an extract from her story of her early years, Childhood at Brindabella, *the novelist Miles Franklin (1879–1954) describes her mother and her grandmother and the pivotal role they played in their families. Franklin herself, however, turned her back on such informal access to power to seek education, work and personal fulfilment as a single woman in urban settings.*[15]

c. 1880s

Among first impressions are winter evenings with the room, as it appeared to me, brilliantly lighted by the grand log fire in the snowy hearth, the kerosene lamp on the round table in the corner with an unfurled peacock tail behind it like a wall panel of fabulous brocade, and my mother at the piano with two sperm candles in their wrought brass holders. These as I grew older seemed to me of pure gold such as the angels would have in their harps. I too sat at the piano. No lap, no pair of arms could lure from that position, when my mother began to play the instrument. This also must have been early, as I could not talk then—and I could say nearly any word in the dictionary at two. Also by eighteen months I would have been amenable to discipline and forbidden such rakish hours. Mother was firm in plan, particular in habits. Times of bedding and rising, meals, week-end routines were adhered to with precision. Mother was too well-regulated and capable for unpunctuality.

I was in my long robes—whether the infant robes, from which we were 'short-coated' at three months, were resuscitated as evening wear, there is no one left to ask; but I would be correctly and daintily dressed. My mother enforced and ingrained a fastidiousness in me, so that later the frowsy habits of others caused me acute discomfort.

Mother was not musical, but she had been stiffly governessed, and played the piano correctly and was a prodigy in her situation. As part of her wedding paraphernalia she brought to the wild gullies the novelty of a sewing-machine and the social glory of a piano. The (pre-fire) Broadwood in a beautiful rosewood case had to come in by bullock dray, in some places down wriggling creek beds instead of tracks. Its survival with no scratch on it in such a passage was due to the resourcefulness, tough muscles, experienced bush-craft and tireless enthusiasm of young men serving a divinity.

My mother was the wonder of her region. She was beautiful and accomplished, clever as a hostess and in all departments of home-making. My father's pride in her was as a poem and a triumph combined, and sustained him to the end of his days. There was open expression of surprise as to how he could have carried off such a prize, but he too must have been irresistible with his slim straight height, his equestrian fame, his blue eyes, dark hair and sharp classical profile, his exuberant and witty though unbarbed humour, his boundless generosity. He was prized by all his contemporaries as 'white throughout'.

Young women were worshipped on the remote stations when men were many and women a rarity. Any normal woman with health and youth, whether in kitchen or drawingroom, was a magnet.

. . .

Men would make to mother if sick or injured. Her presence seemed to comfort them, and she was as competent as a trained midwife or nurse. She could set clean breaks in bones with deftness and surety so that the doctor would find nothing to do but congratulate her. On one occasion she successfully sewed on a toe that a boy had severed from his brother with a tomahawk.

. . .

At the age of two I determined to live in the old home where I had been born. I much preferred life with my grandmother to that at Bobilla.

I loved my grandmother's home above my own out of all proportion. I was passionately and unweanably attached to Ajinby. It was a family head station, a place of maturity and amenities. Bobilla was in the making, and my mother must have passed on to me her own dismay.

At the age of fifteen a reversal in fortune had taken her from the school-room and the home she loved, as I loved Ajinby. Her heart turned longingly towards it to the end of her days. Thereafter she had had to take the leading share in nursing her father, a man over six feet tall, paralysed and blind, a task beyond her strength. In addition she had had to labour as hard as a gardener, a farm hand, laundress, charwoman and general servant combined to retrieve the homestead at Ajinby from a pigwallow. It had been erected as a wayside inn in digging days and when my grandma and family had moved in, one of the doors was hanging on the hinges and pigs were comfortable in the earth of the unboarded floors. The roof had been leaky, bedbugs rioted throughout. Grandma and her children, some of them still infants, had converted it into the home I adored, long so famous for its hospitality, comfort, refinement and joyous associations that up and down the land its name has been perpetuated on numerous cottages by those who at some time had known its charms. My eldest uncle aged nine, under Grandma, had had to be working manager, bullock driver, cattle man, etc. The second uncle, aged six, had somewhat lighter work. As he remarks today, 'A child was quite a fellow at six, and by nine he was an old man.'

. . .

In addition to the gruelling labour, my grandmother maintained the standing of the English better classes and insisted upon her daughters observing the conventions and niceties of well-brought-up young ladies. In the taming of the Australian bush the pattern was the English squire. My mother's technique remained unflawed through all the grinding and tragic vicissitudes of a long, impecunious, unrewarded existence. She loathed the early hardships, restrictions and often complete isolation of Ajinby: to be removed to Bobilla, even more secluded, and wilder, with all its amenities to be introduced and maintained by herself, with the cruel burden of unrestricted child-bearing added, was too much.

At Bobilla I had competition with my own sisters and brothers, and my cousins, who were older and of greater physical hardiness and daring. At Ajinby I reigned alone among six young uncles and aunts, with my grandmother at their head. I grew up with pride in and unwavering affection for my grandmother, aunts and uncles. My satisfaction in them assumed a different character with maturity but it never waned, never was wounded. In my estimation my grandmother equalled God, with benificent resources and powers, and my aunts and uncles ranked as seraphim and cherubim. She had authority and self-reliance gained in running the whole station from the time the eldest of her children had been fifteen years old and she in a more hampered position than a widow's with her husband blind and helpless from an injured spine.

She was not quite five feet tall and composed of energy, determination, generosity, common sense, honesty and courage. She believed God to be a fixed identity as delineated by the Church from the Bible. She never owed a penny or turned a tramp from her door without replenishing his tucker-bags or giving him care if he were ill. She mothered the 'godwits' by patching their clothes, giving them boots and admonishment. She was ceaselessly industrious, had a head for business and was known as a 'good manager'. Her haysheds and other storehouses were always well-stocked for winter with the yield from her orchards, potato and pumpkin paddocks, her fowlhouses, her dairy and vegetable garden. She grew and cured her own bacon as well as her own beef. Her streams were full of native trout and Murray cod. Order, plenty, decency, industry and hospitality were in the home I so loved.

. . .

In the light of early forwardness I was singularly reluctant to progress farther. The precocities or any charms of the tiny tot had vanished in the unattractive stage of a big girl, though one still a child, lost without the family. I loved the old nest with maturing passion, the mountains and hills, its rivers and creeks, its rocks and paddocks, though I could no longer roam about even the nearer precincts without accounting for my time, nor accompany the men farther afield.

The limitations of the company of infants and toddlers now confronted me again in restriction to the women's domain. The artificial bonds called feminine were presented to my understanding. I must become genteel as befitting a young lady. A good deal was attributed to God's will, and did not turn my heart any more warmly to that gentleman. It was the humbug in 'womanliness', the distorting and atrophying of minds on a sex line, the grinding superstition that all women must be activated on a more or less moronic level, the absence of fair play between men and women when the masculine and feminine issue arose that was at the root of the trouble, though I did not know so much in my first decade. I was more bewildered and tormented and rebellious in my second, when preoccupation with sex was discovered to be in excess of all needs for perpetuating the species, and banished logic from human behaviour.

Part 4
Seeking social solutions 1886–1901

The years from the mid-1880s to the end of the century were notable for a peak in colonial prosperity, followed by a severe depression. Various groups made slow and halting efforts to seek protection for those disadvantaged under a capitalist system, and to seek social justice for women. Liberals sought state intervention on a range of issues that were previously not considered to be the business of government. These events affected white women, who were also becoming more active on their own behalf; Aboriginal women experienced afresh the brutality of the white frontier with each new pastoral expansion and each new mining strike. Missions offered Aboriginal women the apparent chance of expanding their prospects by acquiring western skills and education, but even those who were initially keen to do this found that white society offered them few opportunities to use such skills.

Amidst the boom, depression and its aftermath, women contributed to family incomes one way or another—with paid work; with unpaid labour as workers on family farms; as assistants to professional husbands; as thrifty housewives managing the family budget; or, as in the case of Bert Facey's aunt and grandmother, organising all available family members to eke out a subsistence living. One step that wives could take to lessen their burdens was to limit the number of children they bore and reared. The birthrate, extremely high in the mid-nineteenth century, began to fall rapidly as the century closed. Means of artificial birth control, once a forbidden subject, became more widely known through the work of reformers, many of them women.

It was becoming apparent that the white population of the colonies was not about to expand rapidly either by natural births or large-scale immigration, and this strongly influenced national sentiment and government intervention in individual lives as the end of the century drew near. The colonies' plans to federate in 1901 were inspired in part by hopes for increased prosperity, in part by racist fears of being 'invaded' by populous Asian countries to the north. White women as mothers or potential mothers inspired concern about the health of female paid workers and the wage security of male breadwinners.

At the same time an organised women's movement took shape. The Woman's Christian Temperance Union, formed in the colonies in the late 1880s, was concerned with male drunkenness and male violence towards women, as well as with women's liberties. In their demand for the women's vote they were joined by women's suffrage leagues in the cities, in a decade that saw women enfranchised in two colonies, South Australia and Western Australia. The achievement of this vote ensured these women's right to the vote in the Federal Constitution of the new Commonwealth of Australia, enacted to commence on the first day of the new century. In the following year, 1902, this right was extended to all adult white women, but not to Aboriginal women. In 1901 white feminists concentrated on their own partial victory, and their hopes for a bright new future, with women alongside men at the helm of state.

Document 4.1 An Aboriginal woman tells of mission life

Bessy Cameron (c. 1851–1895), a Nyungar, was born in Western Australia in the early 1850s. When very young she was adopted by Henry and Anne Camfield, who ran a school for Aboriginal children at Albany. The school aimed to teach Aborigines Christian religion and western values. As a young woman, Bessy Cameron was sent to Victoria, to Ramahyuck, a Moravian mission run by Friedrich and Louise Hagenauer, and later to Lake Tyers Mission. Her experience there was mixed and ultimately a disappointment to her, as her skills as a teacher and a leader were not recognised. In this letter to the

Melbourne newspaper, The Argus, *she responds to a critical article*
by John Stanley James, 'The Vagabond' (Document 3.8), supporting
the mission and also strongly defending her people against his racist
slurs. For an Aboriginal woman to have the skills and confidence to
write to a newspaper in the nineteenth century was a rare triumph.[1]

April 1886

Having read in the *Australasian* of the 27th March an account of 'The
Vagabond's' impression of the people of Lake Tyers, I was moved to write
a letter in defence.

In the first place, I will not say much on his style of calling us niggers,
as he told us in his address that he was an American. Now, all respect to
Mr Vagabond, but I know the way the niggers have been treated in
America.

Secondly, Mr Vagabond says it was related to him that the Rev. F.A.
Hagenauer knocked down a loafing black fellow three times. Now, I have
lived on Ramahyuck many years, and never in my time did it happen, nor
before as I was told. Besides, Mr Hagenauer is not [of] a fighting nature;
he managed us by kindness.

Thirdly, Mr Vagabond said 'he did not find the houses particularly
clean and well-kept'. He forgot that he went around inspecting at 9 o'clock
on Saturday morning, just in the middle of cleaning.

If Mr Vagabond was a Benedict he would know all about the business
of house-cleaning on a Saturday; but, then, in his own house there would
be a room set apart for visitors, and we have only two rooms, so he must
excuse us at not finding the houses clean and tidy at 9 o'clock Saturday
morning.

In conclusion, I must say the words, 'Very lazy and useless is my
summary of the Lake Tyers blackfellow', are very sad, as there is some
truth in them, yet still there is some work done, or else the station could
not go on as it has done. But, as Mr Vagabond asks himself, 'Would I,
in his place' and goes on to say, 'As I am a truthful judge of my own
character I am compelled to admit I would not', so we will take courage
from that, and go on our way, trying what is in our power to bring up
our children to earn their own living, and be useful members of society,
and ourselves to be grateful to the board and our missionaries for all their
kindness and patience to us aboriginals.

Hoping, Sir, you will excuse my taking up a little of your valuable
time, as I am writing this in the name of all my coloured brethren and
sisters of Lake Tyers.

Document 4.2 A male missionary tells of white male cruelty to Aboriginal women

John Brown Gribble (1847–1893) was a clergyman who arrived in Western Australia from New South Wales in 1885 to establish a mission station for Aborigines in the Gascoyne River area. He quickly became alarmed at the exploitation of Aborigines by the district's large and powerful landowners, but faced hostile opposition when he attempted to make his observations public. In 1886 he published the pamphlet Dark Deeds in a Sunny Land, *which included articles Gribble had written for the local press. The vitriolic reaction to it in Perth—one newspaper described him as a 'lying, canting humbug'— prompted Gribble to take libel action in the courts. He received no support from his church or the government, lost the libel case, and left the colony when he was unable to pay the legal costs of his suit.*

In these extracts Gribble describes the sexual exploitation of Aboriginal women and girls by white men, a common occurrence on the frontiers of settlement and one that, as Gribble's experience shows, authorities did little to prevent.[2]

1886

But that Australia itself, professedly the new home of liberty and light, should also have become the theatre of the dark deeds of oppression and cruelty; that a land not only blessed by the Great God, with cloudless skies and wide-spread prosperity and happiness to those who have been privileged to make it their home, and moreover a land which professes to reflect the noble institutions of Great Britain, those godly and philanthropic fabrics, which are not only England's glory and boast, but the envy of all the world beside; that a land so circumstanced and blessed by Divine Providence, should have become the nursing mother of oppression and injustice, and that deeds of infamy should find toleration therein, is not only a cause for the greatest astonishment, but in itself constitutes the foulest blot that could possibly rest upon the escutcheon of Australia's fame.

But the question may be asked by some, 'Is it really so; are deeds of darkness, in the sense of injustice and inhumanity practised in this land of light and blessing?' That such is the case will be clearly shown in the following pages.

. . .

To prove my statement that the native labor system in this district is one bordering on slavery, I must first deal with the way in which they are secured. I do not say that no natives do come voluntarily and offer their services to the owners of stations; but this I do say—that in some cases the native labourers are recruited in a way which does not give the native the least freedom of will.

They are compelled to touch the pen to an assignment paper which it is impossible for them to understand, and, as regards the witnessing of such assignment, the parties so acting are doubtless interested, so that in such case the poor natives becomes a bondservant by force. But there is an advanced phase of this side of the question which must be disclosed. At times the wild natives are really run down and captured and taken to the stations, and then the assignment as above described takes place; and then, if they run away (which they are almost certain to do), a warrant is issued for their arrest, and then the police are set in motion, and if run down or ferreted out they are taken to the Junction Police Station and there chained up for a few weeks.

. . .

But yet another reason for my defining the native labor system as a species of slavery is the sad fact of the assignment of native women and girls to white men, the great majority of whom are single. This, to my mind, is the most sad association of the whole native labor question. On every station women and girls are engaged, principally as shepherds, and these creatures are entirely in the hands of the owners; I say owners, because certain settlers have told me that they owned all the natives on their respective runs, and these natives women and girls are, when away in the bush with their flocks, placed under the care of young white men, who camp out with them, their duty being to go from flock to flock to see that the natives are watching the sheep. I was informed that some of the females had their native husbands with them. One of the settlers told me he had hard work to get husbands for all the women. Many of these native shepherds are mere girls. Doubtless some of these females are voluntary servants; but I got to know of one case in which the poor creature was not, and because she ran away she was in the 'black book' of her owner, and I afterwards found her at the camp of a young man to whom she had been lent because his girls had run away; and these same girls I discovered at another station, and they had run away, they said, because they could not get enough damper. I also found that women and girls were fully assigned to teamsters. It is quite a common thing to see them even in Carnarvon with such. Upon asking some of these men why they had girls and not boys attached to their teams, some said they 'preferred them'; others said they were 'better than boys', and that 'boys always run away', but others frankly admitted that they had them for immoral purposes. And although this is bad enough, I have in my possession facts which are so exceedingly repulsive in their character as to be unfit for the columns of a family newspaper. I ask every right-thinking person whether such a feature of bondservice is not shocking to contemplate, especially when professed Christian men are connected there with? Assignment of native females against their will for purposes of immorality is a sign of slavery.

. . .

In the year 1874 when at Cossack [New South Wales], I saw two dead native women, they had died from eating poisoned flour which they got from a station near the George River, and I was told by the natives that three others had died from the same cause. The owner of that self-same station afterwards poisoned himself, as commonly reported.

. . .

In 1883 I met the Bishop of Perth at Cossack, and told him of the slavery and cruelty existing. I pointed out to his lordship several native children not more than eight years old whom I was then protecting, and who I had good reason to believe had been criminally abused by white men. And I said, pointing to the police station. 'That house is no better than a b——, and the authorities will not give the natives justice.' His lordship said in reply, 'I am sure that Mr. — will give everybody justice.' I said, 'My lord, I am sure he will not, bring me to the test, and I will prove it.'

Previous to this circumstance I had reported to Captain Smith, the head of the Police Department, that a certain constable had, whilst drunk, dragged a native girl named Fanny to the lock-up, the girl crying out while being so dragged that she was being locked up for carnal purposes. I received no reply to this report.

. . .

In addition to this hideous list of dark deeds I must briefly state a few facts which have occurred since I arrived in this colony, some of which have come under my own observation.

On a certain station several native men declared aloud in the presence of their owner that a young native girl about 15 years of age was their master's wife. On hearing this unexpected bit of information the settler adroitly smuggled the girl out of sight and hearing, and I saw her no more. At the same station I was informed by a white overseer that in certain places the choicest bit of hospitality that could be tendered to a visitor was the finest-looking black girl.

At another station when retiring one night I stumbled over a white man in the act of debauching a native girl, and that, too, on the very verandah of the master's house; the vile offender was not ashamed to acknowledge his conduct, and in excuse he said, 'The masters do it and why can't we?' I told the master of the shocking circumstance, and with a laugh he said, 'I don't see much harm in that kind of thing.'

On reaching a police station I reported the case, and a constable told me that the man to whom I referred was well known to the police, that stealing native girls for carnal purpose was his favorite game, and that he had stolen the girl he then possessed when she was in charge of a flock of sheep, the property of a neighboring settler. This case I reported directly to the Governor.

. . .

The Clerk of the Court at Carnarvon told me he knew that little native girls, only seven or eight years old were the victims of white men.

. . .

During our return journey to the Coast, when about 22 miles from the Mission Station we halted at a sheep camp, and the white man in charge gave me the following particulars. A white man from a station up the river had sent a native lad to his camp during his absence, to get a young native girl, whose friends were on this particular station. But as the girl would not go he gave her a great beating, and then rode away. But about a week after, just on the Sunday previous to my call, he came again bringing with him a rope, and the girl still refusing to comply with his request, he deliberately tied the rope round her neck, and fastened the other end to his horse. He then mounted, and rode away, dragging the poor creature along the ground. When she was nearly choked by this brutal treatment he stopped, and having untied the rope, he gave her a sound thrashing and then rode away. His pretence was that the girl had been promised to him, but the girl declared that he had no claim on her, and that what he had done to her was at the instance of the white man who required her for carnal purposes. The girl was brought into my presence, and she related her sad story, and a Malay who witnessed the outrage confirmed the girl's statement. The white man, my informant, stated that when he returned in the evening after the occurrence, he plainly saw the track along the ground caused by the dragging.

On reaching the Mission Station, I reported the case to the police at Carnarvon, but I have heard nothing more of it.

. . .

In the preceding pages quite sufficient has been adduced to show unmistakably that even in Australia, under its sunny skies, deeds, the most dark and horrible in their nature, have been committed, and are still being practised, and that, too, not only under the British flag, but even in the

face, so to speak, of the representative of the greatest Sovereign the world
has ever seen, and who emphatically declared that the justice and righteousness of the Word of the Living God constituted 'The Secret of
England's greatness'.

Document 4.3   The making of a woman temperance advocate

*One of the earliest and largest women's associations in Australia was
the Woman's Christian Temperance Union (WCTU). Established by
members from the American WCTU in the mid-1880s, the organisation rapidly found support among Protestant women in Australia who
opposed alcohol consumption. In particular, the WCTU appealed to
women who associated male drinking with violence against women
and who were frustrated with women's inability to take political and
legal action to remedy their plight. Members of the WCTU, like Bessie
Lee, often became involved in advocating a wide range of women's
rights.*

*Bessie Lee (1860–1950) grew up in a small Victorian mining
town and at nineteen she married a railway worker, Harrison Lee.
Her autobiography,* One of Australia's Daughters, *describes how this
self-educated, reserved young woman was horrified by social inequality and women's sufferings and became a prominent public figure
whose speaking tours attracted large audiences. Her autobiography,
a self-dramatising work, is written in both the first and third-person
voices.*[3]

c. mid-1880s

It was a surprise, too, one day to be asked to speak at a meeting for the
Young Women's Association, but she accepted the invitation simply, and
began to prepare a Bible reading for the young members . . .

With her little Bible in hand she sallied forth on the appointed evening,
and duly reached the building. She entered, blissfully happy, expecting to
find about a dozen young ladies there, but the bliss turned suddenly to
unutterable dismay as she beheld about 300 ladies present, and learned it
was not an ordinary meeting of the members but the Anniversary of the
Young Women's Christian Association. Her aunt's training stood her in
good stead again. With quiet face, though throbbing heart, she mounted
the platform and took the proffered chair till her turn came to speak.

    . . .

No earthquake was at hand, but the helpless sinner's friend was. And there came a sudden question: 'Bessie Lee, what are you here for, to speak of yourself or of Christ?'

'Of Christ,' I answered.

'Then speak,' sternly said the voice. And with a new power thrilling my whole being, and taking entire possession of soul and body, I stepped forward and spoke. No need of the table for support now. God's strong arm was there, and instead of a shrinking woman, there stood a messenger from the King. I don't know what I said, nor how I said it, but that very week a minister called upon me to ask, 'Would I preach for him on Sunday?' Of course I unhesitatingly refused, and asked him how could he, a clergyman, ask a woman to do what Paul had forbidden.

'But you spoke on Wednesday night, to women.'

'Ah! but they were women. Paul suffers us not to usurp authority over the man.'

'Suppose you do not usurp, but simply accept the authority offered you by the man?'

I shook my head decidedly.

'Have you ever read the parable of the talents, Mrs. Lee?'

'Yes, many times.'

'What excuse will you give to God for neglecting the talent He has evidently endowed you with?'

I stared bewilderedly. He continued—

'You speak to mixed audiences of boys and girls at the Sunday School, you have spoken to a large audience of women, now why will you not speak to men in a church? Do you think they are not in as much need of salvation as women and children?'

Always at a loss in argument, my perplexity grew deeper as the minister reasoned in a way I had never heard before, and at last utterly vanquished, I consented to go to his church and preach for him on the Sunday.

The little wooden church in Burnley, where I preached my first sermon, stands exactly opposite the girlhood's home of Australia's famous nightingale, Madame Melba—then Nellie Mitchell—whose rich voice was often heard, ringing out on the evening air in Burnley. My sermon was on 'Prayer'. I crept up into the pulpit, a frightened, perplexed woman, with a dark cloud over me heavily, that I was doing wrong by daring to stand upon such holy ground, but the moment I stood up to speak the fear fell off like a wet cloak, and I spoke as the Spirit gave me utterance . . .

. . .

As a district visitor and church worker, she could not fail to note drink's share in the poverty and degradation of the people around, but was too accustomed to the sight of drink and drunkenness to do more than deplore its dire consequences. She never thought of asking the victims to give up drink's use, but ventured once or twice to urge—moderation. That was as far as she dared go, and even that was a failure, so she sighed over the poor people, and, leaving the cause untouched, did all she could to minimise its effects.

. . .

In November the W.C.T.U. Annual Convention came round again. Delegates, timid, retiring, home-loving women, most of them, gathered from every part of the colony for spiritual up-building and grace for service. The first Colonial President was one of God's stars of the earth, Mrs. M. M. Love, a Virginian lady, and a woman of saintly character. She had also been one of the early Crusaders in America. Under her loving guidance the Woman's work had prospered greatly in Victoria, and calls were daily coming from all parts for an organizer to visit and band the women together, in each town and village, under their banner, with its beautiful motto, 'For God, and Home and Humanity'.

Unfortunately there was no fund for this pressing and expensive work, neither had the Union a woman, except Mrs. Love herself, capable of taking up such a very important department as organizing and evangelistic work. It was the first meeting after the Convention that the women sat around the Council table with prayerful anxious hearts and besought God to send them the right woman. The qualifications required were so many and varied, that they were puzzled to find anyone to come even near the mark.

For instance, she would have to be physically strong, for long, difficult journeys by rail, boat, coach, and horseback lay before her; she must be a Christian of highest character in whom ministers and others could have perfect confidence; she would need to have a thorough knowledge of Temperance work, else she would fail in the very objects of her journeys; she would need to be tactful, wise, discreet, brave, quick, and bright, and last of all she must ask no salary from the Colonial Executive, for there was not a pound in the exchequer to give her. In fact, she would have to go on faith without purse or scrip, expecting the manna to be provided each day, as God saw best.

The women looked from one to another in silence as all these special qualifications loomed before them, and all sighed at the hopelessness of getting the right woman for that vacant position. Mrs. Love looked through her glasses, and her gentle voice broke the painful silence.

'Mrs. Lee, will you take up the work?'

The lady addressed nearly capsized from her chair, and looked in astonishment at the sweet, spiritual face of the president, to see if her ears had deceived her. But no, gentle, quiet and serene, Mrs. Love waited, looking with those kind eyes at the perturbed face before her.

'My husband would never consent,' was the reply, at last.

'Is that the only hindrance in the way?'

Mrs. Lee stared, feeling that Mrs. Love did not know her strong-willed partner, for surely that would be hindrance enough. Well did she know that if her husband gave one of his decided negatives, it would be as unalterable as the laws of the Medes and Persians, Mrs. Love notwithstanding. She simply bowed, finding no words with which to reply.

'Go home, my dear,' the quiet voice said, 'and before you reach there an angel will have rolled away the stone.'

It was hard to believe that anything on earth would make her husband consent to give his wife up to a public life. But she went home, resolving to lay the matter before him . . . The husband was very thoughtful for a little while, and like a wise woman she did not hurry him. When he did speak, she found the angel had indeed rolled away the stone.

'My dear, I think you had better accept the position, you love the work, the frequent changes will do your health good. Try it for a time, and see how you like it.'

Document 4.4 A journal opposes a feminist's views on marriage

The Bulletin, founded in Sydney by the journalist J.F. Archibald, shaped an influential style of masculine national identity in the 1880s and 1890s. Its championing of male camaraderie, whether exemplified by the bushman or the bohemian, valued the life of the free-wheeling male over domesticity and companionate marriage.

In 1888 Bessie Lee wrote a letter to The Herald *in Melbourne, affirming friendship and companionship between husbands and wives, playing down the role of sexual relations within marriage, and advocating abstention as a method of limiting family size. Such ideas of voluntary motherhood were common among reformers in the late nineteenth century when other means of birth control were expensive or haphazard.* The Bulletin, *however, ridiculed this with the following response, indicating its hostility towards independent women's claims, especially those involving any check to male sexuality.*[4]

October 1888

Melbourne *Herald* has had its soul shattered and its soft emotions torn by
the great marriage question which is, during the present season, going the
rounds of the press in default of well-authenticated perjuries from valued
correspondents concerning the over-worked snake. Ladies have rushed
headlong into the fray and poured their sweet convictions into Editor
Winter's [the editor of the *Herald*] columns with a persistency and
callousness worthy of a tax collector: soulful sylphlike things with appeal-
ing eyes and lips of the rose-petal pattern who want to be married, and
tough and leather skinned old maids who protest they would die before
linking themselves to a 'horrid man', and dames who have bloomed in
wedlock into florid maturity, and soured, crabbed wives who have been
thrashed and starved into man-haters, and parson-loving females whose
hearts have been turned against the 'old man' by the voice of the pietistic
turtle, and whose dreams of connubial bliss have been rudely shattered by
the ecclesiastical kiss of peace with which church-going ladies disturb the
set of their friz. Amongst others who have plunged their little feminine
pens into the ink-bottle of controversy is that well-known champion of
'Women's Rights', Mrs. Harrison-Lee (with a hyphen), who solemnly
paints a frigid picture of polar moonbeam happiness by marriage according
to the tenets of the Abelites [members of an early Christian sect which
forbad sexual relations between husbands and wives]. The letter is such
a funny one that it deserves immortality—as an early specimen of unconscious humour in an Australian woman. List to the wailful strain of the
Abelite, 'Bessie Lee':

> The general reason given by the gentlemen for not proposing
> seems to be the one of small salaries, and I know that in many
> cases this objection holds good; but have we not often been told
> that two can live as cheap as one? And this has been clearly
> proved. But, says one, what about a possible family? My advice
> to those who cannot afford a family is not to have one. Marriage
> should be a union of souls, a sweet companionship, a mutual help
> and sympathy; but marriage, as it is—

Well, the end of the matter is that Mrs. Lee advises poor people to
live together platonically and 'know what genuine love and happiness
means'. And she concludes by . . . 'Trusting that my views may lead many
to regard marriage in a new light. I will close, first assuring my readers
that it is because I so dearly love the girls and boys of our fair land, that
I have, after much consideration, decided to write as I have done.'
After reading this letter over one would naturally ask: 'Why marry
at all?' Or, 'Why should not women marry each other, the old maid joined

in icy wedlock to the other old maid?' Or, on the above basis: 'Why should a man not have a dozen wives, or a woman a dozen husbands, seeing it is purely platonic and thoroughly make-believe?' The truth is that not thus will the difficulty be bridged. There is no reason why a man should not have dummy wives, but he will always probably yearn for one, or a fraction of one, of a *bona-fide* and provokingly real description. As woman has become purely a specialist (for you don't find now a days many of those homely old-fashioned wives who could not only sing but also cook) there is really no reason why a man should not have several in order to thoroughly experience what it means to be married. He thus might have a wife to dress and a wife to keep house, a wife for the carriage, and a wife for drawing-room receptions. Indeed there is no limit to the number. He might have a walking-costume wife, a winter-costume wife, a wife for fancy dress carnivals, and a wife for the apparel of the ordinary ball. To make him perfectly happy he would require a button-sewing wife and a chop-grilling wife, one whose speciality was warming slippers and another whose strong point was the wearing of a spring-bonnèt, and even then, perhaps, he would be miserable. We are told that in Heaven there is neither marriage nor giving in marriage. The cynical man would admit that that *would* be Heaven indeed.

Document 4.5 A new journal claims a new voice for women

In 1888 Louisa Lawson, who was prominent in Sydney labour circles, began a lively monthly journal for women which she called The Dawn. *Produced by female typesetters and printers,* The Dawn *aimed to publicise women's issues, fight their battles, and give them advice on subjects ranging from the campaign for suffrage to household hints.*

Louisa Lawson (1848–1920) grew up in poor circumstances in rural New South Wales, married young, and had four surviving children, one of whom became the poet Henry Lawson. She separated from her husband and moved to Sydney in 1883. The Dawn *was not only a vehicle for Lawson's political convictions but her means of livelihood.*

The campaign by liberals such as Catherine Spence to make divorce easier for women bore fruit in 1888 in New South Wales where a Divorce Extension bill, which would extend the grounds of divorce beyond adultery to include desertion, was under consideration. Louisa Lawson makes this the occasion of an editorial in which she supported marriage, but asserted strongly a woman's right to withdraw from her marriage if it became destructive.[5]

May 1888

There are few questions so important for the consideration of women as those of the laws of marriage and divorce, since full half the sorrows of women rise from marriages foolishly made, or from nuptial ties which being made cry out for severance. Thank Heaven there are many happy marriages—many men and many women who have found a matrimonial partnership double their stock of content, and whose ties of association are made up of so many mutual memories, so many joys shared and sorrows divided, that no legal tincture could bind them closer. But you men and women who have not—and we pray never may have—cause to name the hideous word 'separation', are those who should take up the first weapon and fight in the front ranks for the liberation of unhappy spirits tied upon connubial racks. That man who being content, and finding life and his home a blessing and a day-to-day comfort, cares nothing for surrounding sorrows, nor longs to see this whole world happy as he, is one of those who must thank their fortune, not their deserts, for the pleasure they enjoy.

If there is one thing most calculated to make the blood of honest and manly hearts boil over, it is to see a woman bound by ill made laws, and by the cruel pruderies of public opinion to a life of hourly sorrow and perennial torture.

Have we not all seen women striving to do patiently and well their ordinary tasks, smiling on their friends and visitors; laboring with a noble persistence along the road they have thoughtlessly or blindly entered, while their hearts secretly bleed from the hidden stabs of continual marital unkindness[?]

Freedom through divorce is a method of escape scarce thought of by women. There is every guarantee that on their side at least every case where divorce is sued for is a genuine one. Publicity they hate and fear with a shuddering inconceivable to men; the dread of comments of acquaintances and the unkindly criticism of outsiders, as well as the well-grounded fear that the world has no sustenance to lend them, prove such barriers to women, that most will rather bear on and die than fly to such a remedy.

For these reasons the fact that Sir Alfred Stephen's just and admirable Divorce Extension Bill has been again postponed occasions both sorrow and indignation. Her Majesty's Ministers have not seen fit to recommend Her Majesty to grant her assent to the measure. The Bill must, therefore, be again sent home for approval, and at the next general election the readiness to support this measure must be made one of the test questions.

Then will fall the opportunity for women to work, and write, and use their influence in its favour. For the act, though not solely designed for the benefit of woman, will in effect be for her good almost exclusively, for of its provisions men rarely need to make use.

The provisions of this Act are briefly that any person resident in this colony for two years and upwards may present a petition for divorce.

I.   On the ground of desertion without just cause or excuse for three years.
II. On the ground that the respondent has by continued habits of drunkenness during two years left his wife without the means of support, or being petitioner's wife has rendered herself unfit for her domestic duties.
III. On the ground that at the time of presentation of the petition the respondent has been 12 months in gaol, and is still confined under sentence for a capital crime, or under sentence for seven years or upwards for some other crime, or that being a husband has by frequent convictions left his wife for two years without the means of support.
IV. On the ground that within the the previous six months the respondent has been convicted of an attempt to murder the petitioner, or has been repeatedly guilty of assaulting and cruelly beating the petitioner, or that the respondent has during a period of two years been repeatedly guilty of cruelty.

If the petitioner's own habits or conduct contributed to the wrong complained of, the petition for divorce may be dismissed nor does this act allow the respondent in the suit to re-marry for a period of two years.

These are just reasons, and some day they certainly will be embodied in our Statute Book. Women have power; they must use it to make this time come quickly. There is not one pure-minded woman but has longed at some time to be of more use in the world, and to benefit the universe by some noble act. Well, here is one chance. Spread justice, widen the boundaries of happiness, help your sorrow-laden sisters. Men are more rarely the victims of connubial ties than women, and except in the case of drunkenness it is improbable that any man ever feels the need of more aids to freedom. But the anomalies of the law as it stands, and the cruelties inflicted on women under its protection are horrible.

The woman whom a brutal husband has attempted to murder finds herself doomed to support herself as best she may during the long period of years during which her husband pays the penalty of his crime in gaol, and finds moreover when the brute is released that she is still the felon's legal helpmeet and companion. Legally, and in the eyes of Society, bound to again entrust her life to him—to run the gauntlet of his blows and offer him another opportunity for a more surely delivered thrust. So, too, a deserted woman is called upon to live alone, constant to the blackguard who has left her, though he, curbed by no restraints, roams what part of the world he pleases. In almost every case of desertion the wife is left practically with no means of support, and she has then to toil in that most difficult of paths—the single woman's way to monetary competence. Should she be desperately poor, and should there happily be some good fellow of a worthier sort ready to marry her it avails nothing. The choice lies between immorality on the one side and on the other continued poverty and allegiance to a deserter.

On the horrors of a drunken housemate (surely wife and husband are not fit terms to use here), we will not descant. There are few who have not at some time or place seen the trace of this domestic serpent. Its deadly track is artfully concealed—with loving patience its insidious attack is combated—strength, health, hope, gladness, wealth are all devoured in time.

Is it asserted that these cases are rare? What then? The hideous injustice of them is such that did they occur, but once in a hundred there would be reason enough for the preparation of a legislative thunderbolt fit to exterminate on the instant the intolerable wrong.

The sacredness and strength of marriage ties can never be weakened by the severance of bonds which women's tears have already rotted, nor can any sanctity remain in marriage bonds which only bind to torments.

Document 4.6 A clergyman's wife describes their plight

Ada Cambridge (1844–1926) arrived in Victoria with her husband, the Reverend George Cross, in 1870. His appointments to various rural parishes took them around the countryside, experiences she describes in her autobiography, Thirty Years in Australia. *Her dissenting views on the self-sacrificing role expected of women married to clergymen made her unpopular in church circles, but she maintained her independence and forged a successful career as a novelist and poet.*

In this passage she gives vent to her frustration at the unsung work carried out by clergymen's wives—often more able than the men themselves—and at the terrible toll this work could take.[6]

mid-1870s to 1880s

It was about this year (1873) that I began to write for the *Australasian*—trifling little papers, at long intervals—not because I found any fascination in such work to dispute the claims of the house and family, but to add something to the family resources when they threatened to give out. I had no time for more, until one day the editor of the *Australasian* wrote to inquire what had become of me and my contributions, when it occurred to me that it might be worth while to make time.

The Sunday school was at the further end of the township—it was the common school on week-days—and I used to rush thither morning and afternoon on Sundays, and return breathless to attend to my baby and play the (American) organ in church. I trained the choir, visited every parishioner within reach, did all that hard work unfairly demanded of the parson's wife under these democratic systems of church government; besides the multifarious work at home—making and mending, cooking and nursing, and, as it appears, building sideboards and dining-tables. Moreover, the Free and Compulsory Education Act had come into force (January 1873), and as the State had to be satisfied that our little nursemaid, who was within school age, was being educated according to law, I charged myself with this job also, rather than lose her services for the greater part of the day. And I may add that the baby in arms was rarely trusted to this functionary, except for airings in the garden under my eye. All other attentions that it required I gave myself. So there was enough occupation for one not-over-robust woman, without the addition of literary work.

Touching upon this matter, I am reminded of a conversation that I had with Bishop Perry soon after our arrival. It was not the hardships of the clergy that troubled him, he said, but the killing strain upon their wives—literally killing, for he quoted figures to show the disproportionately high rate of sickness and untimely death amongst them. I rather think I have heard Bishop Moorhouse express himself to the same effect. Certainly my own long and intimate acquaintance with the subject leaves me in no doubt as to which of the clerical pair is in the shafts and which in the lead. It is not the parson who, to use the phrase so often in his mouth, bears the burden and heat of the day, but the uncomplaining drudge who backs him at all points, and too often makes him selfish and idle by her readiness to do his work as well as her own. Under colonial and 'disestablished' conditions, he is not largely representative of the class from which our home clergy are drawn; as a general rule he comes from that which, while as good as another in many ways, and perhaps better in some, is not bred to the chivalrous view of women and wives—regards them, that is to say, as intended for no other purpose than to wait upon men and husbands. The customs of the profession accord so well with this idea that it is not surprising to find a pious man killing his wife by inches without having the slightest notion that he is doing so.

Amongst my colleagues of those days was a lady of exceptional culture and refinement. Her husband, a Bush clergyman like my own, was poor, of course, and they averaged a baby a year until the baker's dozen was reached, if not passed. The way she 'kept' this family was such that I never saw a dirty child or a soiled table-cloth or a slatternly touch of any sort in her house. She taught the children as they grew old enough; I know that she did scrubbing and washing with her own hands. In addition, she did 'the parish work'.

One day, when she was run down and worn out, her husband told her that the organist, from some cause, was not forthcoming, and there was no time to procure a substitute. 'So, my dear, you will have to play for us.' He knew that she could do it, for she had often done it before; it was the merest trifle of a task, compared with those she hourly struggled with; but it was the one straw too many that breaks the over-loaded back. She looked at him in silence for a moment, flung out her arms wildly, and, exclaiming 'I can do no more!' went mad upon the spot. She had to be put into an asylum, and the parish and the husband and the growing young ones had to do the best they could without her. The husband, I may say, was—apart from being the inadvertent accomplice of the parish in her destruction—one of the very best of husbands and of men . . .

. . .

But very early in the day I evolved opinions of my own as to the right of parishes to exact tributes of service from private individuals in no way bound to give them. And I came to a conclusion, which I have never since seen reason to alter, that the less a clergyman's wife meddles with her husband's business (except between themselves) the better, not only for her but for all parties. After I could plead the claims of a profession of my own, my position in the scheme of things was finally and comfortably defined. Parishes, like clerical husbands, when they tyrannise, do it unconsciously, from want of thought, and not from want of heart. At any rate, my parish, for the time being, never, so far as I can see, bears me any malice for my desertion of the female-curate's post, but quite the contrary . . .

Document 4.7 A judge supports the battle for contraception education

In 1888 Justice Sir William Windeyer (1834–1897) brought down a landmark decision in the Supreme Court of New South Wales to allow the sale of the British activist Annie Besant's pamphlet on contraception. While many women fought for access to information on contraception. men held all the power in the judiciary and legislature, and the success of women's campaigns depended on supporters like Windeyer.

Windeyer begins his judgement by confidently quoting the Rev. Thomas Malthus, whose population theories were, however, by no means accepted as indisputable fact. Malthus had argued in his Essay on the Principle of Population *(1803) that population growth, if not kept in check by misery or self-restraint, would soon outstrip the means of feeding it. He held the poor responsible for their own plight and blamed them for worsening their situation by 'overbreeding'. Socialists like Annie Besant were careful to disassociate their advocacy of birth control from the taint of Malthusian ideas about controlling the size of working-class families, but Windeyer, with remarks such as 'the masses likely to over-breed', makes at least a conservative link. He also invokes the eugenics movement and controversial notions about selective breeding with his concern about 'the seething mass of degenerate and criminal humanity'.*

Windeyer was a well-known politician and judge whose wife, Mary, and daughter, Margaret, were prominent in women's associations in Sydney, being founders of the Womanhood Suffrage League, and involved in the Woman's Christian Temperance Union's suffrage department, among other activities.[7]

1888

This case comes before us on the motion to make absolute a rule *nisi* granted by me, calling upon a stipendiary magistrate to show cause why the conviction of the applicant of selling an obscene pamphlet, under section 2 of the Obscene Publications Prevention Act of 1880, should not be set aside upon the ground that the work in respect of which he had been convicted was not an obscene publication . . .

The pamphlet before us, by Mrs. Annie Besant, is entitled 'The Law of Population: its consequences and its bearing upon human conduct and morals'. The work starts with a statement of the theory first propounded by Malthus, now as Lord Cockburn says, accepted as 'an irrefragable truth', that population has a strong and natural tendency to increase faster than the means of subsistence afforded by the earth or that the skill and industry of man can produce for the support of life. It shows in clear and powerful language all the miseries which result to mankind from the unchecked operation of this law, and it discusses whether it is not possible for man to avert the consequences of this inevitable tendency by such means as medical science and an enlightened understanding of the laws of nature place at his disposal. As it cannot be denied that the question propounded for discussion is of enormous importance, and that it is right to advocate in the abstract the expediency of checking the advancing tide of population, it appears to me impossible to contend that language which tells how this may be done is obscene if it goes no further than is necessary for this purpose. Having carefully read the third chapter of the pamphlet, it appears to me to be written with all decent sobriety of language. I see nothing in its language which an earnest-minded man or woman of pure life and morals might not use to one of his own sex, if explaining to him or her what was necessary in order to understand the methods suggested by which married people could prevent the number of their children increasing beyond their means of supporting them. There is nothing which points to the conclusion that any language is used with the intention of exciting feelings of wantonness and lust; and it requires but slight acquaintance with the medical profession to discover that the advice given in this chapter is frequently given by them to women suffering from over child-bearing, and to those to whom parturition is dangerous. The information afforded in the third chapter of the pamphlet, if given by a medical man to a patient suffering from over-maternity, or if whispered in matrimonial confidence, or imparted in the privacy existing between the author and the reader of her pamphlet, is not obscenity; though the public proclamation of the same information on a placard in George Street or Piccadilly, so that all who ran might read, would be an obscenity of the grossest kind, so clearly do the circumstances of a publication alter its character. If admitted, as it is, that the information, physiological and otherwise, given in chapter III can be found in medical works of an expensive kind, it cannot affect the character of the information for obscenity that it is given in a cheap form. Information cannot be pure, chaste, and legal in morocco at a guinea, but impure, obscene, and indictable in a paper pamphlet at sixpence. The information, to be of value in a national point of view as a safeguard from the miseries of over-population and over-crowding, must be given wholesale to the masses likely to over-breed. The time is past when knowledge can be kept as the exclusive privilege of any caste or class . . .

A further argument urged before us, as showing that the work was obscene, was that its advice as to the adoption of scientific checks to population involved a violation of natural laws and a frustration of nature's ends. The argument that nature intends every woman to conceive as often as is possible would, if carried to its logical conclusion, result in the Indian custom of marrying every female child upon reaching puberty in order that no opportunity of conception should be lost. In all other matters of breeding but the all-important one of the breeding of the human race, the aim of man is to defeat the effects of nature's laws of reproduction, and to limit the number and kind of animals produced to the amount required for the use of man. The forces of nature, blind and ruthless in their effect, we control and defeat in their operation by all the means that science places at our command. To protect churches and hospitals from the operations of nature's laws, we put up conductors to arrest the inexorable effects of lightning, which would remorselessly destroy what piety and humanity would protect. The course of nature is to kill a noble woman, a devoted wife and loving mother, if her pelvis is too small to admit the delivery of a child with an abnormally large head. The practice of civilised man, aided by science, is in such a case of parturition to destroy the infant and to save the mother. The interference with the course of nature is direct, the practice in no way condemns it. But if the pelvis of a woman is so unusually small that she never can be delivered of a child but at the peril of her life, where is the immorality in the husband and wife resorting to any preventive checks that may preserve a life that is dear and perhaps valuable to the world? It is unreasoning prejudice alone that starts the objection that such prevention of all the physical agony involved in a painful and dangerous delivery and possible loss of life is immoral and unnatural. Or, take the case of a woman married to a drunken husband, steadily ruining his constitution and hastening to the drunkard's doom, loss of employment for himself, semi-starvation for his family, and finally death without a shilling to leave those whom he has brought into the world, but armed with the authority of the law to treat his wife as his slave, ever brutally insisting on the indulgence of his marital rights. Where is the immorality, if already broken in health from unresting maternity, already having a larger family than she can support when the miserable breadwinner has drunk himself to death, the woman avails herself of the information given in this book, and so averts the consequences of yielding, perhaps under threats of violence, to her husband's brutal insistence on his marital rights? Already weighted with a family that she is unable decently to bring up, the immorality, it seems to me, would be in the reckless and criminal disregard of precautions which would prevent her bringing into the world daughters, whose future outlook as a career would be prostitution; or sons, whose inherited taint of alcoholism would soon drag them down with their sisters to herd with the seething mass of degenerate and criminal humanity that constitutes the dangerous classes of great cities. In all these cases the appeal is from thoughtless, unreasoning prejudice to conscience, and, if listened to, its voice will be heard unmistakably indicating where the path of duty lies.

Document 4.8 Women who are not members of trade unions are questioned about their work

Women's paid work was concentrated in areas notable for the absence of union activity. This was partly because Australian trade unions consisted of members who possessed knowledge of a skilled craft and such skilled work was considered the province of men. In addition, many women workers were young and part of the waged workforce for only a short period of their lives. Married women who worked usually had dependents to support and were desperate for work no matter what the conditions.

Progressive, liberal politicians initiated inquiries into the conditions of women's work largely because of the health risks and dangers to those who were to be the mothers of future Australian citizens. Here are some Queensland women describing their working lives to members of a parliamentary Royal Commission.[8]

1891

MRS REID EXAMINED, 16 MARCH 1891

1675. *By the Chairman*: Your husband keeps a store on Bowen Hills? Yes.
1676. Do you attend in the shop yourself? Yes.
1677. Have you been an employee yourself in any of the shops? For just about a month, a long time ago . . .
   . . .
1679. How many employees have you in your own store? None.
1680. You and your husband work it? Yes.
1681. You wish to give evidence as to early closing, I presume? Yes.
1682. At what hour do you open your store? About 7 o'clock a.m.
1683. And you close when? At 8 p.m.
1684. You do not find these hours too long? They are.
1685. You and your husband, being your own master and mistress, can close when you like? Yes.
   . . .
1696. *By Mr McDonnell*: You are not a constant attendant at the shop? You do not stay there the whole day? We live on the premises.
1697. You can stay inside and watch customers come in and so on?

Yes; certainly . . .

. . .

1723. *By Mr Chapman*: How are you appearing before the Commission and not your husband—you have a husband? Yes.

1724. He is well? Yes.

1725. Why does he not come? Is he in favour of late hours? I was asked to come.

. . .

1730. *By Mr McDonnell*: Was your husband aware that you were coming here to give evidence? Oh, yes!

1731. I suppose it was more convenient for you to attend than him? Yes.

. . .

1735. *By Mrs Edwards*: Have you got a family? Yes.

1736. How many children? Two.

1737. Little children? Yes.

1738. Do you keep a servant? Not just now.

1739. Do you believe in individual effort or individual sacrifice? In what way?

1740. Would you think it a sacrifice to close your shop early so that you might have time to put the buttons on your children's clothing, hear them their prayers, and put them to bed? It would be better.

1741. As you are employed now you cannot do these little things in the same way as you would like to. If you had your little ones round you and were hearing them say their prayers and putting them to bed, and someone came into the shop, you would have to leave them and serve in the shop? Yes.

. . .

At Peacock's Jam Factory, Kangaroo Point, 5 May 1891: Mrs Welson examined

11490. *By the Chairman*: Are you on piecework? Sometimes on piecework and sometimes on weekly wages . . .

. . .

11492. How long have you been here? Two years.

11493. Have you far to go home when you leave work? Three miles every night and three miles every morning.

11494. Is your husband alive? No, he has been dead for two years.

11495. *By Mr McDonnell*: Have you any family? Yes, six children.

11496. *By the Chairman*: Are any of them working? One of the boys, in the canning-room.

11497. *By Mr McDonnell*: Do you take the 'bus to go home? No, I walk both ways.

11498. Are your hours of labour from 7.30 until 5.30? Yes.

11499. You never make more than 12s. a week? Not unless I am on piecework.

. . .

11503. How long has your son been at work? Four years.

11504. What is his age? Eleven years.

11505. What wages is he getting now? 8s. a week.

11506. What did he start with? 4s.

11507. Is he the only help you have got? I have another boy working at Alfred Shaw and Company's.

11508. What is his work? Labouring work.

11509. What is he paid? 10s. a week.

. . .

Still at the Jam Factory; Alice Gibson examined

11517. *By Mr McDonnell*: How long have you been working here? Three years.

11518. What is your age? Seventeen.

11519. What wages are you getting? 12s. a week.

11520. Do you work the same hours as the other girls? Yes.

11521. How long have you been getting 12s? A little over six months.

11522. What were you paid before that? 8s. 6d.

11523. How long were you getting 8s. 6d? About twelve months and I got 7s. before that.

11524. How long were you getting 7s. a week? About eighteen months.

11525. What is your father? I have no father.

11526. Is your mother alive? Yes.

11527. Does she work? No.

11528. Are you the only support she has, or have you any brothers? I have two sisters and two brothers; one brother and one sister at work.

11529. What does your sister do? She is at service.

11530. How much has your mother coming in to her altogether? 12s. a week from me; 6s. from my sister; 7s. from my brother, and she minds a little baby, and gets 6d a week for that.

. . .

Mrs Rose Hussey, newsvendor, examined, 8 May 1891

12453. *By the Chairman*: You are a newsvendor? Yes.

12454. Have you been long selling papers? About six weeks.

12455. Are you able to make a living at it? It is very hard at the beginning. I have three children to keep.

12456. What do you make per week? I generally sell about seven dozen altogether. I sold only three dozen today.

12457. What does that bring in? Ninepence; 3d. on every dozen.

12458. Do you find the boys prevent you from selling papers? No; but there is a woman at the same corner who does her best.

12459. What corner do you sell at? At Hunter's; corner of Edward and Queen streets.

12460. What forced you into this business? Because my husband left me with three children. I am a cripple and not able to work for myself.

12461. Your husband has left you? Or rather I left him through ill-treatment.

12462. Is he in town now? No; he is at Bundaberg, I believe.

12463. Do any of your children sell papers? Yes; two little girls. Seven dozen is all we manage to sell between us. The other woman tells people not to take papers from me . . .

12464. *By Mrs Edwards*: Have you tried to get your children into the orphanage? No, I have not.

12465. Don't you think you could earn a living for yourself if you got your children into the orphanage? I am very delicate; and it is only my children who keep me up. I should not like to part with them all.

12466. Would you not try and get two of them in? Yes, I might try to do that. The eldest girl could take a place now, if anyone would be kind enough to take her.

12467. Do you belong to any church? The Wesleyan. I clean out the Wesleyan Church in Grove Street, and get 1s. a week for doing it.

12468. Do you often feel weary at night? Yes.

. . .

12471. *By Mr Hunter*: What occupation does your husband follow? He is a labourer.

12472. Has he been in employment? He is too lazy.

12473. He could get work if he chose? Yes. He wanted me to keep him, and I did not see why I should keep a lazy man.

12474. *By Mr Salton*: What ages are your children? Eleven, nine and seven.

12475. Have they ever been to school? Yes, until I commenced selling papers.

12476. Have you any other means of support? Only the 1s. a week for cleaning the church.

12477. Have you house rent to pay? Yes; but the landlady has been very good to me, and has never troubled me since my husband left.

   . . .

12484. *By Mrs McConnell*: Do you manage to pay your rent and keep your children on 10s. a week? I have to since my husband left.

Document 4.9 A woman chemist advocates contraception

Justice Windeyer's decision (Document 4.7) meant that druggists' shops, such as that run by Brettena Smyth in North Melbourne, could stock contraceptive devices and literature without fear of prosecution.

Smyth (1842–1898) combined an interest in women's suffrage with a recognition of the liberating potential of birth control for women. Unlike reformers such as Bessie Lee who advocated self-restraint as a means of fertility control, Smyth maintained in her pamphlet, Limitation of Offspring *(1893), and in her well-known lectures to female audiences, that it was important to dispel women's ignorance about their bodies and to publicise effective techniques to limit family size. Brettena Smyth risked censure and ridicule in her efforts to spread knowledge about birth control, and was an important figure in the fight to free white Australian women from the constraints and dangers of repeated childbirth.*

On the other hand, the fertility levels of many Aboriginal women were falling, due to venereal diseases introduced by Europeans and the trauma of dispossession. They also had to deal with the pain of having their children forcibly removed from their care to mission stations and reserves.

Smyth's arguments, like Windeyer's, have eugenicist overtones when she refers to hereditary 'weaknesses'.[9]

1893

Scientific checks are necessary to control the population, for as long as poor men have large families, pauperism is a necessity, and from pauperism grow crime, vice, misery, and disease. It is much more moral to prevent the conception of children than after they are born to desert or slowly murder them by want of food, air, and clothing. It is not too much to say that hundreds of infants are ignorantly murdered in this city every year. It is a crime of crimes to bring children into the world doomed to

misery and death, while the woman's health and life are embittered by
having too many children. No child should be allowed to come into the
world unless it was welcomed by loving parents. Parents have no right to
bring children into the world unless they can give them a good constitution,
and this is what mothers cannot give when they have them too often. Let
us enquire if there is a possibility of having too many children in a family.
Unquestionably there is; its disastrous effects on both mothers and children
are known to every medical man who has any kind of practice in women's
diseases. An eminent medical author on Women's Diseases says—'Two-
thirds of all womb diseases are traceable to over-much child-bearing.
Hardly a day passes that a physician in any kind of practice does not see
instances of debility and disease arising from excessive child-bearing.' Dr.
Hillier, whose authority is unquestionable, says that the children of parents
who indulge in over-production are specially susceptible to rickets, &c.

Worse than this, statistics show that such children are peculiarly liable
to idiotcy. Weakly herself, she brings forth weakly children, born but to
suffer and die. Then are the accumulated evils of an excessive family
manifested. Even the lower animal illustrates this. Every farmer is aware
of the necessity of limiting the offspring of his mares and cows. How
much more severe are the injuries inflicted upon the delicate organisation
of woman[?] Dr. Duncan says a very great mortality attends upon con-
finements when they become too frequent. Apart from these
considerations, there are certain social relations which have been thought
by some to advise smaller families. When either parent suffers from a
disease which is transmitted, and wishes to avoid inflicting misery on an
unborn generation, it has been urged that they should avoid having
children. Such diseases not unfrequently manifest themselves after marriage, which is answer enough to the objection that if they did not wish
children they should not marry. Pregnancy is a nine months' torture to
some women, and to others it is nearly certain to prove fatal. Such a
condition cannot be discovered before marriage, and therefore cannot be
provided against by a single life. Can such women be asked to immolate
themselves? How often do we hear that medical men have said to some
women, you must not fall in the family way again for at least three or
four years, or if you value your life you must never become pregnant
again[?] Yet they do not tell them how to prevent pregnancy. They lay
down no rules to guide them. All is left to blind chance, or to abstinence
from sexual connection. Now, when some women are so constituted that
they cannot give birth to healthy or even to living children, is it desirable,
is it moral, that such women should become pregnant? Others who ought
never to become parents, because if they do it is to transmit to their

offspring hereditary diseases which render such offspring mere subjects of misery throughout their sickly existence. Yet such women will not lead a life of celibacy. They marry, they become parents, and the sum of human misery is increased by their doing so. Those who suffer from hereditary diseases, consumption, or insanity in the family, might marry if they so wished, but they should not have children. The whole race would gain in vigour, in health, in longevity, if only healthy parents gave birth to children.

. . .

Look at the mother of a large family, whose husband is a working man, tugging at the oar of incessant labour from morning till night, toiling to live and living but to toil; whereas if she had only half that number of children she would have enjoyed better health and a little more comfort, and would have produced a healthier and stronger type of humanity. By her having so many children she is compelled to toil on even at those times when nature imperiously calls for some relief from daily drudgery. How often is the mother's health, nay, even her life sacrificed? Suppose that the father dies, she is left with a large family to face the world for a living; unable with the most virtuous intentions to save her fatherless offspring from becoming degraded objects of charity and profligate votaries of vice. If a woman has a right to decide on any question it certainly is as to how many children she shall bear. Wives have a right to demand of their husbands at least the same consideration which a breeder of cattle extends to his stock.

Every woman should say so many and no more, and when she will have them. Marriage should protect her freedom, not make her a slave. This is a law of nature respected through the whole animal kingdom. No female in the world, except the human female, is required to submit to the sexual embraces during pregnancy, and this law is respected and observed in some countries, and broken by great numbers in others. Women who get into feeble health should give over having children, and try to build up their constitution; go away for three or six months in the country.

Document 4.10 A worker for women's suffrage reports on the progress of the cause

Following the achievement of women's suffrage in New Zealand in September 1893, South Australia was the first Australian colony to give women the vote. This report of the Women's Suffrage League of South Australia was written in 1894 when women were at last

granted the right to become electors. Its secretary, Mary Lee (1821–
1909), was one of the many women in Australian cities involved in
establishing suffrage leagues in the 1880s and 1890s. These bodies
were not always large, but included prominent women who had often
been involved in other women's organisations, like the Woman's
Christian Temperance Union, and they formed part of an interna-
tional movement. This comradeship helped to sustain them against
the ridicule and attacks to which women reformers were subjected.[10]

July 1894

At a meeting of the Women's Suffrage League held in the Albert Hall,
Adelaide, on above date, Mrs. Mary Lee, Honorary Secretary to the League
read the following Report:

It has been well said, that 'the footsteps of Liberty are slow but she
never turns them backwards'. This applies most surely to the efforts of
the Women's Suffrage League of South Australia which grew out of that
memorable meeting of June 6th, 1888, when the ladies of the Adelaide
Social Purity Society for urgent reasons pledged themselves to the cause
of Women's Suffrage. This principle has patiently, slowly and surely been
making conquest of public sentiment, and, although our young State may
not, as was then hoped, lead the nations of Christendom in this greatest
reform of our century, we may still fairly claim that in these colonies
South Australia has led the way in this noble struggle . . .

In March of this year, 1894, a new petition in a more simple form
was agreed upon, this is now being actively circulated, the W.C.T. Union
co-operating, and it is hoped that the signatures will be so numerous as
to give emphatic denial to the plea so often urged as an excuse for
withholding this right, 'that the women do not want it', a plea which an
honestly patriotic statesman should blush to urge, since it proves if it prove
anything, that some women are too supinely selfish to recognise their duty,
while others are too crushed and careworn to listen to its call . . . Some
New York ladies have recently entered a strong protest against the granting
of the Suffrage to Women—with every luxury and privilege which boundless wealth can bestow—any change must mean to them, restriction of
privilege, curtailment of luxury, but the change is coming and they will
ere long have to give an account of their stewardship. On the other hand
there are women struggling intensely for their right to live—for the means
to cling to a mere animal existence; these, owing to the ingrained cow-
ardice engendered by long oppression and misery, fear any change, lest it
should bring a death-grapple with starvation. Well may those who day by
day witness these awful contrasts, cry out in agony of soul 'How long, O

Lord', but 'The Lord will come and will not keep silence' . . . Let the *women* arise and answer this—women, the great reserve force of the army of Peace, Love, and Order. The world waits for its women—prepared for this crisis by centuries of wrong and humiliation, of faith and patient endurance. It is wrong to say that women desire to take men's work out of their hands, but it is time that we insisted on good true men to help us to do our work and to do their own.

They tell us that we women are sufficiently represented by proxy! Methinks voting by proxy is very much like praying by proxy. It seems safe to say that the man or the woman who leaves his or her praying to be done by other people is long past praying for, and the same applies in a degree to voting. In New Zealand women are advocating the election of men on the basis of character, irrespective of party. It does not seem that we have much to dread from the influence of party here. Outspoken honourable foes may be persuaded or outgeneraled by the sagacity and discretion of those at the helm of the movement, but what the League has most to dread is the influence of false friends and the machinations of those who would exploit the organization for narrow selfish ulterior ends. We understand that it is 'in the air' to wed the Women's Suffrage Bill with a new partner this session—a Bill to lower the property qualification for the franchise for the Upper House. If this be so, an identical experience with that of last session may be safely predicted, and the advocates of the parliamentary vote for women must possess their souls in patience . . . Other speakers will tell you of the advance of women in art, science, and academic achievements all over the world since this agitation for women's enfranchisement began, but I must give here part of a resolution carried a few months since in the Legislature of the Great American State of Wyoming, which has had Women's Suffrage for upwards of a quarter of a century. 'The exercise of the suffrage by women has largely aided in banishing crime, pauperism and vice, and this without any violent or oppressive legislation. It has secured peaceful orderly elections, good government and a remarkable degree of civilization and public order. We point with pride to the facts that after twenty-five years of Women's Suffrage not one county in Wyoming has a Poorhouse; our jails are almost empty; and crime, except that by *strangers* in the State, is almost unknown. That an authenticated copy of this resolution be sent by the Governor of this State to every legislative body in the world and we request the press throughout the civilized world to call the attention of its readers to these resolutions.' As a result of this encouraging example, in the neighbouring State of Colorado, a body of male voters recently decided by a majority of six thousand to admit women to precisely the same political privileges as themselves. In these colonies New South Wales and Victoria are following us closely, while Queensland, Tasmania and Western Australia are moving in the same direction. The women of the British Isles are bravely bestirring themselves and also the nations of Europe.

Document 4.11 A male journalist discusses the woman question and the social question

The socialist and journalist Henry Hyde Champion (1859–1928) counterposes in this article from Cosmos *Magazine the struggle between employers and workers and that between men and women, and argues that the two oppressed groups should support each other. Champion, who married Elsie, the sister of the feminist political activist Vida Goldstein, founded the National Anti-Sweating League (against sweated labour). He was also the leading organiser of the appeal for funds for women doctors which led to the opening of the Queen Victoria Hospital in Melbourne.*

This piece also raises issues that prompted the demand for suffrage by many women—issues that provoked their anger about domestic violence and assault. They had much to do with male sexual demands, and as Champion points out, this was a topic that few women felt able to speak about publicly.[11]

May 1895

No matter is discussed with so much alike of heat and futility as the Woman Question. Yet it is high time that it was temperately examined and clearly understood—in Australia at any rate. South Australia has bettered the instruction of New Zealand. The Government of Victoria is publically pledged to make the removal of the sex-disqualification on voters its first legislative reform. New South Wales cannot be far behind. No one can doubt that the postponement of the time when women will wield great political power over all Australasia is only a matter of months.

. . .

Little of what is now to be said is to be heard on the platforms of Woman Suffrage. Go to the meetings and you will hear plenty of excellent reasons why women should vote. They are intelligent, they pay taxes, they should not be classed with paupers, criminals and lunatics, and so on. But you will not hear why they *want* the vote. Yet people do not demand enfranchisement on grounds of abstract justice. The right to mark a ballot-paper is not to be coveted for its own sake. It is but a means to an end. The vote is always desired for the sake of tangible advantages to be gained by its use, though that end itself is not always very clearly defined in the mind of the rank and file. In the case of woman these ends are not easily dealt with in public meetings addressed by speakers naturally unwilling to take the odium of plain speech on delicate topics. For if these are touched on by unmarried women, there is an outcry about their shamelessness. If they are dealt with by the married, the inference is at once drawn that they are publishing their own experiences. It may be said in fact that a woman who put her name to this article would have to pay a crushing penalty. Yet I make bold to say that, excluding the noisy, flippant and hysterical who swarm to every reform movement and would, if allowed, turn it into a ridiculous fad, the vast majority of women who ask for the franchise hold the following views and will, privately, endorse them.

There is a curious analogy between the two great movements that are absorbing the interest of this generation—the revolts of the class and of the sex that think themselves oppressed. Together they constitute a denial of the postulate on which past sociological theory has been based, namely, that all the energies of man are motiv[at]ed by the desires for self-preservation and re-production. 'Thou shalt want ere I want', says the possessor of the means of life to the proletariat. The proletariat everywhere is protesting with all its force, though often enough in a blundering, incoherent way, that we have reached a stage of evolution at which the blind, savage struggle for existence must be replaced by a reasoned co-operative effort to conquer hunger. This *is* the Labour question, stripped of all local and non-essential characteristics. The protest of woman is equally blundering and incoherent, but less loudly uttered for the reasons stated above. But it is, in its essence, a claim that we have attained the point of civilization at which the desire for reproduction can be and should be controlled by reason.

. . .

The workman is quite prepared to do the necessary work of the world. But he insists that his function shall not be allowed to obscure his rights as a man, that he shall no longer be regarded by society and its laws primarily as a 'hand', and only incidentally as a human individual. So there may be women who give point to the assertion that their watch-word is 'Liberty, Equality and no Maternity', but the majority are untouched by the taunt. They are by no means inclined to belittle the sacredness or dignity of their special social function. All they ask is that their rights as human individuals shall not be ignored, that they shall no longer be regarded by social law and custom as existing *solely* to satisfy the instinct of reproduction in its modern degraded developments.

It will be hotly denied that any such wrong is done to woman in civilized societies. But the careful and temperate observer of her grievances has no difficulty in tracing them to this one source. It is pointed to in her most energetic recent protests, not from the platform, but in the 'Is marriage a Failure?' controversy [Document 4.4], the correspondence on 'The Revolt of the Daughters', and in the swarm of novels written by women for women. These articles, letters and books, with their astounding popularity amongst thousands of women who would never contemplate ascending the platform or even attending a meeting, show the true meaning of the movement. It is to assert the recognition of women as human individuals as against the tolerance of them as child-producers and the satisfiers of a distorted primal appetite.

What force is there in this protest? Let us first take the case of women in social circumstances that put them beyond the necessity of entering the labour market.

From her birth the girl is, so she feels, cramped and fettered by the idea that only the one career—marriage—is open to her, and must be the aim of her training and education. Though more sensible notions are now slowly spreading, thanks to the advocates of woman's emancipation, her physical development is still injured, as compared with that of her brothers, by the restraints that are supposed to make her womanly but only make her ill. Later she recognizes that her disabilities are largely due, not to sex, but to sex-training, and that a freer dress and more open air exercise in her growing years would have reduced the lack of strength and endurance she feels so bitterly. She was denied them because it was her mission, primarily, to become the wife of some man who wants a small waist, a pink face and small hands at the end of his dining-table. For the same reasons, expressed or implied, she is condemned to fancywork and scales when her brother is learning history and geometry. Maidenly accomplishments, not common sense and useful knowledge, are required in the marriage market. When, later, she is compelled to admit that she is nearly a fool, she sees that, given equal opportunities, her brains would have been as good as her brothers, in many cases better, and in all good enough to have given her pecuniary independence and an interesting career. Thus her health and strength of body and mind have been artificially lessened—but she is a candidate for orange-blossoms.

. . .

But her brothers (and the other girls' brothers) have other things to think of than marriage. They have pursuits, occupations, professions and interests which absorb their time and energies. They have not been brought up with the sole idea of becoming husbands and fathers. So Prince

Charming is not engaged in climbing the briar hedge into the palace. He too, unfortunately, has in his way become the victim of current theories about the primal instincts and is very often 'sowing wild oats'. At best he is aware that he cannot make a friend of any girl of his own set without at once raising false hopes that he is going to give her an opportunity to fulfil her career and, as her mother will tell him, 'spoiling her chances and getting her talked about'. So he keeps out of the way until he is prepared to settle down. He may flirt with girls he would never think of marrying, but Miss Innocence and he have not many subjects in common. Besides, all things conspire to tell him not to marry, to cling to his freedom and to give no hostages to fortune.

Yet all things conspire to tell the girl to marry. Deep in the sacred recesses of her heart, fostered by influences she is forbidden to understand, and fed by a good deal of miscellaneous reading of the romantic kind, there is a spark waiting to be blown into a flame. She ponders over her own ideals and thinks of 'Two souls with but a single thought, Two hearts that beat as one'. Still no one who could possibly be taken for Prince Charming comes along. 'The light that never was on sea or land' fades from her eyes. Her companions who marry warn her that it is well not to expect too much from life. She begins to think of matrimony as the less of two evils. If there were any satisfactory alternative—if the girl were able to achieve pecuniary independence and social freedom by her own efforts—she would regard marriage unaccompanied by ideal love on both sides as much the greater of the two evils. As it is, she does what is so obviously expected of her. If her marriage is a failure, is it not because, in the absence of opportunities for any other career, she has been practically forced into this one by the compulsion not of affection but of circumstances?

The modern woman does not deny that some marriages are very happy and that a great many—since most people are, luckily, very easily pleased—are fairly satisfactory. To do so would be idle in the face of the facts. She has no quarrel with the institution, but a great one with its abuse. Intelligent married women, from whom comes most of the strength of the agitation, have no desire to pose as *femmes incomprises* and to wear their hearts upon their sleeves for daws to peck at. But they know too well the tortures that await the wife who has other hopes than 'to suckle fools and chronicle small beer', dully accepting the position prescribed for her by the theory that woman has but one function and must sacrifice everything to that. The double standard of morals for the two sexes that turns upon her a raging appetite where she looked for a sacred aspiration; the knowledge that the love (which was never love at all) has disappeared with the honey-moon; the chilling assurance that her function is certainly not to be a comrade and a helpmate; enforced maternity that turns the crown and glory of womanhood into a degradation that crushes the mother and blights the child; the absolute dependence in all pecuniary matters on another, with all that means; the eternal harassment of cares multiplied past endurance by rapid child-bearing and ill-health; the absence of sympathy for any kind of self-development; the premature ageing and weakening of mind and body; the impossibility of making the man understand what is the matter; the hopelessness of finding any way of escape:—all these things they trace, and rightly, to the one underlying theory that the instinct of reproduction need not be controlled by man before or after marriage, and that the woman who is not its minister has missed her vocation.

. . .

Women will use their political power, eventually, to uproot the evils indicated above. But they have much to learn and will require all the patience which has been instilled into them by their treatment in past ages. It will be the work of many generations and the best part of it will have to be done in the home and especially in the nursery. But much must be done in the senate and in public life. In that portion of the task the oppressed sex must needs make common cause with the oppressed class. It will have the assistance and good will of many a man who, like myself, lays no pretensions to be classed either with Sir Galahad or with Mr. Chadband.

Document 4.12 A woman replies to another woman's doubts about suffrage

This article by the feminist Rose Scott (1847–1925) was a reply to one by Emily Badham in the journal, The Australian Economist. *In the 1890s Scott was rising to prominence as the leader in New South Wales on women's issues. In 1891 she became secretary of the Womanhood Suffrage League, and was active in many causes to promote the welfare of women and children. She came from a socially prominent and wealthy family, and influenced several liberal politicians, but in this case turned her attention to a woman who could not see the advantages of suffrage for women. Scott's article is an example of how radical ideas could be successfully promulgated by women active in public life.[12]*

June 1895

Miss R. Scott: In answer to the fear that women may, in recording a vote every few years, neglect their domestic duties, we can point to dozens of noble women who have done work outside their homes, and yet never neglected them, but rather, through that work, brought into their homes a wider and more exalted influence. In many classes in life women have more time than men, and yet it is never argued that the father of a family, who is also a business man, should not vote, or even become a member of Parliament or an alderman, because it will interfere with his home duties or his business. For my part, I think it is not women, but men, who need to be reminded not to neglect their families and their home duties, duties which often sit too lightly on the male conscience. Miss Badham affirms that in any art or science where the work of men and women collectively is on the same plane of excellence, and represents the same amount of training, both sexes receive the same wages. I doubt this statement, but even if it is the case, what a small number of woman workers it embraces. Certainly, as teachers, as mistresses of post offices, with the same training, the same or even greater responsibility, women are paid less than men, and are not allowed to rise to the highest position in the service, as men are. This question is in other respects so much regulated by the present law of demand and supply, that it is not easy to fathom in some respects. But it is a far more important thing to be one of a represented class than Miss Badham is aware of; and had working women the vote, they would, I believe, very soon gain that eight hours a day and other reforms which working men have already secured for themselves, for 89 000 women earn their living in New South Wales alone, and I believe 6000 of them are supporting their husbands and children. [The number of white women in New South Wales at the end of 1894 was estimated to be 578 500.] Are women weaker than men? A vote is a protection to the weak; otherwise, why has it not remained the privilege of the rich and the highly educated? Do not the taxes, the bad or good government of the country, concern these working women as much as, sometimes even more than, they do men? And should future electors be trained by mothers ignorant of the duties of citizenship, and untrained in the spirit of patriotism? Miss Badham asks what remedy woman suffrage can bring which will not rather aggravate the evils connected with women workers. Have I not answered this? And she asks the promoters of the league to state any practical plan in their minds, and so silence their opponents. We have one very practical plan, and that is—to get the vote for women. History shows what the vote has done for men, and history will yet show what it will do for women. All men and women who have worked for social reforms connected with women, have invariably declared that the foundation stone of all social reform is the education and enfranchisement of women. The position of women, historians and philosophers agree, is the best criterion of the civilisation of a people and an age. The vote is not compulsory. [The first election in New South Wales with compulsory voting was held in 1930.] Let those men and women who do not desire to use it let it alone, but it is quite another thing to endeavour to debar other men and women from voting, and from having the liberty to do as they think best. Miss Badham dreads interference with 'a man's inherent right to order his private life as he pleases'. I agree with Miss Badham in certain limits. Why, then, should she not dread interference with a woman's right to do the same? Miss Badham appears to be more fearful of interfering with the evil and selfish individuality of men as displayed in drink, gambling, and immorality (which all have their share in injuring poor children), than she is of interfering with (what she is pleased to set forth as) the weak and foolish individuality of women. Why should foolishness be restrained and wickedness allowed to run riot? Surely what is sauce for the gander is sauce for the goose also, and here we come to the foundation stone of this question—the bedrock, as it were—what is a vote? It is a certain factor in the system of our government. Does Miss Badham suppose that we are merely fighting for this piece of machinery, which may be here today and gone tomorrow? No, we are battling for the liberty, the freedom of women. We claim that as a human being, she should have from the parent State the same rights and privileges as that other section of humanity called men, and we affirm that the sex of a human being is, like race and colour, a secondary matter, and that it has never been the highest vocation of women to be wives and mothers any more than it has ever been the highest vocation of men to be husbands and fathers. The highest vocation of either sex is to be a noble, honest, loving human being, and it follows that if they fulfil their vocation, they will also nobly fulfil the duties which their individuality decides may or may not belong to them as creatures of sex. It was fortunate there was no law to prevent a woman going out to save a shipwrecked crew, or Grace Darling would never have been heard of. It was well for the world that there was no law forbidding Florence Nightingale to bring order and decency into the chaos of neglect that had grown up round medical men and staff officers. Who are we, either men or women, that we should arrogantly meddle to map out the path of any human being, or limit the ascent of their individuality. Even the Almighty leaves us to direct and guide ourselves—so true it is that 'fools' rush in where angels fear to tread . . . I claim that in Miss Badham's paper, with all its wit, sarcasm, and literary ability, there is not one logical reason against woman suffrage. The vote is not given to men on an intellectual basis, or because of their many brilliant achievements in the way of climbing, running, playing cricket, writing books, or generally mismanaging financial affairs upon which the prosperity of the country depends. The vote is given to the men of the country in spite of their follies, wisdom, or mistakes, because they are human beings with an interest in the country and its government. On this ground the vote is given to men—on this ground do we demand it for women. It is given to men on logical grounds—it is withheld from women on sentimental grounds. 'There comes a time in the history of the world,' says Sir George Grey, 'when the machinery of national life gets played out, and when it must be remodelled.' We affirm that this time has come, and that with us are all the noblest women workers in the world, from Florence Nightingale to Josephine Butler. With us are all the greatest statesmen, and many of the noblest intellects of the British Empire and America. Those who work for this cause are human, but the cause itself is divine, for it is the cause of freedom. Ancient wisdom depicted Justice standing with scales in her hand, endeavouring to secure a perfect balance. In political matters, men have all scrambled into one scale (except perhaps policemen!) and the scale has gone down, down-weighted, no doubt, by men's superior intellect and creative power! But where is the balance? How can it be secured till you put women in the other scale? Those wonderful creatures called men and women are the complement of each other, and owe to each other more than words can say. Evil is only subjective, and all we require is a faithful balance.

Document 4.13 Women and children still struggle for subsistence

A.B. (Bert) Facey (1894–1982) wrote a remarkably interesting auto-biography, A Fortunate Life *(1981). He began with his memories of the 1890s when his father left Victoria for the goldfields of Western Australia but shortly after died. Facey's mother then joined her two elder sons there, leaving the young Bert and his other siblings with their grandparents. When their mother failed to send back any money for their support, their grandmother, now widowed, took the children to the goldfields to find her, but their mother had remarried and was unable to offer them a home.*

The extract here shows how all family members had to be marshalled to eke out a subsistence living. This life of rural poverty harks back to earlier descriptions of women making do, and highlights the fact that, not withstanding liberal politicians' advocacy of women's rights, poor women's problems with basic survival had not been solved.[13]

1899

Just before midday we arrived at Kalgoorlie and Aunt Alice was there to meet us. We had been unable to see what the country was like as we had travelled during darkness for most of the way and slept during daylight. Aunt Alice had her two older daughters with her. Grandma, Aunt Alice and Myra left the two girl cousins to help the rest of us take the luggage out to Aunt Alice's place. Grandma and Aunt Alice went to see our mother. We found out later that Mother wouldn't have us at her place but was glad to keep our sister Myra. Grandma said our mother was going to have another baby.

When we arrived at Aunt Alice's place we were dog-tired and hungry. Aunt's place, which was only a hut, was built near a big hill. It consisted of bush poles for uprights with hessian pulled tight around the poles making an enclosed space of about thirty-six feet by twelve feet, sub-divided into three big rooms. The outside walls were white-washed with a solution of chalky clay mixed with water which stiffened the hessian and made the inside private. The roof was bush timber and galvanised iron. The three rooms of the hut were used as bedrooms. A few feet away from the hut was another structure, the kitchen, and this had a fireplace at one end and a large table with a long stool along one wall. The kitchen was fourteen feet by sixteen feet. We were to have all our meals in this room.

We had been there about an hour when Aunt Alice and Grandma arrived. They had left Myra with Mother. We were told that our older brothers, Joseph and Vernon, were no longer living with Mother. Joseph had left Kalgoorlie to work with a surveyor and Vernon had joined the Australian navy.

Grandma said that she had had a long talk with Mother about our situation and that Mother was very ill and would see us when she was well enough. So until then we were to make Aunt Alice's place our home. The house and furniture showed that Aunt Alice didn't enjoy a surplus of money. There were many families living in similar circumstances.

The surface gold was just about prospected out, and the men had to find other means of employment to keep their families. Aunt Alice's husband, Archie, was away chopping wood for the mines at Boulder, and for the many condensers that were condensing the water for all the Goldfields people. In those days there was no fresh water, and it became too costly to have water carted. There was plenty of salt water underground so this was pumped up from wells and bores and converted to drinking water by the condensers. There was a large condenser about a mile from Aunt's place and the water obtained from there had to be carried home in buckets. It cost two shillings a gallon if you carted it yourself, or two shillings and sixpence a gallon if you had it delivered. The condenser people wouldn't deliver less than fifty gallons at a time and as Aunt Alice couldn't afford to buy that much at one time we had to go and get it.

Uncle Archie used to come home every two or three weeks, and we had been there for about a week when he came home. That was the first time I had seen him. He would come home on Saturday and go away again on Sunday afternoon. When he went away this time he took Eric and Roy with him. Eric was nearly fourteen years old and Roy was nearly eleven. Uncle said Eric could help with the wood stacking and Roy would be useful around the camp boiling the billy, washing-up the dishes and doing many other little jobs. So my brothers could not go to school.

Aunt's three older girls—Alice, Daisy and Mary—went to school in Kalgoorlie and they had to walk nearly eight miles each school day.

We lived there with Aunt Alice until 1902. Uncle and my brothers came home for a weekend once a month and two Christmases came and went.

We used to have a lot of fun when a heavy shower of rain came and made the ground very wet. We would all go out into the diggings looking for gold that had had the earth washed off it, and between us we found quite a few pieces. It was worth twenty shillings an ounce.

Aunt Alice found another way to make a few shillings—she took in washing and ironing. She made us kids—May, Bill and myself (she now had another child, Jim, but he was still a baby)—go to the camps and get the washing, and after it was washed and ironed, take it back to the owners and collect the money.

Also, Grandma and Aunt Alice used to take all us kids, who were too young to walk the long distance to school, to hunt miles around for places where prospectors had camped. The prospectors lived on tinned foods. When the tins were emptied they were just thrown into heaps near the camps.

Aunt and Grandma gathered the tins, then we would gather bushes, scrub and sticks, spread them onto the ground, and pile the tins on top. A pile would be left for a few days until the bushes and scrub, which were mostly green, dried enough to burn. Then we would come back and set it alight. The heat from the fire would melt the solder that was in the tins, and it would fall down into the ashes and onto the ground. Then, when the fire finished burning and cooled off we used to sieve the ashes and the ground under the ashes, to get the solder that had melted into small lumps. We put these into a bag and took them home. When we had enough Aunt Alice would melt them in an iron pot. Then she would wet a small piece of level ground, make impressions in the damp soil to the size of a stick of solder, and pour the melted solder into them. When the solder cooled she used to wash it and take it into Kalgoorlie where she got five shillings a pound for it. A fairly large heap of tins would be worth about thirty shillings. All this used to help, and, as Aunt Alice said, it gave us something to do.

Document 4.14 A woman writer claims a national identity for Australian women

At the turn of the century, as the British colonies of Australasia were moving toward greater political independence from Britain, there was much preoccupation with national identity, which was mostly discussed in terms of the colonial white male. White women's experiences were rarely included in generalisations about what it meant to be 'Australian'. Aborigines were not given a place in this debate at all and were debarred from rights in the Federal Constitution prepared in 1901, not counted in the census, and excluded from citizenship in the new Commonwealth.

This piece is an interesting example of a woman commissioned to write about white Australian women and their separate history and achievements. Mrs Hirst Alexander's chapter, 'Women of Australasia', appeared in 1900. Needless to say, for a volume that was part of 'The British Empire Series', Aboriginal women are not mentioned, while white women are seen as 'pioneers'.[14]

1900

The lives and achievements of Australasian women will, I feel sure, furnish [a] rich theme for many papers and books yet to be written in the centuries to come, when that history has been lived and won, for the absence of which the lusty young colonies at the antipodes are so often twitted and almost scorned, in common with other striplings, having often to bear with its time-wise elders for the irresponsible and withal daily amending fault of its juvenility.

To say that Australasia has no history is, I think, not quite correct. What about the intrepid, fearless explorers and brave pioneers?—a long roll, from Dampier and Cook onward—who sought out new lands, vanquishing the wilderness, undauntedly and successfully surmounting the

great difficulties and obstacles to be encountered in the opening up of a
new world for the overcrowded population of the British Islands, and
adding to the empire a vast continent, teeming with riches, and opulent
with all natural means to man's prosperous existence. In fact, powerful to
produce almost everything under the sun that man needs or luxury can
lust after.

. . .

The young Australians in their short history have much to be proud
of, and the history of the grand old motherland, from whence their parents
migrated, is as much their heritage as it is that of their fathers and
forefathers. Planted in fresh soil, they are scions from the old stock, and
in that new country are each acting out the history of the land of their
nativity far more distinctively than they could among the thronging
millions of Old England.

And what about the women of Australasia? For who shall estimate
the incalculable import of women's influence in the building up of a great
nation and of a worthy national character?

The women of the present are giving most fair and gracious promise
that neither now nor in the future will they do discredit to their pioneer
mothers or to their sisters of the old centres of civilisation and culture.

And those brave pioneer mothers! How they roughed it in the old
days; put their shoulders to the wheel, and worked side by side with their
husbands, toiling from morn till night, turning their hands to anything,
living in tents, some of them helping manually even in the building of
their own houses; making happy home-nests, and rearing stalwart sons
and comely daughters to the nation, thus with their own and their children's
prosperity establishing that also of their adopted land.

Of course I am speaking now more particularly of those who went
out with little or nothing but their own willing hands and honest hearts
to begin the world over again in the new country—not of those who took
out capital with them. The latter, though from the exigencies of life under
primitive conditions having to put up with makeshifts and comparatively
rough living, were still saved much of the hardship, the scraping and
difficulties which the unmoneyed pioneers had to go through.

Away in the bush, the newer settlers are, many of them, going through
much the same sort of battle at the present moment, to emerge, doubtless,
after the first few years of struggle have been won through, into that same
haven of comfort and competency which so many of the enterprising,
laborious pioneers are now deservedly enjoying. Thousands of women
whose names will never be heard of have done splendid work in the
development of Britain's Australasian dependencies by their arduous,

onerous share of the planting and tending of pure, gracious homes throughout the length and breadth of those fair colonies, and in the bringing up
to take their places of children as good, upright, and industrious as
themselves, but with more of this world's oil to grease the starting wheels
of life than fell to the lot of their parents.

. . .

And now to turn to the cities of Australasia and the employments in
which women there engage. Before I go further I had better state that,
according to the latest statistics available, there were 235,000 more men
than women in Australia. I am not quite sure of the difference in New
Zealand, but there also the women are in a minority. Thus the position
numerically is all in favour of the women. Outsiders might suppose in
this state of society that the demand for employment on the part of women
would be small. But such is not the fact. Many thousands of women in
the colonies are gaining their own livelihood, and in not a few cases
assisting their families.

Women are extensively engaged in the government printing offices,
and in the post and telegraph departments. Unlike the American women,
their salaries are inferior to those of men in similar positions. This, I think,
is an injustice wherever it occurs. Women are engaged also by the large
private printing establishments, wholesale stationers and bookbinders of
the city. They are employed almost exclusively in the telephone department
of the stock exchanges, and by some of the merchants in the same posts.
They are extensively engaged in the tram and omnibus companies for
counting the money. To a limited extent they are occupied as clerks and
private secretaries, more largely as copyists and type-writers. A great
number have opened type-writing offices, choosing their rooms where
lawyers abound, and are generally kept very busy by these gentlemen and
others. A few have gone into mining business . . .

In educational callings ladies are prominently represented. Several
made fortunes by private schoolkeeping in the early days when money
was plentiful and good schools were scarce. I am sorry to add that some
of those ladies in the bank collapses of 1893 lost their fortunes, and have
had to turn to work again. But those bank collapses and the mad boom-
time which led up to them have taught the colonies a lesson, which bids
fair to establish them in the future on a firmer and sounder basis of
prosperity than ever before. In the meantime many have suffered, and are
still suffering, from that epoch of commercial rottenness, and many women
were among the victims.

A large number of trained nurses are yearly graduating from the
Australian and New Zealand hospitals, and others are always arriving from

England. Milliners and dressmakers do exceedingly well, and as heads of departments in leading shops get very high salaries . . . The industries of the cities which give employment to women are much the same, though perhaps not so various as those in the cities of Great Britain. Women are numerously found in the clothing and other factories, and also as piece-workers at home, and, notwithstanding, wages and pay generally being better than in England, I am afraid *sweating* is not unknown even in Australasia, especially in the *protected* industries . . .

Socially the Australasian woman enjoys all the advantages of her English sisters, with perhaps a little more freedom and independence. Calm self-possession and the early development of power to assume her place in society are characteristics of the Antipodean girl.

Sir John Suckling thus writes of an Australian girl—

> She's pretty to walk with,
> And witty to talk with,
> And pleasant, too, to think on.

But I would like to remark that she has another and very sober and serious side to her character, as the perusal of the University Calendars will very notably testify.

At the Colonial Universities the Australian girl has proved that her intellectual capacities are sound and vigorous . . .

. . .

At the Sydney University, among a group of distinguished girls, Miss Eleanor Madeline Whitfeldt took, besides first-class honours, a university medal and two professors' prizes, one being for mental philosophy and *logic*. Imagine a young woman, in competition with the sex supposed to enjoy the monopoly of the reasoning faculty, carrying off the prize for logic!

Women generally marry in the colonies between the ages of eighteen and thirty. They marry at all ages, more or less, but notwithstanding the disproportion of the sex so much in favour of the women, some, as in the old world, do not marry at all.

And now a little about politics, in which progressive women at the Antipodes are much concerned, for they have seen that 'every great reform must enter the portal of the law through the portal of politics', and experience has proved to them, as to others elsewhere, that the representations of *non-voters* are disregarded . . .

Evidently Mr. Gilbert Parker during his residence at the Antipodes did not associate or even meet with any member of that large band of women, spread throughout Australia and New Zealand, who for so many

many years—well on towards twenty—have been working and battling, as so many are here battling in England, for Woman's Suffrage.

Men, especially when short residents in a country, in writing of its women are apt, I think, to take the ladies of their own particular 'set' or circle, and create them into representatives of the nation. If to be indifferent to the laws of their country, and the character of the men who make those laws, which so deeply affect the moral and social wellbeing of family life and the community as a whole—if this supineness constitutes 'real' and 'primitive' womanliness, then I recognise that the women of Australasia possess neither the one nor the other.

But I maintain that it is their very *real* womanliness, and love of justice and righteousness, that have moved them to fight so long, so unweariedly and perseveringly to get the franchise, and their efforts have at last been crowned with success in New Zealand and South Australia; and events foreshadow that the time is not far distant when women will be enfranchised throughout all the Australian Colonies. New Zealand led the way, and South Australia followed, but outran New Zealand by giving complete equality to its women, granting them not only the vote but the right to sit in parliament. The rights were won in spite of the bitterest opposition, and in the teeth of a hostile press . . .

Document 4.15 The Federal Constitution inscribes citizenship for some women

In this extract from the Federal Constitution, written in 1900, the first issue discussed is that of allowing all women to stand for parliament—in this instance 'he' was to include 'she'.

The question of voting was more complex. The discussion under the heading, 'Rights of Electors', section 41 of the Constitution, was about protecting the voting rights of women in South Australia and Western Australia; they had the right to vote in their colonies and were now permitted to vote in the elections for the new Common-wealth Government. Section 41 also promised the federal vote to white women in the other colonies, a promise fulfilled in 1902. This same section, however, disenfranchised Aboriginal men and women; in those states where Aborigines did not have the vote (Queensland and Western Australia, where most Aborigines lived), civil rights were uncategorically denied. In the other states, where they had been permitted to vote, section 41 was interpreted in such a way as to gradually remove their names from federal voting rolls. Aboriginal women, then, were not included with their white sisters as citizens of the new nation.

These sections are taken from The Annotated Constitution of the Australian Commonwealth *by the jurists Quick and Garran; the historical note is theirs and refers to the politicians' debates at the constitutional conventions held in the 1890s.*[15]

1901

PART III THE HOUSE OF REPRESENTATIVES

Qualifications of a Member

#129. 'He'
The personal pronoun 'he' here used in introducing the qualification of members, being in the masculine gender, naturally suggests the query whether women are disqualified by the Constitution. This cannot be answered without considering some of the other qualifications required. Thus, a member must be an elector entitled to vote at the election of members of the House of Representatives, or a person qualified to become an elector. Are persons having the right to vote and otherwise constitutionally qualified, entitled to be nominated for election irrespective of sex? If the pronoun 'he' had not been made the subject of an express interpretation by an Imperial Act, there would be little doubt that males only would be qualified. By the Interpretation Act (1889) . . . commonly known as Lord Brougham's Act, it is declared (sec. 1) that 'In this Act and in every Act passed after the year 1850, whether before or after the commencement of this Act, unless the contrary intention appears, words importing the masculine gender shall include females'. The Constitution of the Commonwealth being embodied in an Imperial Act may be fairly considered as capable of interpretation by the anterior Imperial Act . . . If this be the true construction then 'he' includes 'she' unless the contrary intention appears.

. . .

PART IV BOTH HOUSES OF PARLIAMENT

Right of Electors of States

41. No adult person who has or acquires a right to vote at elections for the more numerous House of the Parliament of a State shall, while the right continues, be prevented by any law of the Commonwealth from voting at elections for either house of the Parliament of the Commonwealth.

Historical Note—At the Adelaide session of the Convention, on the discussion of the qualification of electors of the House of Representatives . . . Mr. Holder proposed that 'every man and woman of the full age of 21 years, whose name has been registered as an elector for at least six months, shall be an elector'. This was opposed as being likely to prejudice the prospects of the Constitution in the colonies where women's suffrage had not been adopted, and was negatived by 23 votes to 12.

Mr. Holder then, as a compromise, moved an amendment which contained the germ of the above section; namely, to add the words: 'No elector now possessing the right to vote shall be deprived of that right'. The object was to prevent the Federal Parliament, when declaring a uniform franchise, from depriving the women of South Australia of the right to vote. Without such a provision, the apprehension was expressed that the women of South Australia might be deprived of the franchise by the Federal Parliament, and such a possibility might induce them to vote against the Constitution when submitted to the people. The proposal was at first objected to on the ground that it would embarrass and fetter the Federal Parliament in framing a uniform franchise; that it showed an unreasonable want of confidence in the Parliament; that the Parliament might be trusted not to do anything unreasonable or unjust. After some discussion the proposal was moulded into the following shape: 'But no elector who has at the establishment of the Commonwealth, or who afterwards acquires a right to vote at elections for the more numerous House of the Parliament of a State, shall be prevented by any law of the Commonwealth from exercising such right at the elections for the House of Representatives'. This was carried by 18 votes to 15.

#139. 'Has or Acquires.'

The word 'has' apparently refers to rights in existence at the establishment of the Commonwealth; the word 'acquires' to rights acquired after that time. At Adelaide . . . Mr. Barton endeavoured to secure the limitation of the clause to rights existing at the establishment of the Commonwealth, but was defeated. At Melbourne . . . he endeavoured to limit it to rights acquired, before or after the establishment of the Commonwealth, under a State law in force at the establishment of the Commonwealth. This he ultimately withdrew on the insertion of the word 'adult'.

It is clear that a right under this section to vote at federal elections can be acquired after the establishment of the Commonwealth, but it is not so clear that such a right can be acquired after the passing of a federal franchise law, or under State laws passed after the passing of such federal law. Three possible interpretations may be suggested:—

(1.) That the right may be acquired at any time, under a State law passed at any time.

(2.) That the right may be acquired at any time, but only under a State law passed before a federal franchise is fixed.

(3.) That the right must be acquired by the 'adult person' concerned before the federal franchise is fixed.

It seems clear from the following extracts that the first of these interpretations was not intended by Mr. Holder, the author of the clause:

'There is a stage up to which the franchise is purely a State question, and the regulation of the franchise is within the power and authority of the State. The moment that ends is when the Federal Parliament passes a law fixing the franchise. What I want is that so long as the State is free to fix the franchise, any franchise they give shall be protected afterwards . . . The right of the State to alter the franchise continues, not up to the time of the formation of the Constitution, but up to the time that the Federal Parliament frames a franchise, and I want all the rights granted up to that time preserved in the future. [*Mr. Peacock:* If the Federal Legislature has legislated?] No. I want the States to have their rights with regard to the franchise unimpaired up to the day when the federal franchise is indicated, and that whatever the franchise shall be at that date it shall be preserved, and so that no person having a right up to that date shall have it taken from him, and that this shall apply not only to South Australia, but also to other colonies who may widen their franchise before the federal franchise is provided.' (Mr. Holder, Conv. Deb., Melb., p. 1195.)

'I want the right of the State Parliament to be protected up to the moment when the Federal Parliament moves.' (Mr. Holder, Conv. Deb., Melb., p. 1843.)

These quotations make it clear that Mr. Holder did not contemplate the first interpretation, but his expressions seem to waver between the second and the third. In one passage he speaks of *persons having a right* when the federal franchise is framed—words which seem to contemplate the third interpretation; whilst elsewhere he speaks of protecting *the State franchise* as it existed at that date—words which involve the second interpretation. The latter seems to accord better with his general object of securing the federal franchise to women in those States where adult suffrage might exist when the federal franchise was framed.

Let us illustrate these distinctions. Suppose that the Federal Parliament fixes a federal franchise, such as suggested above, for male adults; and that afterwards Victoria passes a law extending the Victorian franchise to women. In South Australia the franchise was extended to women before the federal franchise was fixed. Then the three questions are:—

(1.) Are Victorian women entitled to vote at federal elections?
(2.) Is a South Australian woman, who has come of age since the federal franchise was fixed, entitled to vote at federal elections; or
(3.) Are only those South Australian women who were qualified voters at the date of the federal law entitled to vote at federal elections?

Mr. Holder's intention was that Victorian women, under those circumstances, should not be so entitled; though if the Victorian law had been passed before the federal franchise, it would have been otherwise. But he probably intended that South Australian women should be entitled to vote, whether actually qualified before or after the federal law, because the franchise under which they claim was in existence before the federal law.

Document 4.16 A feminist embraces women's citizenship

As the new century begins, Louisa Lawson, editor of The Dawn *(Document 4.5), makes a spirited claim to public life for white Australian women.*[16]

1901

. . . Woman's freedom—to do what? Not to cease working for the true, the good . . . Woman does not seek to cast aside life's burdens, to wrest from conservatism and prejudice the right to greater ease, to larger leisure. She seeks for freedom to bear her part of the broader burden of social and political life, to share with her father, husband, brothers, the task of hastening humanity with surer and more certain steps towards the goal of justice, truth and mercy.

Here in Australia the two basic principles 'that true democracy is the government of the whole people by the whole people' and 'that there should be no taxation without representation' seem at last to receive practical demonstration at the hands of both the Federal and New South Wales Parliaments. The Federal Government has promised to introduce at an early date a measure to concede the Federal Franchise to women and the Legislative Assembly of New South Wales is, as we go to press, deliberating upon the provisions of the Women's Franchise Bill.

The chief evils from which the Bill is at present suffering are that no 'argument of weight can be found against the principle of the reform', and 'Women have not clamoured for it'. The cry of our opponents was that we clamoured too much, and, now that they find that we do not, they blame us for it. Ask any mother of the household who reads the newspapers, ask any thinking woman—sister, wife or sweetheart—whether she wants a voice in the election of those who make the laws that govern her, and mark her reply.

Every cause is blamed for the exuberance and over-zeal of its first advocates; every suppressed and down-trodden race or clan has to be educated, to be taught to look for its promised land, by the far-seeing few who initiate a movement of reform—did the slaves cry out for freedom, they knew not what it was; did the people of Australia clamour for Federation, when shewn them they realised its benefits and advantages!

Let women, therefore, educate themselves, let them learn the work they can do in the social and political world, let them claim more and more urgently the right to be allowed to do that work, and let them take their stand in public life, as we trust they have at home, the champions of good and the opponents of injustice and evil.

Notes

Part 1 Women in convict society 1788–1840

1 Lord Sydney's memo of 18 Aug. 1786 to the Lords Commissioners of the Treasury was published in *Historical Records of New South Wales,* vol. 1, part 2, Government Printer, Sydney, 1892, pp. 17–19. The British Government's assumptions about the role of gender in its penal colony are discussed in Patricia Grimshaw *et al., Creating a Nation,* McPhee Gribble, Melbourne, 1994, ch. 2.

2 The story, first published in *Scot's Magazine,* 48, Nov. 1786, was republished in *The Push from the Bush,* no. 17, April 1984.

3 Ralph Clark's journal was published in Paul G. Fidlon and R.J. Ryan (eds), *The Journal and Letters of Lt. Ralph Clark 1787–1792,* Library of Australian History, Sydney, 1981; these extracts were taken from the corrected typescript copy in the Mitchell Library, C219. Anne Summers first wrote Clark and his 'damned whores' into history in her book *Damned Whores and God's Police,* Penguin, Ringwood, 1975.

4 David Collins, *An Account of the English Colony in New South Wales,* vol. 1, Reed, Sydney, 1975, ed. B.H. Fletcher (first pub. London, 1798). The incidents described here are further examined in *Creating a Nation* (see Note 1), ch. 1.

5   Elizabeth Macarthur's letters are published in Sibella Macarthur
     Onslow (ed.), *Some Early Records of the Macarthurs of Camden*,
     Rigby, Adelaide, 1973 (first pub. 1914); these extracts come from
     pp. 28–9, 33, 37–9. Her life is told in Hazel King, *Elizabeth
     Macarthur and her World*, Sydney University Press, Sydney, 1980.

6   Catchpole's letters are amended and reproduced in Helen Heney,
     *Dear Fanny: Women's Letters to and from New South Wales,
     1788–1857*, Australian National University Press, Canberra, 1985;
     details of her life are also told in this source.

7   Kelly's reminiscences were published in K.M. Bowden, *Captain
     James Kelly of Hobart Town*, Melbourne University Press, Mel-
     bourne, 1964, pp. 40–1. See also Lyndall Ryan, *The Aboriginal
     Tasmanians*, University of Queensland Press, Brisbane, 1981,
     ch. 3.

8   Christiana Blomfield's letters are published in *Memoirs of the
     Blomfield Family*, privately published, Armidale, 1926. For bio-
     graphical details, see Helen Heney, *Dear Fanny: Women's Letters
     to and from New South Wales 1788–1857*, Australian National
     University Press, Canberra, 1985, pp. 79–84 and Patricia Clarke
     and Dale Spender (eds), *Life Lines: Australian Women's Letters
     and Diaries 1788 to 1840*, Allen & Unwin, Sydney, 1992, pp.
     97–105.

9   The original of Isabella Gibson's letter is in the Mitchell Library,
     MSS 1416b.

10   Robinson's interview with Sarah is in the Mitchell Library, George
     Augustus Robinson Papers, ML MSS A7066, vol. 45.

11   The depositions for the case of Regina v. Benjamin Hodgen, Chief
     Constable at Windsor, are in the New South Wales State Archives,
     Box 9/6314 AONSW, Windsor no. 59, 6 Jan. 1838. Alan Atkinson
     has investigated Elizabeth Power's story and published the news-
     paper report of her statement in court (*Sydney Gazette*, 24–5 Feb.
     1838, in 'Document: The Tale of an Errant Wife', *The Push from
     the Bush*, no. 16, Oct. 1983, pp. 71–7.

12   Eliza Hamilton's poem appeared in *The Australian*, 13 Dec. 1838;
     it is reproduced and discussed in Elizabeth Webby, 'Reactions to
     the Myall Creek Massacre', *The Push from the Bush*, no. 8, Dec.
     1980.

13   This report was not published; the document is at the Archives
     Office of Tasmania as the 'Report and Evidence of the Committee
     Inquiring into Female Convict Discipline, 1841–43', and Appendi-
     ces, CSO 22/50.

Part 2   Women in a masculine democracy 1840–1860

1   The extract is from *The Temperance Advocate and Australasian Commercial and Agricultural Intelligencer*, 21 April 1841; see also Elizabeth Windschuttle, 'Women, Class and Temperance: Moral Reform in Eastern Australia 1832–1857', *The Push from the Bush*, no. 3, May 1979, pp. 5–25.

2   Gunther's report was published among the papers presented to the House of Commons; it is in *Commons Papers*, 1844, vol. 34, no. 627, 'Australian Aborigines', pp. 157–8.

3   Chisholm tells this story in *Female Immigration considered, in a Brief Account of the Sydney Immigrants' Home*, Sydney, 1842, p. 45; her account is cited at length in Mary Hoban, *Fifty-one Pieces of Wedding Cake: A Biography of Caroline Chisholm*, Kilmore 1973, pp. 85–6.

4   Lucy Frost has published sections of Annie Baxter's journals in her *No Place for a Nervous Lady: Voices from the Australian Bush*, McPhee Gribble/Penguin, Melbourne, 1984; the extracts are from pp. 101–9; Frost is also the author of Baxter's biography, *A Face in the Glass*, William Heinemann, Melbourne, 1992.

5   Peter Cowan published the Browns' letters and told their story in *A Faithful Picture: The Letters of Eliza and Thomas Brown at York in the Swan River Colony 1841–1852*, Fremantle Arts Centre Press, Perth, 1977; this letter pp. 49–51.

6   The records of the Mechanics Discussion Class are in the Battye Library: Swan River Mechanics' Institute records, Oct. 1853: Accession No. 1836?A, Box 205. This debate is discussed in Patricia Grimshaw *et al.*, *Creating a Nation*, McPhee Gribble, Melbourne, 1994, ch. 4.

7   The correspondence received by Susannah Mapleson has been published by her descendants in Elma Drayton *et al.*, *A Lifetime of Letters*, Drouin, 1981; these letters are from pp. 10–13.

8   C.H. Spence, *Clara Morison*, first published J.W. Parker and Son, London, 1854, was republished in Helen Thomson (ed.), *Catherine Helen Spence*, University of Queensland Press, Brisbane, 1987; the extracts are from pp. 394–8.

9   Menie's letters to her father appear in A.W. Martin, *Letters from Menie: Sir Henry Parkes and His Daughter*, Melbourne University Press, Melbourne, 1983, pp. 5–7.

10   The letters have been collected by Alan Atkinson; they are presented, with some discussion of their context, in *The Push from*

the Bush, no. 25, Oct. 1987, pp. 52–8, and no. 26, April 1988, pp. 64–6.

11 Charlotte's letter is reproduced as an appendix to E.O.G. Shann, *Cattle Chosen: The Story of the First Group Settlement in Western Australia 1829 to 1841*, University of Western Australia Press, Nedlands, 1978, (first pub. Oxford University Press, London, 1926); pp. 179–83.

12 *Debates in the Houses of Legislature during the Second Session of the First Parliament of South Australia from August 27 to December 24, 1858*, Adelaide, 1858; pp. 52–3 and pp. 176–7.

13 See Edna Hickson, *Blanche: An Australian Diary 1858–1861*, John Ferguson, Sydney, 1980.

Part 3   Frontiers—rural and urban 1860–1885

1   The extract is from Rosa Praed, *My Australian Girlhood: Sketches and Impressions of Bush Life*, T. Fisher Unwin, London, 1902, ch. 5. Rosa Praed is one of the writers discussed in Debra Adelaide (ed.), *A Bright and Fiery Troop: Australian Women Writers of the Nineteenth Century*, Penguin, Ringwood, 1988.

2   The lecture to the St Benedict's Young Men's Society was reported in the *Sydney Morning Herald*, on 22 Feb. 1861, p. 4, and that at the Temperance Hall on 14 June 1861, p. 5. Margaret Kiddle's biography, *Caroline Chisholm* (1950), was reprinted by Melbourne University Press in 1990 with an introduction by Patricia Grimshaw.

3   Honor Scattergood's story can be traced in the Colonial Secretary's Office files in the Battye Library. See CSO 505, 1862: 1 July & 4 Sept; CSO 523, 1863: 1 April. See also Marian Aveling (ed.), *Westralian Voices: Documents in Western Australian Social History*, University of Western Australia Press, Perth 1979.

4   Rachel Henning's letters have been edited by David Adams in *The Letters of Rachel Henning*, Penguin Books, Ringwood, 1979.

5   Higinbotham's speech is reported in *Victorian Parliamentary Debates*, vol. 16, 1873, pp. 952–5. Higinbotham features in Stuart Macintyre's *A Colonial Liberalism: The Lost World of Three Victorian Visionaries*, Oxford University Press, Melbourne, 1991.

6   The extract is from Mary Gilmore's *Old Days: Old Ways*, Angus & Robertson, Sydney 1986 (first pub. 1934), pp. 21–4. For the Selection Acts, see Stuart Macintyre, *Winners and Losers: The*

Pursuit of Social Justice in Australian History, Allen & Unwin, Sydney, 1985, ch. 2.

7   Charles H. Pearson, 'The Higher Culture of Women. A Lecture Delivered at St. George's Hall, February 11, 1875', Samuel Mullen, Melbourne, 1875. For Pearson, see Macintyre, *A Colonial Liberalism* (see Note 5).

8   From 'A Refuge', in *The Vagabond Papers: Sketches of Melbourne Life, in Light and Shade*, 3rd series, George Robertson, Melbourne, 1877, pp. 75–87. See also John Stanley James, *The Vagabond Papers*, ed. Michael Cannon, Melbourne University Press, Melbourne, 1969.

9   Catherine Spence, 'Marriage Rights and Wrongs', *The Register* (Adelaide), 15 July 1878, and reprinted in Helen Thomson (ed.), *Catherine Helen Spence*, University of Queensland Press, Brisbane, 1987, pp. 499–503. For Catherine Spence, see Susan Magarey, *Unbridling the Tongues of Women: A Biography of Catherine Helen Spence*, Hale & Iremonger, Sydney, 1985.

10   'Report of the Board Appointed to Enquire into, and Report upon, the Present Condition and Management of the Coranderrk Aboriginal Station, together with the Minutes of Evidence', *Victoria. Papers Presented to the Houses of Parliament*, 1882–83, vol. 2, pp. 159–307.

11   *The Age*, 12 Dec. 1882, p. 5, and 13 Dec. 1882, p. 7.

12   H.A. Dugdale, *A Few Hours in a Far-off Age*, M'Carron, Bird & Co., Melbourne, 1883, pp. 5–12.

13   An Old Housekeeper, *The Australian Housewives' Manual: A Book for Beginners and People with Small Incomes*, A.H. Massina & Co., Melbourne 1883, ch. 15, 'On Taking Care of a Husband'.

14   These passages are from the facsimile edition; see Richard Twopeny, *Town Life in Australia*, Penguin, Ringwood, 1976, pp. 82–7.

15   Miles Franklin, *Childhood at Brindabella: My First Ten Years*, Angus & Robertson, Sydney, 1974, pp. 9–12, 22–5, 140–1.

Part 4 Seeking social solutions 1886–1901

1   *Argus*, 5 April 1886, p. 7. Bessy's story is told by Bain Attwood in *The Making of the Aborigines*, Allen & Unwin, Sydney 1989, ch. 2; some of her letters are reprinted in Phillip Pepper, with Tess de Araugo, *What did Happen to the Aborigines of Victoria, vol. 1: The Kurnai of Gippsland*, Hyland House, Melbourne, 1985.

2   These extracts are from the 1987 reprint of the pamphlet, intro-
    duced by Bob Tonkinson; see Rev. J.B. Gribble, *Dark Deeds in
    a Sunny Land or Blacks and Whites in North-West Australia*,
    University of Western Australia Press, Perth, 1987, pp. 2, 33, 35,
    49, 50, 51, 52–3.

3   Bessie Lee, *One of Australia's Daughters: An Autobiography of
    Mrs. Harrison Lee*, H.J. Osborn, London, 1906, pp. 77, 78–80, 83,
    110–12.

4   'Is Marriage a Failure?', *The Bulletin*, 20 Oct. 1888, p. 5. Marilyn
    Lake has written about *The Bulletin* and masculinism in 'The
    Politics of Respectability: Identifying the Masculinst Context', in
    Susan Magarey, Sue Rowley and Susan Sheridan (eds), *Debutante
    Nation: Feminism Contests the 1890s*, Allen & Unwin, Sydney,
    1993, pp. 1–15. See also Patricia Grimshaw, 'Bessie Harrison Lee
    and the Fight for Voluntary Motherhood', in Marilyn Lake and
    Farley Kelly (eds), *Double Time: Women in Victoria—150 Years*,
    Penguin, Ringwood, 1985, pp. 139–47.

5   Louisa Lawson, 'The Divorce Extension Bill', *The Dawn*, vol. 1,
    no. 1, 15 May 1888, pp. 4–5. See also Olive Lawson (ed.), *The
    First Voice of Australian Feminism: Excerpts from Louisa Lawson's*
    The Dawn *1888–1895*, Simon & Schuster, Sydney, 1990. On
    divorce law, see Hilary Golder, *Divorce in 19th Century New
    South Wales*, University of New South Wales Press, Sydney, 1985.

6   Ada Cambridge published her autobiography in 1903. These sec-
    tions are taken from the reprint: Ada Cambridge, *Thirty Years in
    Australia*, New South Wales University Press, Sydney, 1989, pp.
    72–5. For a biography of Ada Cambridge, see Margaret Bradstock
    and Louise Wakeling, *Rattling the Orthodoxies: A Life of Ada
    Cambridge*, Penguin, Ringwood, 1991.

7   An abridged version of the judgement was published as *Mr. Justice
    Windeyer on the Population Question*, W.H. Reynolds, London,
    1891. The extracts here are taken from pp. 1, 4–5, 6–7. On the
    influence of Malthus and the eugenics movement, see Angus
    McLaren, *Birth Control in Nineteenth-Century England*, Croom
    Helm, London, 1978.

8   'Royal Commission Appointed to Inquire into and Report upon
    the Conditions under which Work is Done in the Shops, Factories,
    and Workshops in the Colony', *Queensland Parliamentary
    Papers*, 1891, vol. 2, pp. 927–1321.

9   Mrs B. Smyth, *Limitation of Offspring*, Rae Bros., Melbourne, 1893,
    pp. 8–9, 11. See also Farley Kelly, 'Feminism and the Family:

Brettena Smyth', in Eric Fry (ed.), *Rebels and Radicals*, Allen & Unwin, Sydney, 1983, pp. 134–47; and, more generally, Stefania Siedlecky and Diana Wyndham, *Populate and Perish: Australian Women's Fight for Birth Control*, Allen & Unwin, Sydney, 1990.

10 Mary Lee's speech is in 'Report of the Women's Suffrage League of South Australia. Presented at the Annual Meeting, July 24, 1894', W.K. Thomas & Co., Adelaide, 1894', pp. 1, 3–5. For the suffrage movement, see Audrey Oldfield, *Woman Suffrage in Australia: A Gift or a Struggle?*, Cambridge University Press, 1992.

11 H.H. Champion, 'The Claim of Woman', *Cosmos Magazine*, 31 May 1895, pp. 448–52.

12 Rose Scott, 'Discussion on "Women and the Franchise" ', *The Australian Economist*, vol. 4, no. 16, 21 June 1895, pp. 495–7. For a facsimile edition, see N.G. Butlin, V.W. Fitzgerald and R.H. Scott (eds), *The Australian Economist 1888–1898*, Australian National University Press, Sydney, 1986. See Judith Allen, *Rose Scott: Vision and Revision in Feminism*, Oxford University Press, Melbourne, 1994.

13 A.B. Facey, *A Fortunate Life*, Penguin, Ringwood, 1983, pp. 9–12 (first pub. by Fremantle Arts Centre Press, 1981). See also J.B. Hirst, *The World of Albert Facey*, Allen & Unwin, Sydney, 1992.

14 Mrs Hirst Alexander, 'Women of Australasia', in *Australasia* (The British Empire Series, vol. 4), Kegan Paul, London, 1900, pp. 280–309.

15 John Quick and Robert Randolph Garran, *The Annotated Constitution of the Australian Commonwealth*, Australian Book Company, London, 1901, pp. 475, 483–4, 485–6. For Aborigines and their voting rights, see Pat Stretton and Christine Finnimore, 'Black Fellow Citizens: Aborigines and the Commonwealth Franchise', *Australian Historical Studies*, vol. 25, 1993, pp. 521–35.

16 Louisa Lawson, 'Federation of the World's Workers', *The Dawn*, vol. 15, no. 4, Sept. 1901, p. 9.

Select Bibliography

Adelaide, Debra (ed.), *A Bright and Fiery Troop: Australian Women Writers of the Nineteenth Century*, Penguin, Ringwood, 1988

Alford, Katrina, *Production or Reproduction? An Economic History of Women in Australia, 1788–1850*, Oxford University Press, Melbourne, 1984

Allen, Judith, *Rose Scott: Vision and Revision in Feminism*, Oxford University Press, Melbourne, 1994

——*Sex and Secrets: Crimes Involving Australian Women since 1880*, Oxford University Press, Melbourne, 1990

Allen, Margaret, Mary Hutchison and Alison Mackinnon (eds), *Fresh Evidence, New Witnesses: Finding Women's History in South Australia*, South Australian Government Printer, Adelaide, 1989

Atkinson, Alan and Marian Aveling (eds), *Australians 1838*, Fairfax, Syme, Weldon, Sydney, 1987

Attwood, Bain, *The Making of the Aborigines*, Allen & Unwin, Sydney, 1989

Aveling, Marian (ed.), *Westralian Voices: Documents in Western Australian Social History*, University of Western Australia Press, Perth, 1979

Aveling, Marian and Joy Damousi (eds), *Stepping Out of History:*

Documents of Women at Work in Australia, Allen & Unwin, Sydney, 1991

Bevege, Margaret, Margaret James and Carmel Shute (eds), *Worth Her Salt: Women at Work in Australia*, Hale & Iremonger, Sydney, 1982

Bradstock, Margaret and Louise Wakeling, *Rattling the Orthodoxies: A Life of Ada Cambridge*, Penguin, Ringwood, 1991

Broome, Richard, *Aboriginal Australians: Black Response to White Dominance 1788–1980*, Allen & Unwin, Sydney, 1982

Burgmann, Verity and Jenny Lee (eds), *A People's History of Australia since 1788*, 4 vols, McPhee Gribble, Melbourne, 1988

Clarke, Patricia and Dale Spender (eds), *Life Lines: Australian Women's Letters and Diaries 1788 to 1840*, Allen & Unwin, Sydney, 1992

Daniels, Kay (ed.), *So Much Hard Work: Women and Prostitution in Australian History*, Fontana, Sydney, 1984

Daniels, Kay and Mary Murnane (comps), *Uphill all the Way: A Documentary History of Women in Australia*, University of Queensland Press, Brisbane, 1980

Deacon, Desley, *Managing Gender: The State, the New Middle Class and Women Workers*, Oxford University Press, Melbourne, 1989

Dixson, Miriam, *The Real Matilda: Women and Identity in Australia 1788 to the Present*, (3rd edn), Penguin, Ringwood, 1994

Finch, Lynette, *The Classing Gaze: Sexuality, Class and Surveillance*, Allen & Unwin, Sydney, 1993

Fox, Charlie and Marilyn Lake (eds), *Australians at Work: Commentary and Sources*, McPhee Gribble, Melbourne, 1990

Frances, Raelene, *The Politics of Work: Gender and Labour in Victoria, 1880–1939*, Cambridge University Press, Cambridge, 1993

Frost, Lucy (ed.), *A Face in the Glass: The Journal and Life of Annie Baxter Dawbin*, William Heinemann, Melbourne, 1992

Fry, Eric (ed.), *Rebels and Radicals*, Allen & Unwin, Sydney, 1983

Golder, Hilary, *Divorce in 19th Century New South Wales*, University of New South Wales Press, Kensington, 1985

Grimshaw, Patricia, Marilyn Lake, Ann McGrath and Marian Quartly, *Creating a Nation 1788–1990*, McPhee Gribble, Melbourne, 1994

Grimshaw, Patricia, Chris McConville and Ellen McEwen (eds), *Families in Colonial Australia*, Allen & Unwin, Sydney, 1985

Heney, Helen (ed.), *Dear Fanny: Women's Letters to and from New South Wales*, Australian National University Press, Canberra, 1985

Hicks, Neville, 'This Sin and Scandal': Australia's Population Debate, 1891–1911, Australian National University Press, Canberra, 1978

Hirst, J.B., The World of Albert Facey, Allen & Unwin, Sydney, 1992

Hoban, Mary, Fifty-one Pieces of Wedding Cake: A Biography of Caroline Chisholm, Lowden Publishing Co., Kilmore, 1973

Jones, Helen, In Her Own Name: Women in South Australian History, Wakefield Press, Adelaide, 1986

Kiddle, Margaret, Caroline Chisholm, Melbourne University Press, Melbourne, 1990

King, Hazel, Elizabeth Macarthur and her World, Sydney University Press, Sydney, 1980

Kingston, Beverley, My Wife, My Daughter, and Poor Mary Ann: Women and Work in Australia, Nelson, Melbourne, 1975

——The Oxford History of Australia, vol. 3, 1860–1900: Glad, Confident Morning, Oxford University Press, Melbourne, 1988

——(ed.), The World Moves Slowly: A Documentary History of Australian Women, Cassell, Melbourne, 1977

Kociumbas, Jan, The Oxford History of Australia, vol. 2, 1770–1860: Possessions, Oxford University Press, Melbourne, 1992

Lake, Marilyn and Farley Kelly (eds), Double Time: Women in Victoria —150 Years, Penguin, Ringwood, 1985

Lawson, Olive (ed.), The First Voice of Australian Feminism: Excerpts from Louisa Lawson's The Dawn 1888–1895, Simon & Schuster, Sydney, 1990

Macintyre, Stuart, A Colonial Liberalism: The Lost World of Three Victorian Visionaries, Oxford University Press, Melbourne, 1991

——Winners and Losers: The Pursuit of Social Justice in Australian History, Allen & Unwin, Sydney, 1985

Mackinolty, Judy and Heather Radi (eds), In Pursuit of Justice: Australian Women and the Law 1788–1979, Hale & Iremonger, Sydney, 1979

McLaren, Angus, Birth Control in Nineteenth-Century England, Croom Helm, London, 1978

Magarey, Susan, Unbridling the Tongues of Women: A Biography of Catherine Helen Spence, Hale & Iremonger, Sydney, 1985

Magarey, Susan, Sue Rowley and Susan Sheridan (eds), Debutante Nation: Feminism Contests the 1890s, Allen & Unwin, Sydney, 1993

Oldfield, Audrey, Woman Suffrage in Australia: A Gift or a Struggle?, Cambridge University Press, Cambridge, 1992

Pepper, Phillip, with Tess de Araugo, What did Happen to the Abo-

rigines of Victoria, vol. 1: The Kurnai of Gippsland, Hyland House, Melbourne, 1985

Radi, Heather (ed.), *200 Australian Women: A Redress Anthology*, Women's Redress Press, Sydney, 1988

Reekie, Gail (ed.), *On the Edge: Women's Experiences of Queensland*, University of Queensland Press, Brisbane, 1994

Robinson, Portia, *The Hatch and Brood of Time: A Study of the First Generation of Native-Born White Australians 1788–1828*, Oxford University Press, Melbourne, 1985

Reynolds, Henry, *Frontier: Aborigines, Settlers and Land*, Allen & Unwin, Sydney, 1987

——*The Other Side of the Frontier: Aboriginal Resistance to the European Invasion of Australia*, Penguin, Ringwood, 1982

Russell, Penny (ed.), *For Richer, for Poorer: Early Colonial Marriages*, Melbourne University Press, Melbourne, 1994

Ryan, Edna and Anne Conlon, *Gentle Invaders: Australian Women at Work 1788–1974*, Penguin, Ringwood, 1989

Ryan, Lyndall, *The Aboriginal Tasmanians*, University of Queensland Press, Brisbane, 1981

Salt, Annette, *These Outcast Women: The Parramatta Female Factory 1821–1848*, Hale & Iremonger, Sydney, 1984

Saunders, Kay and Raymond Evans (eds), *Gender Relations in Australia: Domination and Negotiation*, Harcourt Brace Jovanovich, Sydney, 1992

Schaffer, Kay, *Women and the Bush: Forces of Desire in the Australian Cultural Tradition*, Cambridge University Press, Cambridge, 1988

Siedlecky, Stefania and Diana Wyndham, *Populate and Perish: Australian Women's Fight for Birth Control*, Allen & Unwin, Sydney, 1990

Smith, Babette, *A Cargo of Women: Susannah Watson and the Convicts of the Princess Royal*, University of New South Wales Press, Sydney, 1988

Summers, Anne, *Damned Whores and God's Police*, (rev. edn), Penguin, Ringwood, 1994

Teale, Ruth (ed.), *Colonial Eve: Sources on Australian Women in Australia 1788–1914*, Oxford University Press, Melbourne, 1978

Thomson, Helen (ed.), *Catherine Helen Spence*, University of Queensland, Brisbane, 1987

Windschuttle, Elizabeth (comp.), *Women, Class and History: Feminist Perspectives on Australia, 1788–1978*, Fontana, Sydney, 1980

Woolmington, Jean (ed.), *Aborigines in Colonial Australia 1788–1850*, Cassell, Melbourne, 1973

Index

Aboriginal culture, 2, 40–2
Aboriginal family life, 12–14
Aboriginal mothers, 2, 12, 31
Aboriginal Tasmanians, 26
Aboriginal women, 1, 2, 12;
    Christian religion, 130;
    citizenship, 174; fertility levels,
    154; living conditions on
    reserves, 106–11; mission life,
    129, 130–1; no right to vote, 130,
    173; oppression, 74; privation,
    74; racism, 131; sealing trade, 19,
    26–7; sexual exploitation, 132–6;
    venereal disease, 154; white
    male cruelty to, 132–6
Aborigines, missionary's failure to
    convert, 39; national identity for
    Australians, 169; native labour
    system, 133; population, 76;
    separate missions and reserves,
    74, 106; servant problem, 86;
    station life in Queensland, 75–9;
    traditional lands, 74; voting
    rights, 173

adultery, 45, 68–71, 105, 106, 141
Asian countries, 130
assault, 159
Australasian women, 171
Australian Housewives' Manual,
    118–22

behaviour of young men, 71–3
Bennilong, 12, 16
birth control, 115, 130, 139,
    147–50, 154
Blomfield, Jane, 21

Cambridge, Ada, 144–6
career of marriage, 161
career options, 59–61
Catchpole, Margaret, 2, 18
charity for widow, 82–6
charity workers, 100
childbirth, 12, 154–5
children's rights, 104
Chisholm, Caroline, 37, 43–5, 79
cities, 74, 79
citizenship for women, 173, 177

civil rights of women, 75
civilising males, 37
colonial girls, 122–5
colonial social conditions, 100
conditions of women's work, 150
contraception education, 146–50;
    sales, 154
convict, emancipated 18–19; men,
    9–11; mother, 6–9; refractory
    women, 9–11; riots, 33–5;
    servants, 21; society, 1; violence,
    2; women, 1, 18
convicts, bound for Botany Bay,
    6–9; clothing, 5; human interest
    story, 6–9; transportation, 6

Darling, Grace, 165
divorce, 104–6, 141–4
divorce bill, 68–71
Divorce Extension Bill, 141–4
divorce legislation, 68–71
domestic life in Sydney, 80
domestic violence, 28–31, 159
double standard, of morals, 162
dress reform, 115
Dugdale, Henrietta, 75, 115, 118
Dunlop, Eliza, 2, 31

economic independence, 37, 61–4
education for women, 75, 96–100
eligible bachelors, 71
emancipated convict, 18
employment prospects, 23
equal rights of citizenship, 90–3

Facey, A.B., 166
factories, 75, 101, 111, 172
families, large, 45; maintaining ties,
    21
Federal Constitution, 173–7
federal franchise to women, 177
federation, 130
female intemperance, 37–9
female paid and unpaid work, 129,
    130

female settlers, 74
female solidarity, 2
feminist utopia, 115–18
feminist's views on marriage,
    139–41
Franklin, Miles, 125–8
free-selection payments, 95

gentry women, 2
Gilmore, Mary, 93
goldfields, 166–9
gold rushes, 74, 81
Goldstein, Vida, 159

home life, 81
husband's violence, 28–31

illegitimate children, 103
Immigrant's Home, 43
immigrant women, 23, 43
immigration, 130
industrial action, 111
inequality between males and
    females, 36

journal for women, 141–4

Koori women, 12, 15, 16

lady reformer, 43, 79
Launceston Female Factory, 33–5
laws of marriage and divorce, 142
Lawson, Henry, 141
Lawson, Louisa, 141, 177
Lee, Bessie, 136–9, 139
legal emancipation, 125

Macarthur, Elizabeth, 2, 14–17
Macarthur, John, 14
male democracies, 36
male sexual demands, 45, 159
manhood suffrage, 64
marital bliss, 118–22
marriage, 43, 45, 47, 118, 139,

161–3; prospects, 23; rights,
    104–6
married women in suburbs, 75
masculine authority, 1–2
missionaries, 39, 74

national identity for women, 169
native labour system, 133
New South Wales Temperance
    Society, 37
Nightingale, Florence, 165, 166
nurses, 171

Pacific Island women, 1, 3, 4
Parkes, Henry, 61
pecuniary independence, 161–2
penal colony in NSW, 2; plan to
    establish, 2–5; transportation of
    convicts, 6
Phillip, Captain Arthur, 3
piecework, 151
pioneer mothers, 170
political activity, 36, 125
political emancipation, 90
political equality for women, 90–3,
    99
political power, 163
polygamy, 41
Poor House, 83
population, 130, 147, 154
poverty, 47–51, 82, 93–6, 154,
    166–9
power of women, 125–8; to civilise
    men, 37
Praed, Rosa, 75
pregnancy, 155
Presbyterian Ladies College, 96
professions for women, 99
prostitutes, 2, 100–4
Protestant Female Refuge, 100–4
public life, 163, 177

religion, 21–3, 117
rural areas, 74, 79, 166

schoolkeeping, 171
Scott, Rose, 163
secondary education, 75
secularism, 115
Selection Acts, 74, 94
self-sacrificing role of women, 144
servants, 43, 86
settling, 1
sexual exploitation, 132
sheep farming, 66–8
sisterly feeling, 2
slavery, 133
social freedom and independence,
    172
social position of women, 115, 159
social solutions, 129
Spence, Catherine, 59, 104, 141
squatters, 74, 79, 94
strike, 111–14

temperance movement, 37;
    advocate, 136–9
tertiary education, 97
trade unions, 150

unhappy marriage, 45
union, formation, 111
universities, 172
unmarried middle-class women, 86
urban frontiers, 74; life, 79

venereal diseases, 154
Victorian Women's Suffrage
    Society, 115
violence towards women, 28–31,
    130, 136
visiting gentlemen, 71
votes for women, 64–6, 90, 130,
    156–9, 159, 163–6 , 173, 178

widows, 82
wife-beating, 106
wife-desertion, 106, 141
wives' chief goals, 118–22

Womanhood Suffrage League, 147, 163
Women's Christian Temperance Union, 130, 136, 147, 157
Women's Franchise Bill, 177
women's power in family, 125
women's rights, 90, 104, 136, 167

women's suffrage, 156–9, 159, 163–6, 173
Women's Suffrage League of South Australia, 156
women's wages, 111
working-class housing, 79, 81
working women, 111–14, 150, 171